MarketPlace	: AUK
Order Number	: 203-1884228-0731530
Ship Method	: Standard
Order Date	: 2013-01-09
Email	: n14z39ps8wznqf2@marketplace.amazon.co.uk

Items : 1

Qty	Item	Locator
1	Dan Brown's "The Lost Symbol" The Ultimate Unautho ISBN : 0953317226	HOL-3-BX-015-03-11 RY

R:

We hope that you are completely satisfied with your purchase and ask you to leave positive feedback accordingly.

However, if you are unsatisfied with your order, please contact us by telephone or email. We will do whatever it takes to resolve the issue.

Mulberry House, Woods Way, Goring By Sea, West Sussex, BN12 4QY. Tel:+44(0)1903 507544
Email: sales@worldofbooks.com | Twitter: @WorldofBooksltd | Web: www.worldofbooks.com

Dan Brown

The Lost Symbol

The Ultimate Unauthorized

&

Independent Reading Guide

Alex Carmine

Published in 2009 by Punked Books

An Authortrek imprint

Punked Books
C/O Authortrek
PO Box 54168
London
W5 9EE
(FAQ via www.authortrek.com/punked-books)

Cover photo ©iStockphoto.com/Sergey Rusakov

Contents

The build-up to *The Lost Symbol*

Dan Brown's *The Lost Symbol* was the most anticipated novel of 2009, and arguably, the literary event of the year. Random House set up an unprecedented first print run of 6.5 million copies, although this figure is less astounding when you consider that there are now over 80 million copies of *The Da Vinci Code* in print. Readers were most eager to discover whether Dan Brown had come up with a story that is as intriguing as that of Jesus' bloodline and family. Since *The Lost Symbol* is set in Washington, and features freemasonry, and the foundation of the United States, there is a very good chance that he has done so. I will be examining all the themes in depth, and will provide a chapter-by-chapter analysis of *The Lost Symbol*, following in the footsteps of Dan Brown's hero, the Harvard Symbologist, Robert Langdon.

From my examination of the novel, it is very much apparent that Dan Brown has not only been adhering to his own formula, but that he has also been following Joseph Campbell's concept of the 'monomyth', or, as it's better known, *the hero's journey*. So, I have given several chapters the names of the various stages in the monomyth. We know that Dan Brown likes to play with the names of his characters, so I will be exploring these in great detail. In this way, I will reveal the name of the real American family upon whom the Solomons are based, and I will expose what appears to be quite a rude joke on Dan Brown's part with regards to the name of one particular character! I will also show that, following its development within *The Da Vinci Code*, Dan Brown's still very much in tune with his 'sacred feminine' side, with his stunning representation of womb envy, and I will discuss his fascinating depiction of masculinity within this novel too. In addition to this, I will explore the literary devices that Dan Brown employs, and the magical sleights of hand that he uses to make the reader look the wrong way. Indeed, one of my main arguments in this book is that Dan Brown has hidden much of the true meaning of *The Lost Symbol* behind various veils of allegory, much as the Masons do with regards to their secrets, and like the Symbologist Robert Langdon, I will reveal these meanings to you. However, Dan Brown is an author who also likes to reward his readers, so I will examine the clues about the novel that he disseminated prior to publication via Facebook and Twitter. Furthermore, I will consider the various Masonic practices depicted within the novel, and bring to the fore the various conspiracy theories that surround this mysterious fraternity. Indeed, you could say that my very close reading of the novel leaves no stone uncovered, and that it will transform your own interpretation of the text. I will be doing much of this research in real time, so that you will come across my thoughts on what's happening in the novel as I read it. As Dan Brown has described the writing of the novel to be "a strange and wonderful journey", so I have found the reading of it to be also.

First of all though, I will be reporting on the hopes and fears expressed in the build-up to the publication of *The Lost Symbol*, and all the controversies surrounding the novel. *The Lost Symbol* was originally supposed to be published in 2006, so the sequel to *The Da Vinci Code* has been a long time coming. There does, however, appear to be little danger that Dan Brown has missed the boat.

According to Sonny Mehta, Dan Brown's US publisher, *The Lost Symbol* is "a brilliant and compelling thriller" that is "well worth the wait". As Sommer Mathis wrote in *dcist* on July 8th 2009, "get ready to see every damn person on the Metro reading this thing come fall" (1). Admittedly, *dcist* is an city blog covering Washington DC, where most of the action of *The Lost Symbol* is set. However, the image of whole train cars full of people reading *The Lost Symbol* is one that could become quite familiar to commuters internationally in the weeks after September 15th.

Not only were eager readers hanging about for the new Dan Brown book, as the author himself was also doing this literally. According to *The Independent*'s Alison Jury, "When stuck on points of the plot, Brown would dangle upside down from a pair of 'gravity boots' to think it out" (2) – perhaps Robert Langdon could adapt this strategy also when trying to solve a particularly tricky puzzle? As Dan Brown himself said in a statement released by his publishers, "Weaving five years of research into the story's twelve-hour time frame was an exhilarating challenge. Robert Langdon's life clearly moves a lot faster than mine." Make that a helluva lot faster!

Of course, during this time, there was the distraction of a lawsuit brought against Dan Brown in 2006, with the accusation that he had plagiarised *The Holy Blood and the Holy Grail* by Michael Baigent, Richard Leigh, and Henry Lincoln in *The Da Vinci Code*. *The Holy Blood and the Holy Grail* was mentioned in *The Da Vinci Code*, to the extent that one of the main protagonists in the novel, 'Sir Leigh Teabing', was named after two of the authors of the 1982 book (which can be the only excuse for the anagrammatic invention of such an excruciating name). Possibly Dan Brown's biggest error was having *The Da Vinci Code*'s heroine, Sophie Neveu exclaim that she'd never heard of *The Holy Blood and the Holy Grail* upon seeing it in Sir Leigh Teabing's study. If he'd been around in the UK in 1982, then Dan Brown would certainly have heard of *The Holy Blood and the Holy Grail*, as it caused quite a stir upon its publication. As mentioned above, Dan Brown did utilise *The Holy Blood and the Holy Grail* while researching *The Da Vinci Code*, but denied that he had set out to plagiarise "the whole architecture" of the research that Baigent, Leigh, and Lincoln had put together for *The Holy Blood and the Holy Grail*, although both books did promote the startling theory that Jesus had had a child with Mary Magdalene, and that the bloodline had survived.

However, British High Court Judge Peter Smith dismissed the case, after ruling that "it would be quite wrong if fictional writers were to have their writings pored over in the way... (That *The Da Vinci Code*) has been pored over in this case by authors of pretend historical books to make an allegation of infringement of copyright" (3). This was much to the relief of Dan Brown, who believed that the case should not have been brought in the first place, especially as it now enabled him to get back to the business of writing. However, one can only speculate how much this case must have affected him. Indeed, during the court case, he went into great detail about the struggles that he had faced in his early career as a writer. It must have been heartbreaking for the long dreamt for success achieved by *The Da Vinci Code* to be mired by such controversy. If Dan Brown had suffered from too little publicity in his early career, then by 2006 it is most likely that he was beginning to suffer from having too much exposure. Indeed, during his statement to the court, Dan Brown did note how taken aback he was by strength of feelings aroused by *The Da Vinci Code*, especially from fervent Christians, who took his fiction very seriously indeed. Despite Dan Brown's eagerness to get back to writing, it would be very understandable for him to want to take something of a breather, before embarking on the next ride on the merry-go-round. There is also the consideration that the purported theme of *The Lost Symbol* – the Masons' key role in the founding of the United States, was also covered in another Michael Baigent and Richard Leigh book, *The Temple and the Lodge*. Given these links in themes, it would be hardly surprising if the composition of *The Lost Symbol* were delayed by this plagiarism court case. However, having read both books, I know that there is little or no similarity between them.

Dan Brown's UK publishers were equally as enthusiastic as their North American counterparts when announcing *The Lost Symbol*'s publication. Gail Rebuck, Chair and Chief Executive Officer of the Random House Group UK, was quoted in *The Bookseller* saying this about her star author: "The pure adrenalin thrill of reading his novels, combined with the fascinating insights into what might lie below the surface of our lives and our history, make him unique in the pantheon of contemporary writers" (4). As Ben Hoyle reported in *The Times* the next day, this enthusiasm is not surprising given that, "Brown's last four novels (the first three of them republished after the phenomenal success of *The Da Vinci Code*) are now the first, second, third and fourth best-selling adult paperback novels in British history," (5). Seasoned Dan Brown commentator, Simon Cox, noted on his blog "the publishing and book selling business are overjoyed. Indeed, the announcement at the London Book Fair today was met with joy unconfined, on a scale not seen in the business in many years" (6). It would appear that only J. K. Rowling's Harry Potter books would have the power to compete with Dan Brown now, and of course, there's not going to be another one of those (any time soon).

However, Simon Cox may have been overstating the case a bit in the above quote, as there were many people in the British publishing and bookselling industry that didn't welcome the publication of *The Lost Symbol*. Philip Stone's analysis of Dan Brown's sales figures in *The Bookseller* on 8th August 2009 stated that there was no evidence of a "Brown bounce", and that the publication of a new Dan Brown novel would not necessarily lead to more sales for other fiction titles (7). Random House's competitors will doubtlessly be hoping for a lovely dose of schadenfreude from the reviews of *The Lost Symbol*. Although the sales of the novel are likely to be high regardless of what any reviewer writes. Thankfully, Random House saw fit to give five months' notice of the publication date, allowing their panicked competitors to change the releases of their most notable autumn titles. As David Barrett reported in *The Daily Telegraph* on 11th July 2009, authors such as Nick Hornby, Sebastian Faulks, Iain Banks, Margaret Atwood, J. M. Coetzee, Fay Weldon, and Nick Cave, are going to have their books published in the 3 weeks leading up to September 15th (8). September is traditionally one of the busiest months in publishing, as publishers hope to set the charts alight with books during the fourth quarter (i.e. Christmas), although the publication of *The Lost Symbol* seems to have shortened the month somewhat. The strategy seems to be that releasing these books earlier will give them a much better chance of occupying the No.1 slot in the bestseller charts, as they will obviously have no chance when set against Dan Brown's might. Yet such a strategy seems flawed to me, as at best, only 2 of these books will be able to get to this pivotal position before Dan Brown.

According to John Harlow in *The Times*, *The Lost Symbol* has also caused panic amongst American publishers, who have also been changing the release dates of their most prominent titles (9). Harlow cites the "Harry Potter effect" where the release of J. K. Rowling's later books in the series depressed the sales of other children's books by 15% in the following fortnight. He then goes on to write "Sara Nelson, former editor of *Publishers Weekly*, has called *The Lost Symbol* a 'book killer' because it will depress the sales of other novels this autumn". Despite previous reports to the contrary, Harlow also states that British publishers have not been so worried, and have gone ahead with their mid-September publications.

So, something else seems to be happening here. Cahal Milmo may have hit the bull's eye with her article in *The Independent* on July 13th 2009: *Two weeks to save Britain's book trade* (10). Publishing has traditionally been seen as a recession proof industry in the UK, as people still need to buy books even when they can't afford, say, a new fridge or a car. However, this current recession seems to be quite different. Publishers are nervous, because the whole structure of the industry could be undergoing a revolution. With print on demand technology finally reaching of age, it's very apparent that traditional trade publishers could be threatened with the arrival of new upstarts that don't have the huge overheads of say, being based in London, and since they only print books as and when they're required, they don't need have money tied up in unsold stock. As Cahal Milmo reports, book sales have declined in the UK by about 10 per cent from the previous year, so publishers are doing their best to attract the public's attention by publishing all their big-hitters all in one go. So, a lot depends on these two weeks, with Cahal quoting one senior publishing executive as saying it could "mean the difference between caviar or cat food for Christmas dinner", which is surely an unsavoury enough choice for anyone to make. It seems that in these tough times, the real winners will probably be these big name authors, whose advances are increasing in value, as their publishers try to keep hold of these big earners, while dropping their less prominent colleagues.

When the Random House group in the UK released the details for their release of *The Lost Symbol*, their CEO Gail Rebuck was also quoted in *The Bookseller* as saying that "The arrival of this stunning new novel is a publishing event without compare. For us, and for the bookselling community across the world, it is nothing less than the most extraordinary publishing opportunity" (11). Again, I'm not so sure that booksellers across the UK will be so enthusiastic about *The Lost Symbol*. Independent booksellers in the UK certainly don't have the clout that their bigger competitors have in the food chain, and won't be able to afford to discount the novel. That hasn't stopped some of them from offering some exclusive offers of their own – leading independent bookshop The Bookseller Crow's blog posting on the 31st of July offer buyers of *The Lost Symbol* a free sheet of wrapping paper bearing the legend "shit present" (12) - although it's debateable whether they're bitter about presumably making no money from the novel, or if they were making a prejudgement of the book's contents. When the UK's Net Book Agreement ended in 1997, booksellers could legitimately discount books for the first time. There were fears that this could be to the detriment of authors on the mid list and below, as buyers would be attracted to the lower priced titles from bigger authors. So effective has discounting been to getting traffic into bookshops, it's now become a kind of narcotic drug for the UK industry. It's harmful, because it means that publishing's traditional low margins have inevitably reduced even further as a result. As a result, publishers tend to take fewer risks, and focus on fewer blockbusting authors. As Robert McCrum has complained in *The Guardian* (13):

> The most surreal news from the world of books is the trade press report that *The Lost Symbol*, Dan Brown's follow-up to *The Da Vinci Code*, is going to be launched in September from Random House with the biggest ever global first print run (some 6.5m copies) in the publisher's history... In books, the global marketplace seems to have crushed the spirit of innovation, and squeezed the life blood out of literary experimentation. Who are the avant-garde writers today who have retained their integrity as artists to shun the mainstream, but continue to produce new work? It must be a pretty short list, and, with the exception of a few poets, its constituents are almost totally invisible...

So, there are some quite ridiculous prices out there in the UK for *The Lost Symbol*. At the time of writing, Amazon.co.uk is selling the novel at 50% off the retail price at £9.49, as are Waterstone's, Tesco, Play.com, and Asda online. W.H. Smith is selling *The Lost Symbol* at a price of £7.99, and gave those who pre-ordered a book of discount vouchers for novels by other, less-well-known Random House authors. Amazon and other online retailers, with their economies of scale (i.e. no expensive high street shops), can just about afford to do this, although *The Lost Symbol* will be a loss leader for them also. The independent bookshops, meanwhile, will probably resort to purchasing copies of *The Lost Symbol* from whichever retailer is discounting the most, as this will be the cheapest way for them to buy stock! At least, that's what many did following the publication of the later Harry Potter books. As Boyd Tonkin grumbled in *The Independent* on July 22nd 2009, "Yet again, a hype-driven 'event' publication will drive casual readers away from shops that know how to sell books, and towards the cut-price titans whose economies of scale give them the clout to muscle in on bestsellers" (14). As a financially challenged author, I will doubtlessly be heading to the W.H. Smith pre-order deal, as I doubt that will be bettered elsewhere, and it at least does also promote other authors on Random House's backlist. One could argue that this discounting is evidence of very healthy competition in the UK's bookselling market. However, on the other hand, it's very evident that *The Lost Symbol* will be a bestseller no matter what its price, and it's sad to see booksellers literally placing such a small value on its most prized assets. Random House's large initial print run of 6.5 million copies, while being realistic, will only have encouraged retailers to drop prices, to ensure that they'll be able to get rid off effectively worthless stock (there's no sign yet that Random House will be doing a limited deluxe edition of *The Lost Symbol*). One of economists' main fears about the current recession is that it could lead to deflation, with buyers holding off making purchases until the retailers blink and lower their prices. Since this has already been happening in bookselling for years, it's difficult to see how prices could be further deflated!

Random House in the UK certainly pulled out all the stops to ensure that the publication of *The Lost Symbol* catches the public's imagination, with an advertising campaign that ran for a fortnight from 7th September 2009. They also cannily hitchhiked Sony's advertising campaign for the DVD release of *Angels and*

Demons, as *The Bookseller* reported on 7th August 2009 (15). However, an indication that Dan Brown is not as big an author as J. K. Rowling is indicated by the fact that W. H. Smith did not change its opening hours for the release of *The Lost Symbol*. Maybe adults are too sensible to queue up at midnight, as opposed to children? Random House couriered copies of the novel to journalists immediately after midnight. I considered asking for a review copy, but I'd already plumped for the W. H. Smith pre-order offer, as I wanted to participate in the consumer experience of reading the novel. And also because I love my sleep, as no doubt do my neighbours, and I couldn't be arsed to wait up for the courier. Having written that, it's a short trip up the Uxbridge Road to my flat from the Random House imprint Transworld... Well, they'll probably be coming from the warehouse anyway, and I want to see how the W. H. Smith staff react when I turned up at 08.30 waving my pre-order receipt, and how many other people will be queuing there also. In the end, I turned up a bit later that morning, but W. H. Smith staff still seemed confused as to how the transaction was supposed to be enacted.

Jodi Picoult's slating of Dan Brown On 7th May 2009, Jodi Picoult had a mini interview published in the *Daily Mail*, in which she attacked *The Da Vinci Code*, saying "I don't understand the hype over such a poorly written novel" (1). Which I think is rather a case of the pot calling the kettle black. Don't get me wrong, I really enjoyed Jodi Picoult's novel *Nineteen Minutes*. However, despite having written a review about *Nineteen Minutes*, I really can't remember anything about it, despite this being quite a big novel (in terms of length). Whereas I really remember several images from Lionel Shriver's similarly themed novel, *We Need to Talk About Kevin*, probably because Shriver is a much better writer than Picoult, and maybe Picoult's voice is a bit anonymous and plain? Although many people find Picoult's narratives to be quite involving, I'd argue that this is usually because she's mainly chosen to write about the big moral issues of the day, and some may argue that the whole reason why *The Da Vinci Code* was so popular was that people were fascinated by the whole idea behind it, that Jesus had a child and a surviving bloodline. As soon as you read a second novel by Picoult, you notice that she does very much have a repetitive formula that she adheres to. I read *My Sister's Keeper* recently, and from that, I deduced that her writing style is not entirely unlike say, John Grisham, and not a million miles away from her fellow master of popular fiction, Dan Brown... Jodi Picoult also has a tendency to have some really awful closures to her novels, so she's far from being a master of her craft. For instance, I was really enjoying *My Sister's Keeper*, until I got to the god-awful ending.

In the same interview, Jodi Picoult went on to further criticise Dan Brown by saying "as an author who does all her own research, I know better than to consider myself an expert in the field I am writing about. I believe this was an error in judgment for this particular author". This is presumably a reference to the British plagiarism legal case against Dan Brown that I discussed earlier. Presumably, Jodi Picoult hasn't read Dan Brown's defence, in which he stated that he wasn't an expert on all the conspiracy theories portrayed in his novels, and was sometimes taken aback by the deep probing into *The Da Vinci Code* by readers he encountered while promoting the novel, which forced him to re-read his research notes, so that he could adequately defend a book that he had written a year earlier. To be fair to

Jodi Picoult, I know that at least one of my friends is addicted to reading her novels, and has read every single one of them. But I also know many other readers who've disliked their first Jodi Picoult novel, and won't read any others.

The change of title Way back in October 2004, Stephen Rubin, the then President and Publisher of Doubleday, told reporters that the title of Dan Brown's follow-up to *The Da Vinci Code* was going to be called *The Solomon Key* (1). Before this announcement, Dan Brown fans had been scouring the cover of the *Da Vinci Code* for clues concerning Robert Langdon's next adventure, following the author's statement that such clues were deliberately hidden there. However, the announcement of the title was seen by many Dan Brown followers to be the biggest clue of all. I would agree, as I think that nouns were probably the first structure of spoken language to be used by our ancestors. More importantly, Dan Brown has attached a great deal of importance to the names he has created in his previous novels (such as the already discussed Sir Leigh Teabing).

The announcement of the title, combined with the knowledge of Dan Brown's concerns from his previous books, and the clues on *The Da Vinci Code* cover, encouraged several writers to release books about *The Solomon Key/The Lost Symbol* many years before it was released! One such writer who was caught out by the change in title was Greg Taylor, author of *The Guide to Dan Brown's The Solomon Key*. Writing on his blog, *The Cryptex*, Taylor stated on 28th June 2009 "a few people have asked whether I'm bothered by the decision by Dan Brown and his publisher to change the title of his book to *The Lost Symbol*. In short, not at all... If anything, the change of title indicates to me that my book, *The Guide to Dan Brown's The Solomon Key*, may well have been so close to the mark that they decided to change the title of Brown's book to *The Lost Symbol*" (2). While this may seem boastful on Taylor's part, there would appear to be an element of truth in this. Ben Hoyle, the arts correspondent of *The Times*, quoted from an unnamed source at the publishers, that the "new title was deliberately chosen to be 'as opaque as possible.... only in the past few days has he settled on a title bland or enigmatic enough to give away none of his new subject matter... Dan Brown is so phenomenally successful that anything he says in relation to his books can spawn a whole publishing industry in itself'" (3). Or, as the anonymous author of the *Dan Browns The Lost Symbol* blog puts it, "*The Solomon Key* was only the working title of the book, and we all know how tight secrecy is around Dan Browns work, so the minute the working title was leaked, people began speculating about the contents of the book and mixed news were published misleading the public and creating some sort of turmoil around the novel" (sic, 4). Of course, although the book you're reading is a part of this industry, it will only be published after I've had the chance to read the novel. Although that won't stop me from providing some good informed speculation about the more opaque parts of *The Lost Symbol* beyond its title!

So, Greg Taylor has now followed suit with Dan Brown, and has renamed his book *The Guide to Dan Brown's The Lost Symbol*. Having written that, this isn't the first time that Greg Taylor has had to rename his book to keep up with Dan Brown, since it was originally called *Da Vinci in America*. Oscar Wilde's famous quote springs to mind: to lose one title is unfortunate, to lose two seems careless!

The publication date In 2005, Stephen Rubin, the President of Doubleday, announced, "Dan Brown has a very specific release date for the publication of his new book, and when the book is published, his readers will see why." However, when the release date of September 15 2009 was announced, some commentators were puzzled with this choice, as the date doesn't seem to have that much of a resonance with the public. As Greg Taylor has written, "Now, it's only been a few hours since I've heard the publication date of September 15th, but at this stage I can't see the significance of the release date... Was Brown originally aiming at a date linked to the Presidential election or inauguration (which would have tied into the originally-claimed topics in *The Solomon Key*), but simply missed the boat?"

The Inquisitr website has noted that "Some hardcore Langdon-fans are certain that the plot will [sic] freemasons in Washington D.C., but the early release date of the book could be undermining that. Many fans expected *The Lost Symbol* to be released on September 18, which has always been an important date in Masonic history. It was on September 18, 1793 President Washington led a Masonic parade down Pennsylvania Avenue to lay the cornerstone of U.S. Capitol" (1).

However, September 18th 2009 was a Friday, so was probably not a good date to launch a novel. Having written that, with all its many pre-orders, I'm sure that *The Lost Symbol* would be at the top of the Sunday book charts no matter what. Although book reviewers for the weekend newspapers might have been a bit disgruntled at only having one day to review the novel, since they have been unlikely to have been sent advanced review copies, due to the strict embargoes surrounding the release of *The Lost Symbol*. So, if the publishers had published on the 18th, then they may well have received review coverage over an extra weekend than they would have done otherwise. Of course, there is one date in September that does have greater resonance than the laying of the Capitol Building cornerstone, which may have been withdrawn on reasons of taste – September 11th anyone?

The social networking clues When the publication date of *The Lost Symbol* was announced, the publishers also revealed that they'd be using "social networking sites such as Facebook to release codes, puzzles and teasers" (1). So, I will be examining the most prominent clues, to see what they reveal or maybe even conceal about *The Lost Symbol*. It's curious to see that was some interaction between whoever posed these teasers, and ordinary Facebook and Twitter users, which makes me wonder if the person behind these clues was Dan Brown himself? Certainly, no one else would know the contents of this strictly embargoed book better than him. In his witness testimony during the Baigent/Leigh plagiarism court case, Dan Brown mentioned how his father would give him clues, so he could discover the whereabouts of his Christmas present by himself, so could Dan Brown himself have been rewarding us, his 'children', in the same manner? After all, this has already worked its way into Dan Brown's fiction, as Sophie Neveu's grandfather Saniere played similar games with her when she was a child, as related in *The Da Vinci Code*.

The first noteworthy clue contained a reference to the Perfectibilists, the original name of the Illuminati (the secret society that featured in *Angels and Demons*). According to the book *Perfectibilists* by Terry Melanson, **the Yale Skull and Bones club** (amongst whom members have been a recent US President of considerable notoriety), based some of their ceremonies on the Illuminati's (2). So, this clue may have been designed to give the impression that there could be some Illuminati involvement in *The Lost Symbol*, as Robert Langdon stated in *Angels and Demons* that this organisation had very successfully infiltrated the Masons. Another clue on the 24th June asked who had stolen William Wirt's skull. William Wirt was a nineteenth century US Attorney General. Indeed, Wikipedia credits him as being the first to Attorney General to have turned the role into "one of influence". More importantly, with regards to *The Lost Symbol*, is the fact that he was later a presidential candidate for the Anti-Masonic Party, which Wikipedia considers to have been quite ironic, as he used to be a Mason, and is alleged to have actually defended the fraternity at an Anti-Masonic convention! His skull was found to have been in the possession of a recently deceased collector a few years ago, although it's unknown when and indeed who actually stole his skull from his tomb. However, *Washington Post* staff writer Peter Carlson jocularly suggested in an article about the recovery of the skull that the theft could have been committed by Scottish Rite Freemasons or a Skull and Bones Lodge (3).

The following clue was a quote from Francis Bacon "If we begin with certainties, we shall end in doubts; but if we begin with doubts, and are patient in them, we shall end in certainties". Francis Bacon is regarded having laid the foundations of modern scientific research, and featured in *The Lost Symbol* with the mention of his book *The New Atlantis*, which will be further discussed on pp. 25-27. The eighth Tweet, "MAEIETCTETAOTHPL" was solved by Dan Brown fans to mean, "Meet at the Capitol", which is likely to be a reference to Langdon's false summoning to DC by Mal'akh. The tweets then reveal that famed Renaissance artist Albrecht Dürer trained as a metalworker in his youth, which at first, second, and third sight was not all that exciting, but then I didn't know that Dürer was to play such a huge role in the novel when I came across this clue.

The 13th Twitter clue referred to a "Hell's Legionnaire" who can turn lead into gold. The goal of turning lead into gold, alchemy was one that many men understandably sought to achieve in history. Despite the fact that their aims were so obviously deluded, the efforts made by these alchemists did pave the way to the modern science of chemistry. However, Mark E. Koltko-Rivera has stated that he believes that there is a more obvious link to the novel in his blog, *Key to the Lost Symbol clues* (4). According to Kolto-Rivera, the Legionnaire is a reference to the famous incident in the Book of Matthew where Jesus encounters a mentally ill man (probably a schizophrenic) who claims, "My name is Legion, for we are many". In Biblical times, such mentally ill people were regarded as being possessed by demons. Kolto-Rivera claims that the identity of the demon that can turn lead into gold can be found in the rather occult medieval magic textbook *Goetia*, which, as Kolto-Rivera points out, has the rather interesting subtitle *The Lesser Key of Solomon*. Kolto-Rivera quotes from the Samuel MacGregor Liddel Mathers/Aleister Crowley translation of *The Goetia*:

BERITH. -- The Twenty-eighth Spirit in Order, as Solomon bound them, is named Berith. He can turn all metals into Gold. ... He governeth 26 Legions of Spirits.

The second clue on June 29th gave the coordinates for Newgrange, a megalithic tomb in the Republic of Ireland. The clue asks, "Did they really know?" The inevitable question is did they know what? According to Wikipedia, Newgrange was built more than 500 years before the great pyramids at Giza. Wikipedia states, "Newgrange was built in such a way that at dawn on the shortest day of the year, the winter solstice, a narrow beam of sunlight for a very short time illuminates the floor of the chamber at the end of the long passageway" – which is presumably what the question in the clue refers to. So, this clue would seem to indicate the almost universal practice of sun worship in primitive cultures. Interestingly, the burial chamber was built in a cruciform shape more than 3,000 years before the crucifixion of Christ.

There's another seeming reference to a pyramid with the Latin quote "Totum maior summa partum" ("The whole is greater than the sum of its parts"), which now looks to have be an allusion to the Masonic Pyramid that featured in the novel. One of the clues asked us how a precious stone could have destroyed 20 years' of Isaac's research? Since **Sir Isaac Newton** featured in *The Da Vinci Code* in his apocryphal role as a Grand Master of the Priory of Sion, it's reasonable to assume that he's the Isaac being referred to. It's a short step from there to guess that the precious stone is the most obvious candidate: diamond. And so it turns out that Sir Isaac Newton's dog was called Diamond, who once exasperated his owner by knocking a candle over, which did indeed burn 20 years of the great alchemist and scientist's work. Sir Isaac Newton proposed that the world would end by 2060, so far later than the Mayan prophecy that is mentioned in *The Lost Symbol*.

The next clue is a hyperlink to an online encyclopedia entry on the Christogram, which is a combination of letters that forms an abbreviated version of Jesus Christ's name. The most famous Christograms are IHS and INRI. There's another one called the Chi-Ro, which incorporates the Greek version of the letter 'X', which we now employ whenever we write 'Xmas'. The Chi-Ro was most famously adopted by the Roman Emperor Constantine as a battle standard, the 'Labarum', after he'd seen it in a celestial vision. As part of this vision, Constantine saw the Greek words "Ἐν Τούτῳ Νίκα... The Latin translation is *in hoc signo vinces* — 'In this [sign], conquer'" (5). According to the online *Masonic Dictionary*, "By this sign thou shalt conquer" is a motto that has been adopted by the American branch of the Freemasons, but its utilisation by the Knights Templar is probably apocryphal. Of course, in *The Da Vinci Code*, Constantine's role in the Council of Nicea, which laid the foundations of the Bible we have today, was very much debated, as the Council was accused of excising any Gospel that related Jesus' special relationship with Mary Magdalene, and any Gospel that conveyed him as a mortal man, rather than a divine being. Sir Leigh Teabing tells Sophie Neveu in *The Da Vinci Code* that the Council of Nicea was convened to vote on the divinity of Christ, as prior to that, Christians had viewed Christ as a mortal man.

Next, there's a hyperlink to a Twitpic (a platform that allows you to show pictures via Twitter). This Twitpic is an ambigram, and most of the feedback from fellow Twitters suggests that the first word is "Silvia" followed by "&", but nobody seems to be able to read the second word. Yet the "&" could be a form of the Christogram, with an emphasis on the Greek letter P "Rho", rather than the whole "Chi-Ro" of the Labarum symbol (6). The Twitter clue states, "This Apennine was a member". Well, the most famous inhabitant of the Apennine mountains was Saint Francis of Assisi, so this may have something to do with him. Saint Francis was well-regarded in the Holy Land, and had good relations with the Muslim world, so much so that, as Wikipedia states, "after the fall of the Crusader Kingdom it would be the Franciscans, of all Catholics, who would be allowed to stay on in the Holy Land and be recognised as 'Custodians of the Holy Land' on behalf of Christianity". Incidentally, Saint Francis adopted the Tau Cross as the emblem of the Francisan Order, because when "commenting on the scriptures of Israel, the early Christian writers used its Greek translation, the Septuagint, in which the last letter of the Hebrew alphabet, the tau, was transcribed as a 'T' in Greek. Prefigured in the last letter of the Hebrew alphabet, then, the stylised Tau cross came to represent the means by which Christ reversed the disobedience of the old Adam and became our Savior as the 'New Adam'" (7). According to the Masonic Dictionary, in the ancient Hebrew alphabet, Tau was the figure "X" or "+", so did indeed resemble a cross. The *Masonic Dictionary* states that Tau was also an ancient Egyptian monogram of the god Thoth (who was concerned with writing, magic, science, and judging the dead), and that it's debateable whether the Knights Templar utilised it as a symbol of the phallus, although Masons employ it in a non-phallic way (8). Wikipedia states that the Cross of Tau is also used to represent Taurus in astrology, and is the symbol of the Sumerian God Tammuz, and equates him with Christ, since Tammuz was also associated with fishing and shepherding, and his death and resurrection was celebrated every year. Indeed, as Wikipedia notes, the 'T' used to represent Tammuz is one of the oldest letters known (9).

The next clue regards the **Invisible College**, which as Wikipedia states, was a precursor to the UK's **Royal Society** (10). The members of the Invisible College were dedicated to scientific progress via experimentation. Amongst its members were Robert Boyle, Robert Hooke, and Christopher Wren. The Invisible College was a kind of social network for scientists, where they could exchange ideas, by say, writing in the margins of books that they sent each other. Nowadays, of course, they'd be using the Internet! But what has this to do with *The Lost Symbol*? Well, Robert Lomas has written a book called *The Invisible College: The Royal Society, Freemasonry, and the Birth of Science*, in which he claims that the members of the Invisible College were actually Freemasons, and that their move towards the foundation of modern science was very much supported by King Charles II following the Restoration. Dr. Robert Lomas has written other books on Freemasonry, such as *The Hiram Key*, so I've no doubts that Dan Brown consulted *The Invisible College* in the writing of *The Lost Symbol*.

The 22nd clue referred to an artist whose subjects included Adam and Eve, blessed Jerome and horned ungulate (hoofed animal). Thankfully, other fans have came up with a very likely solution on the Dan Brown Facebook page, that Albrecht Dürer is the artist, since Adam and Eve, Saint Jerome, and a rhinoceros were indeed amongst his subjects. So, from this second mention of Albrecht Dürer amongst the online clues, it became obvious that his artwork would play some role in *The Lost Symbol*.

The 23rd clue stated "GM of the KT. Burned for money". The 'KT' must be the Knights Templar, and the 'GM' most likely stands for "Grand Master". The last Grand Master of the Knights Templar, Jacques de Molay, was indeed burnt at the stake in the purge of the Templars ordered by Pope Clement V on Friday the 13th of October 1307, which was described in *The Da Vinci Code*. The Templars were believed to have been destroyed because they refused a loan to Phillip IV, King of France.

Then there was a link to a YouTube video about the Mayan Chichen Itza site in Mexico, where the shadow of a plumed serpent appears on the steps of the temple at every equinox in an amazing feat of engineering. The 25th clue is a Twitpic of a cross composed of roses. A search online for **"Rosy Cross"** reveals that this was a symbol adopted by **Christian Rosencreutz**, alchemist and founder of the **Rosicrucian Order** (11), something which was quite quickly spotted by followers on Twitter. However, there are some additional aspects of the Rosicrucian Order that seem to be of note with regards to *The Lost Symbol*. For instance, Christian Rosencreutz (whose surname means 'Rose Cross') is believed by many to have been an alter ego for Francis Bacon. The Rosicrucian Order (the Order of the Rose Cross) is also believed to have been a forerunner of the Invisible College, mentioned in a previous Twitter clue. They produced two manifestoes in the early 17th Century, which stated that they "speak unto you by parables, but would willingly bring you to the right, simple, easy, and ingenuous exposition, understanding, declaration, and knowledge of all secrets". According to Wikipedia, "two Rosicrucian-inspired Masonic rites emerged towards the end of 18th century, the Rectified Scottish Rite, widespread in Central Europe where there was a strong presence of the 'Golden and Rosy Cross', and the Ancient and Accepted Scottish Rite, first practised in France, in which the 18th degree is called Knight of the Rose Croix" (12).

The following Twitpic shows a gravestone featuring some quite unusual names: "Alpaca Blithe, Garcon Espies, Quince Esse Kye". Although these would appear to be some quite individualistic Scottish names, there is no reference to them on Google beyond *The Last Symbol*; so one can safely assumed that these names were photoshopped on the gravestone. Twitter followers cracked these anagrams to read "Alphabetical", "Ignore Spaces", and "Sequence is key" (13). A few days later, someone posted 3 comments on the *Belfast Telegraph's* announcement about the UK cover of *The Lost Symbol* using these names in quick succession (14). This article was unusual because it ended with the words "So mote it be", and because it stated that *The Lost Symbol* would be released on "15+09+09". As LexiePyatt commented on the article, "So mote it be" is the closing phrase in Masonic prayers, I guess their equivalent of "Amen", and "15+09+09" equals 33, a Masonic number that offers guidance to the world. So, could this be the reason why *The Lost Symbol* was published on 15th September 2009? It could very well be that the anonymous author of *The Belfast Telegraph* article knows something of freemasonry, and just chose to add these details in him/herself. But then most of the reader comments are a bit bizarre. One reader, under the pseudonym of Andrew Jackson (presumably a reference to the 7th US President and the last one to have fought in the Revolutionary War), wrote the following quote "God prosper and protect them all...in the land or on the sea. Success to all those knighted men...And the Sons of Liberty". This quote seems to be a reference to Freemasons (followers of the Knights Templar perhaps), but I can't find a reference to this quote elsewhere online). Another reader, called Snake, simply writes "Don't Tread on Me", which is related to one of Benjamin Franklin's political cartoons. Maybe the *Belfast Telegraph* had a special deal done with the publishers of *The Lost Symbol* to reveal the UK cover in this enigmatic way?

Anyway, I now want to take a look at the **Masonic number 33**, as this is the best explanation that I've yet come across for why *The Lost Symbol* will be published on the 15th of September 2009. The first article I came across online regarding the Masonic number 33 was a 2001 one by Robert Howard entitled *11, 13, and 33: The Illuminati/Freemason Signature*, which, for obvious reasons, seemed like a very good place to start (15). Howard states that 33 is the highest degree in Masonry, but he also declares that he believes that "33 is also Satan's number". Robert Howard also relates the Masonic numbers to 9/11. While the ideas that Howard expounds require some suspension of disbelief, it's likely that such seemingly offbeat conspiracy theories will feature in *The Lost Symbol*. Howard relates that **Albert Pike**, who created the 33rd degree of Masonry, was a Brigadier General in the Confederate Army, and was the founder of the Ku Klux Klan. Howard also provides a rather interesting quote from Pike: "Magic is the science of the ancient magi.... ``Magic unites in one and the same science, whatsoever Philosophy can possess that is most certain, and Religion of the Infallible and the Eternal. It perfectly ... reconciles these two terms ... faith and reason ... those who accept [magic] as a rule may give their will a sovereign power that will make them the masters of all inferior beings and of all errant spirits; that is to say, will make them the Arbiters and Kings of the World....", which is the kind of message that Mal'akh takes on board from his research into the Masons. I also found this quote interesting because the founder of the Rosicrucian Order, Christian Rosencreutz, was supposed to have been taught by the Zoroastrians (i.e. Magi), so there may be some kind of link here. Indeed, Wikipedia's entry on the Rosy Cross quotes extensively from Albert Pike regarding the 18th degree of Masonry:

The Degree of Rose Cross teaches three things;—the unity, immutability and goodness of God; the immortality of the Soul; and the ultimate defeat and extinction of evil and wrong and sorrow, by a Redeemer or Messiah, yet to come, if he has not already appeared... But [the cross's] peculiar meaning in this Degree, is that given to it by the Ancient Egyptians. Thoth or Phtha is represented on the oldest monuments carrying in his hand the Crux Ansata, or Ankh, (a Tau cross, with a ring or circle over it). [...] It was the hieroglyphic for life, and with a triangle prefixed meant life-giving. To us therefore it is the symbol of Life—of that life that emanated from the Deity, and of that Eternal Life for which we all hope; through our faith in God's infinite goodness.... The ROSE, was anciently sacred to Aurora and the Sun. It is a symbol of Dawn, of the resurrection of Light and the renewal of life, and therefore of the dawn of the first day, and more particularly of the resurrection: and the Cross and Rose together are therefore hieroglyphically to be read, the Dawn of Eternal Life which all Nations have hoped for by the advent of a Redeemer

This is all very interesting, as it suggests that a Messiah (or Antichrist) may not have already appeared.

The next Twitpic shows the Library of Congress's record for the first edition of *Angels and Demons* for some reason, with the sample text coming from the beginning of the novel, with Robert Langdon's nightmare featuring the Pyramid at

Giza. So, as we know now, this clue was suggesting that Langdon would make a visit to the Library of Congress. Next there's a reference to Latin in the clue "Our favored endeavor in the language of the Tiber". However, since we still call Rome's main river the Tiber in English, that language could also be modern day Italian, as well as Latin. I tried to translate this phrase into Latin, but couldn't find an easy fit. Some of the commentators on Dan Brown's Facebook Fan page pointed out that the Latin phrase "Annuit cœptis" appears on the reverse of the Great Seal, and is therefore on every $1 bill. However, "Annuit cœptis" translates as "He approves our undertakings" ("He" presumably referring to God), although that's not an exact translation of "Our favored endeavor". According to Wikipedia though, the artist appointed by Congress to draw up the national seal, William Barton, originally wanted to use the motto "Deo Favente Perennis" – "Enduring by the Favour of God" (17). Wikipedia also states that "Annuit cœptis" is derived from Virgil's *Aeneid*, from by a prayer by Aeneas's son to Jupiter to "favour my daring undertakings" ("audacibus annue cœptis"), which would be a neat fit, as the *Aeneid* is a mythical poem depicting the foundation of the Roman state. Indeed, I've often thought that ancient Rome could be an ideal analogy for modern America. In fact, Dan Brown stated in *The Lost Symbol* his belief that the builders of DC were intent on founding a 'New Rome'. Virgil used the same phrase in another poem, the most pastoral *Georgics* (18), which could be seen as a veiled reference to George Washington. The next clue referred to Alexander Hamilton's grave in New York, which has an obelisk on top of it, which was most likely meant as a subtle allusion to the Washington Monument.

Then there was a Twitpic of the face of God painted by Michelangelo in the Sistine Chapel with Roman numerals around his head. According to Twitterer Shugarius, this Twitter clue referred to **Deism**. As Wikipedia states "Deism is a religious and philosophical belief that a supreme being created the universe, and that this (and religious truth in general) can be determined using reason and observation of the natural world alone, without a need for either faith or organized religion... Deists typically reject most supernatural events (prophecy, miracles) and tend to assert that God (or "The Supreme Architect") has a plan for the universe that is not altered either by God intervening in the affairs of human life or by suspending the natural laws of the universe" (19). The mention of a 'Supreme Architect' suggested Freemasonry to me, and indeed, this is a notion of God that Freemason employ, so as not to give offence to the various religion beliefs of their members. Another tie with *The Lost Symbol* clues is the Wikipedia statement that the notion of the 'Supreme Architect' was also utilised by the Rosicrucians (20), although Max Heindel's seminal book on this topic was only published in 1909. More importantly with regards to *The Lost Symbol* is the Wikipedia revelation that many of the Founding Fathers, including Benjamin Franklin, Thomas Jefferson, Alexander Hamilton, and Thomas Paine, are regarded as having Deist beliefs (21).

The next clue was a Twitpic of a museum flyer at the **Smithsonian**, for a show of artwork inspired by Julius Caesar. At the bottom of the flyer are admission codes, which Twitterer kasikirby has revealed reads as "Reverse alphaorder word dash letter". Fellow Twitterer bgates87 commented that, "This might also be referencing a Caesar Cipher or a 4-Square Cipher". As we know, the Smithsonian was very much part of the novel. The Smithsonian was founded after the British scientist **James Smithson** bequeathed funds to the United States government for the "increase and diffusion" of knowledge (22), despite the fact that Smithson had never visited America. Smithson was the youngest man to have ever been elected to the Royal Society when he was voted in 1787 at the age of 22 (23). The logo of the Smithsonian is a sun, so it's quite appropriate that the head of the institution gets his sister and Langdon to do a bit of sun worshipping at the end of the novel. According to an interview that Dan Burstein did with *New York Magazine* on the 6th of September 2009, Dan Brown had been "bugging them [Smithsonian workers] for details about the museum to the point that people were getting frustrated" (24).

Washington DC was also very relevant to the next clue, which was a Twitpic of an ambigram that reads "L'Enfant". Since this was an ambigram, I presumed that John Langdon, the artist who created the ambigrams for *Angels and Demons* (and provided the inspiration for our hero's surname), must have created this image. However, Fellow Twitterer Greg Taylor handily provided the link to a website (wowtattoos.com) that can generate ambigrams – no doubt the Illuminati would have benefited from having such a tool in their day! So John Langdon was possibly not required to create the ambigrams for the clues. The clue refers to **Pierre Charles L'Enfant**, the architect who drew up the plans for Washington DC. L'Enfant, as his name suggests, was a Frenchman, who had been brought up in royal circles (25). He served as a military engineer in the Continental Army with Lafayette at first, before becoming George Washington's Captain of Engineers. After the war, he set up a civil engineering firm in New York. L'Enfant told Washington that he was interested in becoming the new capital's architect, and was duly appointed. However, L'Enfant was notoriously short of temper, and drew up plans that were far too grandiose for the money available. Washington dismissed L'Enfant in 1792, with Congress still owing him the fee for his work. L'Enfant did not endear himself to Congress with his repeated requests for the tens of thousands of dollars that he claimed were owed him. He eventually died in poverty, effectively disgraced. L'Enfant's achievements were only properly recognised in the Twentieth Century, after some prompting from the French government. In 1909, his remains were removed from Maryland, and reburied on a hill in Virginia that overlooks Washington DC. There is a well-known conspiracy theory that claims that there are **Masonic symbols built into the street plan of Washington DC**, specifically the pentagram. According to an article on the Grand Lodge of British Columbia and Yukon website (26, *Washington DC, a secret Satanic plot revealed?*), these claims first originated in Michael Baigent's and Richard Leigh's book *The Temple and the Lodge*. However, the author of the article disputes Baigent and Leigh's claims, and states that there is no evidence that L'Enfant was ever a Mason. Since this article is on a Masonic website, conspiracy theorists would be entitled to comment that Well, they would say that, wouldn't they? Besides, as we know from *The Da Vinci Code*, Robert Langdon has a more enlightened view of the pentagram, arguing that it was a symbol for the sacred feminine, long before the Church associated it with Satanic rites. Although L'Enfant's name is presented in the Twitpic as an ambigram, it's unlikely that this means that he was ever a member of the Illuminati, the Church hating cult that infiltrated the Masons according to Langdon in *Angels and Demons*.

Then there is a Twitpic of a gold coin that bears the legend "Britanniarum Regina fid def", which means "British Queen, Defender of the Faith", which was the seal of Queen Victoria. Accompanying this picture is the clue "100,000 immortalized him in the halls of science", which is a bit of a puzzle, as the coin doesn't seem to refer to any scientists. However, I then searched online to find out if there were any links between the Royal Mint and a scientist, and the name that popped up immediately was Sir Isaac Newton, who became Master of the Royal Mint in 1699, and profited handsomely from it. Newton's tomb, of course, played a pivotal role in the finale of *The Da Vinci Code*, as he was supposedly a Grand Master of the Priory of Sion. One can only presume that he has recently won a popular vote to place him in something akin to the Science Hall of Fame. The next Twitter clue read "Betrayer of double agents", and linked to a lengthy news story about Robert Philip Hanssen, an FBI operative who fed secrets to the Russians. No doubt this clue is one of several that is meant to make the reader think that Sato is a double agent in the novel.

The following Twitter clue featured six Washington DC coordinates, the first of which belongs to Dupont Circle. The next one was the White House, then Logan Circle, followed by Washington Circle, then Mount Vernon Square (home of the Historical Society of Washington DC), and then back to Dupont Circle. Dupont Circle is the home of the **House of the Temple**. This Masonic temple contains the remains of **Albert Pike**, the former Confederate general who wrote *Morals and Dogma of the Ancient and Accepted Scottish Rite of Freemasonry*, which depicts the 33 ranks of Freemasonry (27). Some observers believe that these coordinates form a pentagram, and in occultist terms, this is referred to as the **Goathead**. As the author of the website *The Revelation* (28) states, "According to occultic/Satanic doctrine, the upper four points of the Goathead (left) represent the four elements of the world, Fire, Water, Earth, and Air. The bottom fifth point represents the spirit of Lucifer. In the above photocopy of the Goathead Pentagram, the fifth point extends down into the mind of the goat, who represents Lucifer". So, those who see a pentagram in the map of Washington, see that at the bottom of the fifth point is the White House! So, Dupont Circle and Logan Circle form the top two points of the pentacle, while Washington Circle is the left hand point, and Mount Vernon Square is the right hand point. *The Revelation* goes on to point out that Dupont, Logan Circle, and the intersecting Scott Circle below them each form the crossroads for 6 roads, which together forms 666, the Number of the Beast. The House of the Temple is also apparently 13 blocks north of the White House, which supposedly means that Masons who become President have to obey the orders of their Master Masons. In *The Lost Symbol*, the House of the Temple's location north of the Washington Monument was quite important. *The Revelation* quotes an account by General Gordon Granger of a meeting between President Andrew Johnson (who was a Mason), and Master Mason Albert Pike, in which Granger was amazed that President Johnson considered himself to be subordinate to Pike. *The Revelation* goes on to report that it's important that the House of the Temple is north of the White House since "North is the place, occultists believe, where Governmental authority dwells". According to ancient lore, the Antichrist will dwell in the North, as that's the region traditionally inhabited by the lost Jewish tribe of Dan. As JewishEncyclopedia.com (29a) reveals –

But Dan became the very type of evil-doing. He was placed to the north... this being the region of darkness and evil... because of his idolatry which wrapped the world in darkness... Still further goes a tradition which identifies the serpent and the lion... with Belial..., and other Church fathers have a tradition, which can not but be of Jewish origin, that the Antichrist comes from the tribe of Dan...

The author of *The Revelation* states that the Masons who created the layout of Washington were secretly Satanists, and that the city plan proves this. So, could the Antichrist be found amongst the tribe of Dan (Brown), i.e. Dan Brown readers!
There's a fascinating article going round on the Internet that states that Albert Pike was one of the Illuminati who infiltrated the Masons. Apparently, the Illuminati wanted to overthrow all governments as well as religious bodies, and to replace them with one ruling government. They say that Albert Pike, who died in 1891, predicted that 3 World Wars would be required to create the Illuminati world order. According to the lore, Pike wrote about this to Guiseppe Mazzini on the 15th of August 1871 –

> The Third World War must be fomented by taking advantage of the differences caused by the "agentur" of the "Illuminati" between the political Zionists and the leaders of Islamic World. The war must be conducted in such a way that Islam (the Moslem Arabic World) and political Zionism (the State of Israel) mutually destroy each other. Meanwhile the other nations, once more divided on this issue will be constrained to fight to the point of complete physical, moral, spiritual and economical exhaustion...We shall unleash the Nihilists and the atheists, and we shall provoke a formidable social cataclysm which in all its horror will show clearly to the nations the effect of absolute atheism, origin of savagery and of the most bloody turmoil. Then everywhere, the citizens, obliged to defend themselves against the world minority of revolutionaries, will exterminate those destroyers of civilization, and the multitude, disillusioned with Christianity, whose deistic spirits will from that moment be without compass or direction, anxious for an ideal, but without knowing where to render its adoration, will receive the true light through the universal manifestation of the pure doctrine of Lucifer, brought finally out in the public view. This manifestation will result from the general reactionary movement which will follow the destruction of Christianity and atheism, both conquered and exterminated at the same time.

Albert Pike's prediction of World War II specifically mentioned the Nazis, an organisation that obviously didn't exist in 1871. The author of the website *ThreeWorldWars* states that the reason why Pike was able to predict the name of Hitler's party was because the Illuminati invented the Nazis (29b). Unfortunately, I can't find any mention of this story on the Internet in any article prior to 2008, so I think we can accept that Pike's supposed prediction of this Third World War is nothing but a modern hoax. If it isn't a hoax, then why didn't this prediction emerge in say, 1939?
The next clue reads as "Levi's Goat: a symbol used to accuse the righteous of evil deeds". As Nick Johnson writes on his blog, *The Millennial Freemason*, this is a reference to Eliphas Levi's famous image of **Baphomet**, "which some Anti-Masons believe is a deity revered by Freemasons, another complete untruth" (30).

Baphomet, was, of course, the occult deity that the Templars were accused of worshipping, and it was this that partly justified their burning at the stake during the purge ordered by Phillip IV of France, as Langdon related in *The Da Vinci Code*. Although Nick Johnson interprets that it's modern Freemasonry that's being accused of evil deeds, the clue probably refers to this persecution of the Templars, Freemasonry's supposed forebears. According to Wikipedia, Eliphas Levi was inspired to start his magical writings after meeting the English novelist Edward Bulwer-Lytton, who was the president of a Rosicrucian order. Levi created the most famous image of Baphomet in 1854 for his book *Dogmas and Rituals of High Magic*. According to About.com's entry on the demon, the name 'Baphomet' is derived from the name of the Prophet Muhammad (31), so it seems that one of the main charges against the Templars was that they had become too enamoured of Islam during their time in the Holy Land. Levi described the image of Baphomet thus –

The goat on the frontispiece carries the sign of the pentagram on the forehead, with one point at the top, a symbol of light, his two hands forming the sign of hermetism, the one pointing up to the white moon of Chesed, the other pointing down to the black one of Geburah. This sign expresses the perfect harmony of mercy with justice. His one arm is female, the other male like the ones of the androgyn of Khunrath, the attributes of which we had to unite with those of our goat because he is one and the same symbol. The flame of intelligence shining between his horns is the magic light of the universal balance, the image of the soul elevated above matter, as the flame, whilst being tied to matter, shines above it. The beast's head expresses the horror of the sinner, whose materially acting, solely responsible part has to bear the punishment exclusively; because the soul is insensitive according to its nature and can only suffer when it materializes. The rod standing instead of genitals symbolizes eternal life, the body covered with scales the water, the semi-circle above it the atmosphere, the feathers following above the volatile. Humanity is represented by the two breasts and the androgyn arms of this sphinx of the occult sciences.

According to Catherine Beyer, author of the About.com article, the image conveys the nineteenth century occult concept of polarity, dividing the world into male and female energies. The image also represents the four Platonic elements: earth, water, air, and fire. This very much reflects the themes of *The Da Vinci Code* and *Angels & Demons* (i.e. the cardinals murdered in Robert Langdon's first adventure were branded with the words *Earth*, *Water*, *Air*, and *Fire*). Indeed, I believe that Mal'akh intends to become all that Baphomet symbolises.

Catherine Beyer goes on to write that, "Levi describes Baphomet as the sphinx of the occult sciences... They originated in Egypt, where they were probably connected with guardianship, among other things. By Levi's time, the Freemasons were also using sphinxes as symbols of guardians of secrets and mysteries". Indeed, there are some sphinxes outside the House of the Temple. Eliphas Levi was briefly a Mason himself and, as the website of the Grand Lodge of British Columbia and Yukon relates, following his initiation, Levi announced that, "I come to bring to you your lost traditions, the exact knowledge of your signs and symbols, and consequently to show you the goal for which your association was constituted" (32). Such a pronouncement would have greatly intrigued a symbologist such as Robert Langdon. Unfortunately, the other Masons present at this meeting were none too impressed at Levi's claims that their symbols derived from the Kabbalah. After his ideas were dismissed, Levi left Freemasonry, stating that since the Pope had excommunicated the Fraternity, they could not be as tolerant of Catholics as they were of all other religions, so the Catholicism of his youth was obviously still close to his heart.

Probably the most damaging allegations of Satanic practices within the Mason came in the 1890s from French writer Leo Taxil, in a series of pamphlets entitled *La France chrétienne anti-maçonnique*. His publishers used an edited version of Levi's image of Baphomet to promote his work. However, Taxil later admitted that he had fabricated the Satanic allegations against the Masons in a bid to bait the Catholic Church, which was well known to be anti-Masonic. It would appear that Taxil found his Catholic upbringing to be far less favourable than Levi's. Unfortunately, Taxil's hoax caught the public imagination, and the stories he invented are still circulated in anti-Masonic literature (33).

Wikipedia relates that Eliphas Levi had a great influence of the **Hermetic Order of the Golden Dawn** (34), the organisation founded in the late nineteenth century in Britain that had, in its turn, a huge impact on twentieth century occultism. As Wikipedia states, the Golden Dawn was founded by three Freemasons, who were also members of a Rosicrucian order (35). Although the initiation ceremonies and hierarchy were similar to that of Freemasonry, they were obviously more enlightened, as women were allowed equal status with men in the Golden Dawn. Amongst its members were such luminaries as Bram Stoker, Arnold Bennett, E. Nesbit, Maud Gonne, Arthur Edward Waite, and William Butler Yeats. Levi certainly had a huge impact on probably the most controversial Golden Dawn member, **Aleister Crowley**. The movement's founding documents were written in ciphers, which would undoubtedly excite a symbologist such as Robert Langdon. At the time, I thought that the Anglocentric Golden Dawn would unlikely to make an appearance in *The Lost Symbol*, since I knew that Langdon would be spending much of his time in DC. I also thought that the Hermetic Order of the Golden Dawn no longer existed in any practical form. However, their writings do live on, and certainly influenced Mal'akh to a considerable degree.

The next Twitter clue contained a hyperlink to a picture of George Washington laying the cornerstone for the Capitol in a Masonic ceremony on September 18th 1793. The clue also asks where the cornerstone is; since it's current location is unknown. The succeeding Twitter clue is a Twitpic of a handwritten letter, with the legend "Apply heat", which may be a reference to invisible ink and probably the incandescent clue on the Masonic Pyramid. We're back on the espionage theme with the next clue, which is a Twitpic of six men, who are described as conspirators. The clue asks for the name of the leader of these conspirators. After putting a couple of the men's names into Google, I found that they were both members of the Duquesne Spy Ring, a bunch of German spies captured in America during the Second World War. However, this clue is probably a sly reference to Aleister Crowley's activities in the US during the First World War, when it was claimed that he was a British spy.

After that is a similarly puzzling image of the infamous Blue screen of death that afflicted all Windows users prior to the release of XP. There's a sequence of numbers that don't appear to mean anything, "0402 0701 0101 0201" etc. However, Twitterer avalonssari has pointed out that the words are also significant, particularly "fatal sequence", which is another name for the "Tytler Cycle". The Tytler cycle is believed to have been derived by Alexander Fraser Tytler, Lord Woodhouselee, a British writer and lawyer and writer who died in 1813, although the authorship of the whole cycle is still debated (36). The Tytler Cycle reads as follows:

A democracy is always temporary in nature; it simply cannot exist as a permanent form of government. A democracy will continue to exist up until the time that voters discover that they can vote themselves generous gifts from the public treasury. From that moment on, the majority always votes for the candidates who promise the most benefits from the public treasury, with the result that every democracy will finally collapse due to loose fiscal policy, which is always followed by a dictatorship. The average age of the world's greatest civilizations from the beginning of history has been about 200 years. During those 200 years, these nations always progressed through the following sequence:

From bondage to spiritual faith... From spiritual faith to great courage... From courage to liberty... From liberty to abundance... From abundance to complacency... From complacency to apathy... From apathy to dependence... From dependence back into bondage.

Tytler was believed to have been writing about the causes of the downfall of Athenian democracy over 2,000 years ago. Yet it's not surprising that this Cycle still has such currency in America, whose democracy is, of course, just over 200 years old. Such fears of the downfall of American civilisation are part of the background of *The Lost Symbol*.

Following this is a Twitpic of a six-pointed star with a cross in the background. The clue refers to an order of "Ascended Masters". According to Wikipedia, Ascended Masters "are believed to be spiritually enlightened beings who in past incarnations were ordinary humans, but who have undergone a process of spiritual transformation" (37). One organisation that propounds this idea is The White Eagle Lodge, and as other Twitterers have pointed out, you can still see the name of this organisation in the Twitpic, so it must be the one that the clue is referring to. The White Eagle Lodge was founded by the British medium Grace Cooke, and was named after her Native American spirit guide. Her belief in reincarnation was very much influenced by the writings of Eliphas Levi (38). It's possible that Mal'akh was intending to become the ultimate Ascended Master.

Another Twitpic formed the basis of the next clue, which featured a saint-like man against a fervent purple background. The text clue mentioned an "inspirer of the constitution", and I came up with the name of the Seventeenth Century English Philosopher John Locke, whose liberal ideas did help fan the flames of the American Revolution. However, the clue also refers to the man in the image, who does not look like Locke, as an "Ascended master", so I next searched online for a link between Locke and an "Ascended master", and came up with the name of **Saint Germain**. Apparently, John Locke was greatly inspired by Francis Bacon, and according to occult stories, Saint Germain was really Francis Bacon. Not only that, but Bacon was the secret lovechild of Queen Elizabeth I and Robert Dudley, brought up in secret by the Bacon family. However, Francis Bacon somehow knew of his true royal lineage, which he hinted at through his plays (which are usually ascribed to one William Shakespeare). Other legends state that the Count of St. Germain was (is) immortal, an alchemist with knowledge of the Elixir of Life, and that he was a Rosicrucian. His name is apparently the French version of the Latin "Sanctus Germanus", which means "Holy Brother". C. W. Leadbetter, an early member of the Theosophical Society, claimed to have met St. Germain in Rome in 1926, and described him as wearing a purple cloak with a seven-pointed star on its clasp (39). His legend is also promoted via the White Eagle Lodge, so we can be fairly sure that he is the gentleman to whom this clue alludes. In fact, we can be damn sure that it's St. Germain, as the author of the Twitter clues made the unusual decision to publicly tell a Twitterer that they were correct, and that Saint Germain "was rumored to be the name that Francis Bacon chose as his Ascended Master name".

In 1745, Horace Walpole gave an account of a Count St. Germain who was arrested on suspicion of espionage during the Jacobite rebellion:

The other day they seized an odd man, who goes by the name of Count St. Germain. He has been here these two years, and will not tell who he is, or whence, but professes [two wonderful things, the first] that he does not go by his right name; [and the second that he never had any dealings with any woman... He sings, plays on the violin wonderfully, composes, is mad, and not very sensible. He is called an Italian, a Spaniard, a Pole; a somebody that married a great fortune in Mexico, and ran away with her jewels to Constantinople; a priest, a fiddler, a vast nobleman. The Prince of Wales has had unsatiated curiosity about him, but in vain. However, nothing has been made out against him; he is released; and, what convinces me that he is not a gentleman, stays here, and talks of his being taken up for a spy.

However, it must be pointed out that Horace Walpole was the author of Gothic fantasies, such as *The Castle of Otranto*, which could have led him to embellish the tale. According to other legends, St. Germain was born in 1561, and lived over 350 years, and also used the names Christopher Marlowe, Edmund Spenser, Montaigne, and Cervantes! Oh, and he was Merlin, and Roger Bacon as well as Francis Bacon. The reason why he's so important to the background of *The Lost Symbol* is summed up in a couple of sentences in the most popular Internet site about Saint Germain: "He founded Rosicrucianism and Freemasonry in England. He did this under the name Francis Bacon. It was his dream to create in America a new country free of corruption, greed, and dictatorial monarchies. He was instrumental in formulating the Declaration of Independence and the constitution of the United States as they were being written by his Masonic followers who founded this nation" (40).

The next Twitter clue refers to an airstair escape. From that clue, I found a Wikipedia entry on D. B. Cooper, a man who hijacked an airplane on the 24th of November 1971. As the clue states, he requested his ransom to be paid in unmarked $20 bills, and escaped via an airstair. No one knows what happened to him, as he has never been caught, and the authorities suspect that he did not survive his attempt at a parachute landing. This may be a reference to a fugitive that has evaded capture, like Mal'akh when he first tried to steal the pyramid, or it could be just a reference to a heavenly staircase, an image that also features in the novel.

The Twitter clue master was also unusually helpful with regards to the next clue, which featured a Twitpic of a six-pointed star with a flower in the centre. According to the clue master, the image is of a unicursal hexagram (i.e. a six-pointed star drawn in one continuous line). According to Wikipedia, "Aleister Crowley's adaptation of the unicursal hexagram placed a five petaled rose, (symbolizing the divine) in the center; the symbol as a whole making eleven (five petals of the rose plus six points of the hexagram), the number of divine union" (41). The original clue referred to "His version", so the Twitpic is undoubtedly an image of Aleister Crowley's creation. Aleister Crowley was of course, a notorious British occultist, described by some as "The wickedest man in the World". He was a controversial member of the Hermetic Order of the Golden Dawn, and wrote the *Book of Law* for his religion, Thelema. According to the *Thelemapedia*, the five-pointed star (pentagram) represents the microcosm, while the six-pointed star (hexagram) represents the macrocosm. The Thelemapedia also states that, "closer inspection reveals that the hexagram is the union of elemental glyphs for Fire and Water and, as such, is also a symbol of the Great Work - the union of opposites. The symbol can be further analyzed to reveal the glyphs of Earth and Air as well, indicating that it's not simply macrocosmic, but includes the microcosm too. From this it can be seen that the Hexagram is similar to the Rosy Cross" (42).

After this is a Twitpic of the sun's rays enclosed within a triangle. I hadn't the foggiest idea what this symbol represented, but thankfully fellow Twitterer avalonssari recognised it as belonging to the Hermetic Order of the Golden Dawn. The text clue also stated that, "Their documents are encoded", and indeed the Golden Dawn do keep what they call "Cipher Manuscripts" (43). Then we were given coordinates for, unusually, a place that is under water (25.765267, -79.272451). Nonplussed, I clicked on a little blue square nearby these coordinates in Google Earth, which came up with a reference to "Bimini Road, aka the Road to Atlantis", although it's also known as the Bimini Wall, as many people, like me, think that it does indeed resemble a wall more than a road. The clue also asks whether Man or Nature created this underwater structure. Most experts have concluded that it's a natural geological feature, rather than manmade. More relevant to *The Lost Symbol* is the fact that **Sir Francis Bacon** wrote a utopian book called ***The New Atlantis***. Wikipedia's entry on *The New Atlantis* states that, "Released in 1627, this utopian novel was his creation of an ideal land where 'generosity and enlightenment, dignity and splendor, piety and public spirit' were the commonly held qualities of the inhabitants of Bensalem. In this work, he portrayed a vision of the future of human discovery and knowledge. The plan and organization of his ideal college, '**Solomon's House**', envisioned the modern research university in both applied and pure science" (44). So, this is yet another reason why the Solomons are thus named in *The Lost Symbol*, and you could also argue that in the context of the novel, 'Solomon's House' could refer to the House of the Temple. Indeed, you could argue that the Solomons are representative of modern America, with the materialism of Mal'akh clashing against the philanthropic enlightenment of his father. I clicked on the Wikipedia hyperlink for

Solomon's House, as that sounded like a Masonic reference to the Temple of Solomon, and was intrigued to discover that Bacon's concept of Solomon's House had inspired the creation of the Royal Society in 1660. All this sounds very much like that passage that I quoted from the Saint Germain website: "He founded Rosicrucianism and Freemasonry in England. He did this under the name Francis Bacon. It was his dream to create in America a new country free of corruption, greed, and dictatorial monarchies" (45). So I think this clue about Bimini Road could well be an obscure reference to Sir Francis Bacon. Robert Anton Wilson and Robert Shea's *The Illuminatus! Trilogy* also featured Atlantis, and may well have provided some inspiration for Dan Brown. Ignatius Loyola Donnelly is another writer that expounded greatly on theories of the lost civilisation in his 1882 book *Atlantis: The Antediluvian World*, in which he argued that the Classical World was descended from its Neolithic culture (46). This is how Donnelly summarised the main ideas in his book –

That there once existed in the Atlantic Ocean, opposite the mouth of the Mediterranean Sea, a large island, which was…known to the ancient world as Atlantis. That Atlantis was the region where man first rose from a state of barbarism to civilization… That it was the true Antediluvian world; the Garden of Eden… representing a universal memory of a great land, where early mankind dwelt for ages in peace and happiness… That the gods and goddesses of the ancient Greeks… the Hindoos… were simply the kings, queens, and heroes of Atlantis; and the acts attributed to them in mythology are a confused recollection of real historical events… That the mythology of Egypt and Peru represented the original religion of Atlantis, which was sun-worship… That the oldest colony formed by the Atlanteans was probably in Egypt… That the Phœnician alphabet, parent of all the European alphabets, was derived from an Atlantis alphabet, which was also conveyed from Atlantis to the Mayas of Central America… That Atlantis was the original seat of the Aryan or Indo-European family of nations, as well as of the Semitic peoples… That Atlantis perished in a terrible convulsion of nature, in which the whole island sunk into the ocean, with nearly all its inhabitants… That a few persons escaped in ships and on rafts, and, carried to the nations east and west the tidings of the appalling catastrophe, which has survived to our own time in the Flood and Deluge legends of the different nations of the old and new worlds.

So, *Atlantis: The Antediluvian World* is exactly the kind of pseudohistory that Dan Brown loves to utilise whenever he's researching a new book, as the plagiarism trial revealed. Interestingly enough, in 1888, Donnelly published a book called *The Great Cryptogram: Francis Bacon's cipher in Shakespeare's Plays*, in which he argued that Sir Francis Bacon had written all of Shakespeare's plays. Then the clues began to state that Robert Langdon's adversary would be revealed when his Facebook fan page got 100,000 members, but unfortunately, this target was just missed prior to publication.

The next clue featured an image of the top of the Dome of the Rock in Jerusalem, which contains the foundation stone from where Muslims believe the Prophet Muhammad ascended to Heaven, accompanied by the Angel Gabriel. As the

Dome is on the Temple Mount, Jews believe that it may be the location of the Holy of Holies, the inner sanctuary of the Temple that could only be entered by the High Priest on Yom Kippur (47). The Templars believed the Dome of the Rock was the site of the Temple of Solomon, and called it the "Templum Domini", and featured it on their seals. Curiously enough, The Templars used it as their model when building their churches in Europe, which explains why their churches were round, rather than the customary cruciform. No wonder it was so easy to accuse the Templars of having Muslim sympathies!

The next clue refers to something that 12 inches across and 5 feet high, "bound in silver and fallen from the sky, that a pilgrim should kiss once in his life". "Fallen from the sky" made me think of a meteorite, so I searched on Google for "sacred meteorite", and eventually came across a Wikipedia entry on the Black Stone (or al-Hajar-ul-Aswad in Arabic). It's the eastern cornerstone of the Kaaba, the ancient sacred stone building towards which Muslims pray, in the center of the Grand Mosque in Mecca, Saudi Arabia (48). It is 5 feet off the ground, and 12 inches in diameter, and is encased in silver. Pilgrims do indeed try to kiss the Black Stone during the Hajj. The stone was broken into seven pieces during a theft over a thousand years ago. As Wikipedia states, "According to Islamic tradition, the Stone fell from Heaven to show Adam and Eve where to build an altar and offer a sacrifice to God. The Altar became the first temple on Earth. Muslims believe that the stone was originally pure and dazzling white, but has since turned black because of the sins it has absorbed over the years. Islamic tradition holds that Adam's altar and the stone were lost in the process of Noah's Flood and forgotten. It was Abraham who found the Black Stone at the original site of Adam's altar when the Archangel Gabriel revealed it to him. Abraham ordered his son—and the ancestor of Muhammad--Ishmael to build a new temple in which to imbed the Stone". The new temple that Ishmael built was the Kaaba itself. It's believed that the stone may have come from a meteor impact that destroyed the legendary city of Wabar over 6,000 years ago. The story goes that this fabulous city was destroyed by fire from the heavens due to the wickedness of its king. It's possible that Abraham could also have made the **Akedah knife** that Mal'akh uses from the same meteorite.

The next clue keeps referred to a place 40 miles north east of Lemnos, which turns out to be the island of Samothrace. However, there may have been a mistake in this clue, as fellow Twitterer Greg Taylor pointed out that the building featured in the Twitpic, Simonopetra Monastery, is actually 40 miles north west of Lemnos, not north east, and the Twitter clue master acknowledged that he was correct. The monastery, which must have been named after Simon Peter (St. Peter, the rock of the church), is currently inhabited by brothers from Holy Monastery of Great Meteoron. This latter monastery's name comes from the same root as meteorite, meaning "heavenly rocks", or "rocks suspended in air", as the monasteries in this region are built on seemingly inaccessible sandstone pillars. Coincidentally (or not), another of these monasteries, the Holy Trinity, features in a novel by Chris Kuzneski called *The Lost Throne*, in which a lost treasure is guarded by a secret group of guardians who will stop at nothing to protect it… Oh, and the hero is an academic… However, I believe the real reason why Dan Brown created this clue was to allude to the name of Peter Solomon, because, as above, 'Peter' is derived as from the Greek for 'rock'. I will also argue later in this book that this clue acquires more significance when you consider my argument that the Solomons are based on the Rockefellers.

A more ancient clue followed, as the Twitter clue master mentioned the death of one of Dante's foes in 1303. This foe of Dante must be Pope Boniface VIII, who Dante placed in a circle of Hell in his *Divine Comedy*. Again, this probably an oblique reference to the Templars, as Boniface also had a feud with Philip IV of France, the king who famously ordered the destruction of the Templars. Boniface repeatedly made clear in his papal bulls that he regarded the papacy as having supremacy over kings and princes. Unfortunately, Philip IV of France had a more contrary view, and his army captured Boniface at his Anagni retreat. Philip demanded that Boniface resign the papacy, to which Boniface replied that he would "rather die". Unfortunately, Boniface had rather paved the way for his own downfall by persuading his predecessor, Celestine V, to resign the papacy, and had thus set a precedent. Boniface died soon after his release from captivity, and was probably murdered.

The succeeding clue also had a papal link, as it featured a hyperlink to the Google Map entry on Waterloo Bridge in London, with the text "Hanging there?" Having written that, I think the Twitter clue master's pinpointed the wrong bridge, since it was at Blackfriars Bridge that Italian banker Roberto Calvi was found hanged in 1982, presumably murdered. The British press nicknamed him 'God's Banker', as the Vatican was the main shareholder in his bank, Banco Ambrosiano, which also collapsed in 1982. The Mafia is believed to have been involved in killing Calvi, as they had utilised Banco Ambrosiano for money laundering, and presumably lost funds when the bank collapsed. However, the more relevant link to *The Lost Symbol* is that the bank's downfall was initiated by a police raid in 1981 on the Italian **Propaganda Due Masonic lodge** to arrest the Worshipful Master Licio Gelli, a lodge that Calvi had close links to. Some very powerful Italian men, such as Silvio Berlusconi, were discovered to be members of the lodge. According to some conspiracy theories, Calvi may have played a role in the untimely death of Pope John Paul I, as it was rumoured that the new Pope was intent on clearing up the Vatican finances. The Twitter clue master's geography became somewhat awry during these latter puzzles, so the answer to the question "Hanging there?" is "no"!

The next clue is a riddle that speaks of a "who could carry a child but birthed only words", which was solved by Twitterer bgates87 as relating to George Eliot, the British woman novelist who adopted a male pseudonym in order to publish her work. Of course, many characters in Dan Brown's books adopt pseudonyms for more nefarious reasons. Like Chaucer, she is commemorated in Poets' Corner in Westminster Abbey. George Eliot turned her back on her Christian faith, and was buried in a part of Highgate cemetery reserved for religious dissenters. What probably piqued Dan Brown's interest is the obelisk that sits atop her grave. There's also an Egyptian tone to the next clue, as Twitterer bgates87 identified it as being Nefertiti's cartouche (her name in hieroglyphics). Nefertiti's name means "the beautiful (perfect) one has arrived". She's the most famous Egyptian queen after Cleopatra, and she was thought to have been co-regent with her king, Akhenaten. Nefertiti and Akhenaten made waves in Egyptian culture by only worshipping the sun god, Aten, so their religion was a form of early monotheism. Tutankhamun succeeded them, so this is possibly a veiled reference to the entry in

Howard Carter's diary that features on the Kryptos sculpture. Then there are a series of clues that feature powerful, innovative women with a link to rape. There's Boudicca, whose daughters were raped by the Romans, and the later Baroque Roman artist Artemisia Gentileschi, who was raped. This brings to mind the Hassassin's attempt to rape Vittoria Vetra in *Angels and Demons*, and the fact that Mal'akh symbolically rapes Katherine in *The Lost Symbol*.

The following clue is written in a language I don't recognise "٣-٩-٢٠-٢٥-٢٣-٨-٥-١٨-٥-٤-٥-٣", but Twitterer deetective has written that they are Eastern Arabic numbers (49), which do indeed get a brief mention in the novel. The final clue was an NBC one, which featured the reporter in what appeared to be an indoor tropical greenhouse, so I guessed that this location is the United States Botanic Garden, which is quite close to the Capitol Building in Washington DC.

A critique of *The Lost Symbol*

On the 12th of September, the UK's Mail on Sunday invited its readers to "Be the *first in the world* to read the new book by the author of *The Da Vinci Code*", so I decided to avail myself of this opportunity to read the first couple of chapters a little early.

The extract starts off with one of those Fact boxes that Dan Brown has utilised at the beginning of each of his Robert Langdon adventures. In *The Da Vinci Code,* the Fact box declared that the Priory of Sion was a real organisation, although it's commonly regarded as a hoax. *The Lost Symbol*'s Fact box immediately refers to the Kryptos sculpture, which is in the grounds of the CIA's headquarters in Langley, Virginia. James Sanborn created this sculpture in 1990 with the assistance of a former CIA employee Ed Scheidt, who, appropriately enough, was Chairman of the CIA Cryptographic Center. 'Kryptos' means hidden in Greek, and the sculpture is based on the theme of surveillance work. Only the first 3 sections of the sculpture have been solved, with no solution for the 4th section apparently forthcoming. However, Sanborn did give the CIA director of the time, William H. Webster, a complete solution to the puzzle (presumably it's the document mentioned in the Fact box that contains the phrase, "It's buried out there somewhere"). The first section of Kryptos reads, intriguingly, "Between subtle shading and the absence of light lies the nuance of Iqlusion". The last word, Iqlusion, is spelt correctly, and I guess, could mean "playful intelligence", if you take "IQ" to refer to intelligence together with the Latin for "play". The second section refers to something that was totally invisible, and that they used the Earth's magnetic field. It also states that the information (some secret?) was buried underground. It also gives coordinates that are 200 feet south of the sculpture. Sanborn also placed other sculptures around the grounds, including a slab with a compass rose on it. This may be important, as a lot of the Twitter clues have made references to symbols that feature roses. Even more significant may be the fact that "a compass needle carved onto one of the rocks is pulled off due north by a lodestone that Mr. Sanborn placed nearby" (1). So, the "they" mentioned in the second section of the puzzle could be Sanborn himself, since he has utilized the Earth's magnetic field to have this compass point in a direction other than due North.

The third part of the Kryptos puzzle builds things up nicely by roughly quoting an extract from Howard Carter's diary about the his first impressions of opening Tutankhamun's tomb –

With trembling hands I made a tiny breach in the upper left-hand corner. And then, widening the hole a little, I inserted the candle and peered in. The hot air escaping from the chamber caused the flame to flicker, but presently details of the room within emerged from the mist. Can you see anything?

Dan Brown placed hints on the cover of *The Da Vinci Code* that the Kryptos sculpture would feature in *The Lost Symbol*. However, Dan Brown and his publishers made a deliberate discrepancy on the cover of *The Da Vinci Code* when they referred to the coordinates printed on Kryptos: one digit is different.

The Fact box also refers to a body called the SMSC. However, I don't know which organisation this acronym refers to yet. It also mentions the Institute of Noetic Sciences, which was co-founded by former astronaut Edgar Mitchell in 1973. The institute, or IONS, derives its name from the Greek word 'nous' (i.e. 'intuition'), and seeks to explore "extended human capacities", such as survival of consciousness after bodily death (2). An article on the IONS website entitled *What the Bleep Do We Know?!* describes Mitchell's moment of epiphany (3) –

As he watched the planet Earth floating in the vastness of space he was engulfed by a profound sense of universal connectedness. In Mitchell's own words: "The presence of divinity became almost palpable, and I knew that life in the universe was not just an accident based on random processes... The knowledge came to me directly.

Prologue: the call to adventure *The Lost Symbol* kicks off with an initiation ceremony in the House of the Temple, the Masonic centre in Dupont Circle that I previously mentioned on p.19. Cable-tows are indeed used in Masonic initiation ceremonies, as the website MasonicWorld.com states, "To some of us this non-symbolical idea and use of the cable-tow is very strange, in view of what Masonry is in general, and particularly in its ceremonies of initiation. For Masonry is a chamber of imagery. The whole Lodge is a symbol. Every object, every act is symbolical. The whole fits together into a system of symbolism by which Masonry veils, and yet reveals, the truth it seeks to teach to such as have eyes to see and are ready to receive it" (1) - so, an inspection of a Masonic lodge could keep Robert Langdon very busy indeed! Presumably the use of the skull is just there as a memento mori. I was very interested in the phrase that, "Here all men were equals", and I found an interesting *New York Times* article from the 28th of February 1909 in which the Ohio Grand Lodge was criticised for making President-Elect Taft a Mason on sight, as "Prince and Paupers stand equal in the eyes of Masonry, and I deprecate the lodge that allows Masonry to fall at the feet of power" (2). The speaker, Grand Secretary Ehlers, then stated that the Alpha Lodge of Newark was correct to allow entry to African Americans as they are free citizens, although for some unspoken reason, Ehlers also said that, "I personally cannot extend my own fellowship to the Negro".

The House of the Temple is indeed based on the Tomb of Mausolus at Halicarnassus, which was one of Seven Wonders of the Ancient World. The original mausoleum is now in ruins, partly due to the Knights of St. John of Malta (an institution similar to the Templars) utilising the ruins in the building of Bodrum Castle. The two bodies referred to are those of Albert Pike (see p.16, and pp. 20-21), and John Henry Cowles, who was the Sovereign Grand Commander from 1921 to 1952. The first paragraph describing the Temple Room has a familiar ring to it: "the Temple room was lit by a series of precisely arranged candles... Their dim glow was aided only by a pale shaft of moonlight that filtered down through the expansive oculus in the ceiling and illuminated the room's most startling feature". Could this be a sly reference to *Angels and Demons*, which featured the oculus (i.e. 'round opening' from the Latin for 'eye') in the dome of the Pantheon?

The 'hoodwink' mentioned in the first degree of the initiation is an archaic term for a blindfold, which could have been the name employed to mask birds until ready to strike at prey in falconry. When they're hoodwinked, the initiate is said to be "A poor candidate in a state of darkness", and when the hoodwink is removed, they're said to have been brought "into the wisdom and light of Masonry" (3). For some reason, this reminds me of the opening clue from the Kryptos sculpture, "Between subtle shading and the absence of light lies the nuance of Iqlusion". The words that are employed in the ceremony are based on the traditional First Degree initiation, such as those set down by Richard Carlile in the *Manual of Freemasonry* from 1825.

So it would seem that Freemasons can rest easy, if the Prologue is anything to go by, as it would appear that they are the innocent party being infiltrated by some malicious force, although they probably have some dodgy members. Presumably the initiate is this novel's version of the murderous Silas or Hassassin. Note that despite his nerves, his "muscular frame" is referred to. I'm not quite sure what the initiate is referring to when he thinks, "Tonight... something is taking place within these walls that has never once occurred in the history of this brotherhood". Robert Langdon stated in *Angels and Demons* that the Illuminati had infiltrated the Masons, so it's not the first time that someone has become an initiate for dishonest purposes. Therefore I believe that some violent act will occur within the House of the Temple, as I don't think there's ever been a murder within a Masonic temple. Some Masonic rituals are based around a murder in the Temple of Solomon. A website called *Solomon's Temple* provides a succinct account of this ritual (4) -

The modern Freemasons' Society developed from the Phoenician masons, which is why their rituals are kept secret. The Freemasons' name the chief mason working on the temple as Huram Abiff, son of a Tyrian widow, presumably the same person as Huram the widow's son who did the metalwork. One of the Freemasons' rituals is a re-enactment of the mugging and [murder] of Huram in the temple by Israelite workmen who wanted to extract the secrets of architectural design and construction from him. The ritual drama has his assailants attacking Huram at each corner of the temple with builders' tools before they finally kill him because he won't hand over the secret knowledge.

The assailants' motive was said to be greed, because if they knew Huram's secret skills, they could command higher wages.

I suspect that we'll also see more of the Supreme Worshipful Master, so I'm going to look out for further references to a silver-haired man in his fifties with gray eyes. The initiate's malevolent internal thoughts may be directed to the Supreme Worshipful Master, but I have the feeling that he is more concerned about threatening Freemasonry as a whole.

Chapter 1 Robert Langdon's first appearance in *The Lost Symbol* is similar to his previous adventures, in that he is asleep. As in *Angels and Demons*, he is dreaming, but his dream appears to form part of a memory. Again, as we know from the previous novels, Langdon hates enclosed spaces such as lifts, due to a childhood accident in which he fell into a well, and was trapped for hours. It's significant that he's in the Eiffel Tower, as the designer, Gustave Eiffel, is said to have been a Freemason. Gustave Eiffel also provided the internal structure of the Statue of Liberty, a gift from the French people to mark the United States' centenary. Puddle iron was invented at the end of the Eighteenth century, and its increased carbon content means that it has a higher tensile strength than ordinary wrought iron. Puddle iron was also employed in the construction of the Statue of Liberty. Not surprising then that these monuments crop up in a dream after Langdon had been reviewing Masonic symbology.

There's a huge bit of Masonic symbology present in the name of Langdon's mentor, Peter Solomon. We know that Dan Brown usually tends to have a reason when choosing his character's names, so his mentor's nomenclature is undoubtedly derived from King Solomon, the builder of the temple that Masons revere. His first name also appears intentional, as 'Peter' is derived from the Greek for 'Rock'. There's a Christian element too, as Christ made Simon Peter the 'rock' of his Church, and there is also a casual allusion to building. Peter Solomon would also appear to Langdon's rock in his role as mentor, although, at 58 years old, he's not that much older than Langdon. Note that Solomon's soft gray eyes are specifically referred to, so Dan Brown is leading us to think that Peter Solomon is the Supreme Worshipful Master of the House of the Temple. It's interesting to note that Peter Solomon is also a scientist, so this may lead to some science fictional elements in the novel. His name is also fascinating from the perspective that the original title of the novel was going to be *The Solomon Key*, which I, and no doubt many others, took to be some kind of key or artefact from King Solomon, but which may now derive from the more modern Peter Solomon.

The obelisk referred to is the Washington Monument, built to commemorate the United States' first president. It is the world's tallest obelisk, and was the world's tallest building when it was completed in 1888. Although it took a very long time to build, as Freemasons had marked the laying of the cornerstone in a ceremony in 1848. It's significant that the "meticulous geometry of the streets" of Washington is remarked upon at this early stage in the novel by the narrator, as we know that there is at least one conspiracy rumour about their layout, as mentioned in the Twitter clues.

The novel is not set in September, but in the January of an unspecified year. 'January', is of course, derived from the Roman deity Janus, who was the god of doorways. So, January is a very appropriate month to open a novel about

Freemasons, a society devoted to the secrets of classical architecture. Janus is often depicted as having two heads, which face in opposite directions, and was, of course, the pseudonym adopted by the villain of *Angels and Demons*. Since the novel's set in winter, much of the action will no doubt take place in the dark given the 12-hour timeframe. For some reason, the *Mail on Sunday* has specifically quoted that Pam "spoke with an exuberance that was almost unsettling". Pam goes on to say, "'My book group read your book about the sacred feminine and the church! What a scandal that one caused!'" It appears that she is referring to Langdon's book *Symbols of the Lost Sacred Feminine*, rather than *The Da Vinci Code*!

Pam recognises Langdon from his usual 'uniform' of Harris Tweed jacket, which is akin to what Dan Brown wears himself. Langdon could retort that he's not wearing a uniform, since everyone else wears the casual uniform of T-shirt and jeans. I'm betting that it's not long before Langdon's legendary Mickey Mouse watch is remarked upon. Dan Brown also attended Phillips Exeter Academy, along with other exalted alumni such as President Franklin Pierce, Ulysses S. Grant jr., Gore Vidal, John Irving, Peter Benchley, and some of the Rockefeller clan. The cravat does indeed stem from an article of clothing worn by Croatian mercenaries, although it appears that they wore them all the time, not just before battle. However, an article by Olivia Andrews online, *History of the neck-tie*, states that the Croatian mercenaries originally got this adornment from the fascalia worn by Roman orators (1). I suspect that 'fascalia' is derived from 'fasces', which is the Latin word for 'bundles', most often employed as the 'fasces lictoriae' ('bundles of the lictors'), as a symbol of power in ancient Rome. This ancient symbol of power is present on many Washington DC monuments, as those seeking to represent the concept of governmental power often adopt this symbol. Unfortunately, Mussolini's Fascists derived the name of their party from it. Langdon refers to ties as "little nooses", a metaphor that is often used to describe the cable-tow in Masonic first-degree initiations, so this is probably a deliberate reference to the Prologue.

It seems appropriate that the car that picks up Langdon is named after the United States' most famous presidents, and none too auspicious that he was one that was assassinated. Beltway Limousine is a real company, so Dan Brown may be indulging in some product placement by way of thanks for good customer service. Dan Brown's employment of the cliché "no stone left unturned" is probably a reference to Peter Solomon's rocky first name. It's interesting to learn that Langdon's rendezvous at the Capitol Building is supposed to be a secret one, but one that some nefarious person has prior knowledge of, judging by the "lone figure" eagerly awaiting his arrival some ten miles away from the Capitol.

Chapter 2 The sinister Mal'akh has a very interesting name that could have a couple of meanings. I usually take 'Mal' to mean 'bad', or more correctly, this means a disease or disorder, as in 'malady'. 'Akh' is an Egyptian word meaning 'magically effective one', and relates to the dead, and could even connote 'ghost' (1). So, Mal'akh could mean a bad or disorderly ghost, perhaps a poltergeist? However, according to Answers.com (2), the very similar name Mál'akhî means "my messenger" or "my angel" in Hebrew. The final book of the Old Testament in the Christian tradition is attributed to the Prophet Malachi, and is believed to have been written after the Second Temple had been built. The main theme of the Book of Malachi is to condemn the Jewish people for developing lax moral and religious behaviour. So, despite his Eastern sounding name, Mal'akh may be an agent of Conservative American Christians, wanting to rebuke his fellow citizens for their own lax morals. The words of the Prophet Malachi (who may have not been just one man), is often referred to in the New Testament. Malachi is also an important figure in the Mormon Church (the Church of Jesus Christ of Latter-Day Saints), as they believe that the prophecy at the end of Chapter 4 of the Book of Malachi was fulfilled by the prophet Elijah's visit to the church's founder, Joseph Smith, during Passover in 1836. Mal'akh is obviously employing a pseudonym, much like 'Janus' in *Angels and Demons*.

That quote from Leviticus 19:28 is "Ye shall not make any cuttings in your flesh for the dead, nor print any marks upon you: I am the LORD." Giovanni Battista Piranesi was indeed a famous Italian engraver known for his etchings of 'carceri' (fictional prisons), and he also did an etching of the Pyramid of Cestius in Rome, which was thought to be influenced by the Egyptian pyramids. The Savanorola chair is also known as the 'Dante Chair' (as it became popular in the Renaissance), the 'X Chair', or 'Scissors Chair'. This style of chair was also employed in ancient Rome, Greece and Egypt. So Mal'akh is very rich, and possibly has a love of artefacts derived from the ancient world. The fact that his home has a floor-to-ceiling window suggests that it may have been built for an artist prior to the Twentieth Century, as they needed lots of natural light in their studios.

It turns out that Mal'akh is searching for the United States' "greatest untold secret". So, Mal'akh believes the secret is hidden in Washington, but he could be mistaken about this. It's just as well that it's hidden behind "a veil of symbols, legends, and allegory", or else Langdon wouldn't have much to do in this novel! I was wondering if Mal'akh would turn out to be the initiate featured in the Prologue, and so he is, to the 33rd degree, the highest level. Although Masons are supposed to be equal, one suspects that Mal'akh might have earned their trust a lot earlier if he had not been tattooed, but Mal'akh's thought processes reveals that he does not need their trust to unveil their secrets.

'Lux Aeterna' is Latin for 'Eternal Light', which seems innocuous, but don't forget – 'Lucifer' means 'Light Bearer'. Verdi also composed the Egyptian opera *Aida*, and no doubt Egyptian symbols will feature in this novel. The section of the *Requiem* that Mal'akh turns up – 'Dies Irae' – means 'Day of Wrath', which is, as Wikipedia states, "the day of judgment, [with] the last trumpet summoning souls before the throne of God, where the saved will be delivered and the unsaved cast into eternal flames" (3). So Mal'akh would appear to want to have his own Day of Judgement. Incidentally, the *Dies Irae* section has now been removed from the Catholic Requiem Mass following reforms proposed by the Second Vatican Council. Presumably this "reminder of a previous life" involved Mal'akh being a musician, rather than a castrato, as obviously, once you've been a castrato, you can never go back. Unless you have cosmetic surgery and take hormone injections! Or maybe Mal'akh used to be a conservative priest, in a continuation of the Catholic theme from the previous two Robert Langdon adventures. However, from the Italian antiques in his home, it is obvious that Mal'akh is quite wealthy, unlike a priest. Since Mal'akh's fast has already lasted two days, his body will have already turned to his muscles as source of fuel in the form of glycogen. It would appear that Mal'akh does not suffer from low blood pressure already, as any sudden exertion could lead him to experience dizziness and blackouts.

The narrator of the novel states that Mal'akh has the scales and talons of a hawk on his feet. Yet I could find no specific reference to a Masonic symbol involving a hawk online. According to Wikipedia, 'hawk' is a term that can also apply to an eagle in North American usage (4). So I believe that this is a reference to the Masonic symbol of the Double-Headed Eagle, an image that is continued further up Mal'akh's body, on his chest. Manly P. Hall's book, *The Phoenix: An Illustrated Review of Occultism and Philosophy*, conveys what this symbol means to the brotherhood (pp. 176-177) –

Among the ancients a fabulous bird called the Phoenix is described by early writers ... in size and shape it resembles the eagle.... The body of the Phoenix is one covered with glossy purple feathers, and the plumes in its tail are alternately blue and red. The head of the bird is light in color, and about its neck is a circlet of golden plumage. At the back of its back the Phoenix has a crest of feathers of brilliant color ... The Phoenix, it is said, lives for 500 years, and at its death its body opens and the new born Phoenix emerges. Because of this symbolism, the Phoenix is generally regarded as representing immortality and resurrection ... The Phoenix is one sign of the secret orders of the ancient world and of the initiate of those orders, for it was common to refer to one who had been accepted into the temples as a man twice-born, or reborn. Wisdom confers a new life, and those who become wise are born again.

It could be that Mal'akh is an initiate of one of these pre-Masonic orders. Manly P. Hall is a Masonic writer that is much quoted on Anti-Masonic websites by critics that equate the 'occult' with 'Satanic'. Another of his books (whose title may well have a bearing on *The Lost Symbol*), *The Lost Keys of Freemasonry* states, "These were the immortals to whom the term phoenix was applied, and their symbol was the mysterious two-headed bird, now called an eagle, a familiar and little understood Masonic emblem" (p. 108), so the Phoenix is now represented as a Double-Headed Eagle in Freemasonry. So the talons of the 'hawk' on Mal'akh's body are those of the double-headed phoenix that is represented on his chest. I found these two Manly P. Hall quotes on *The Forbidden Knowledge* website, which is very critical of Freemasonry (5). Continuing on the theme of rebirth, which is symbolized by the phoenix, *The Forbidden Knowledge* goes on to state –

Freemasons like all occultists, refer to their initiates who have completed their initiation, as being "Born Again." In 1988, when George Bush was on the Presidential Campaign Trail; Barbara Walters... asked him a question that caught him off guard. Barbara asked George if he was a Christian. Bush literally stumbled, looked down for a moment, and answered, "If by being a Christian, you ask if I am 'Born Again,' then yes, I am a Christian."

Although I believe that President Bush was being honest in his answer, and that he was referring to his religious beliefs, rather than to any membership of a secret society.

A popular conspiracy theory is that the eagle that currently resides on the United States' Great Seal was originally supposed to be a phoenix. According to another book by Manly P. Hall, *The Secret Teachings of All Ages* (pages XC-XCI) –

European mysticism was not dead at the time the United States of America was founded. The hand of the mysteries controlled in the establishment of the new government for the signature of the mysteries may still be seen on the Great Seal of the United States of America. Careful analysis of the seal discloses a mass of occult and Masonic symbols chief among them, the so-called American Eagle... the American eagle upon the Great Seal is but a conventionalized phoenix...

So, when a Masonic writer states this, it's not surprising that many conspiracy followers believe that the Great Seal was considerably influenced by Freemasonry, especially when one considers that there is a pyramid on the other side of the seal. Dan Brown has obviously been reading Manly P. Hall as *The Lost Symbol* kicks off with an epigraph from *The Secret Teachings of All Ages* –

To live in the world without becoming aware of the meaning of the world is like wandering around a great library without touching the books.

Funnily enough, I found this same quote on the Deland Institute of Noetic Sciences website, so this is very much in the same spirit as their mission statement (6).

The two pillars carved onto Mal'akh's legs, *Boaz* and *Jachin*, were once found inside the porch way of King Solomon's Temple, which the Masons worship. *Boaz* stood on the left, while *Jachin* stood on the right. According to Wikipedia, *Jachin* means 'founding' in Hebrew (7), while the meaning of *Boaz* is unclear, and could be an acronym (8). These two pillars are always present in Masonic buildings, although their location varies from lodge to lodge. There's also some debate as to from whose perspective is *Boaz* on the left and *Jachin* on the right? From the person entering the Temple, or from the person leaving it? W.Bro William M Larson, a 33rd Degree Mason, has written a popular essay regarding them called *Those Mysterious Pillars: Boaz and Jachin* (9). In the essay, Larson states that the two pillars are thought to be memorials of God: "But why two pillars, if but one Deity is represented?... Let us suffice to say that in the times of primitive people, that the gods went in pairs, male and female. Quite possibly this ancient custom was to retain their identity with the past, and therefore stood for male and female, who were the active and passive principles in nature". This is interesting from the point of view of the sacred feminine, which was a major theme of *The Da Vinci Code*. It could also explain why the Anti-Masonic Mal'akh is utilising the brotherhood's symbols against them, if they had a different meaning pre-Freemasonry. The narrator doesn't explain what Mal'akh's cock and balls mean though!

According to Wikipedia, a 'sigil' is a "symbol created for a specific magical purpose" (10). 'Sigil' is derived from the Latin for 'seal' ('sigillum'), and could also come from the Hebrew 'segulah' meaning 'word, action or item of spiritual effect'. A good example of such a magical symbol is the hexagram. The best-known list of sigils is *The Goetia: The Lesser Key of Solomon the King*, the most famous edition of which was edited by Aleister Crowley (I previously mentioned this book on pp. 12-13). So Mal'akh must have a few hexagrams and other magical symbols tattooed on his body, and would therefore appear to be in the process of casting a spell with them. It's interesting that Mal'akh refers to himself as an 'artefact', as this technically means 'something made by human beings' (11).

It's hard to find evidence that the ancients regarded angels and demons as being identical, as any search for these terms are dominated by Dan Brown's previous novel, *Angels and Demons*! No doubt this was intended to be a subtle reference to Robert Langdon's first adventure. Wikipedia states that Christianity views demons as being fallen angels, who rose up in revolt against God, and were defeated by God's army, commanded by the archangel Michael (12). However, according to Wikipedia, some commentators believe that this view only arose in the 6th Century AD, in the writings of St. Augustine and others. There are some demons, like the destroying angel that brings pestilence, that while monstrous, are considered to be good, as they are doing the bidding of a wrathful God. In more recent times, good demons have appeared as characters in narratives such as Joss Whedon's *Angel*. Mal'akh is probably referring to jinn or genies, as these could be good or bad in Arabian folklore. Mal'akh obviously sees himself as a good angel, as his assumed name, as argued earlier, could mean "My Angel".

Since the untattooed top of Mal'akh's head is pale, he must be Caucasian, despite his adoption of an Arabic pseudonym. One can only presume that this 'virgin skin' is awaiting the mysterious lost symbol of the novel's title. It's just as well that Mal'akh is carrying out his operations in winter, as I doubt he'd fool anyone at all wearing that much concealer in summer! The man who can help Mal'akh find the missing piece of the puzzle can only be one Robert Langdon… Note that this missing item is specifically referred to as being 'buried'.

Chapter 3 The Arlington Memorial Bridge was commissioned in 1925 as part of scheme to restore Pierre Charles L'Enfant's plan for the capital (1). This neoclassical bridge includes eagles and fasces, which could be considered to be Masonic symbols. According to Wikipedia, Foggy Bottom is just a 19th-century district of Washington DC, west of downtown (2). It's foggy because low lying, and susceptible to being flooded with industrial air pollution as well as fog, whereas Capitol Hill is far more elevated, as its name would suggest. So, Dan Brown appears to be in error here in implying that Foggy Bottom was the original name for the whole of DC. The US Department of State is nicknamed 'Foggy Bottom' because their HQ is here. The Watergate Hotel, infamous for its role in President Nixon's downfall, is also located here. Just on the edge of Foggy Bottom is the World Bank and the US Department of the Interior.

John Russell Pope, the architect of the Jefferson Memorial, did refer to the Roman Pantheon is his plans, which is no doubt why this monument is often called 'America's Pantheon'. There were objections to the location of the Jefferson Memorial, as it did not fit in with L'Enfant's original plans. The interior of the monument contains many quotes from Thomas Jefferson's writings, such as "I have sworn upon the altar of God eternal hostility against every form of tyranny over the mind of man", by which America's third president meant that he was opposed to the country adopting a state religion. Wikipedia agrees with Robert Langdon's assessment that this land is quite swampy, as "the Washington

Monument, just east of the axis on the national Mall, was intended to be located at the intersection of the White House and the site for the Jefferson Memorial to the south, but soft swampy ground which defied nineteenth century engineering required it be sited to the east" (3).

Robert Langdon's day begins at the ungodly hour of 4.45 a.m. on a Sunday. So, not all of the action in the novel takes place within 12 hours (or else the novel would have finished by now!) So I guess the 12 hours is meant to start from the time that Langdon arrives in Washington. I know that Dan Brown likes to play around with names, but I couldn't find the etymology of the surname 'Jelbart'. Although Langdon doesn't know it yet, this phone call from Peter Solomon's assistant is literally his 'call to adventure' in Joseph Campbell's concept of the *hero's journey*. So, Langdon met Peter Solomon at Princeton, and Solomon's historical lecture led to Langdon's love of symbols. Since Peter Solomon is 58, and 12 years senior to Robert Langdon, then Langdon must be 46 at the time of *The Lost Symbol*. However, before the publication of this novel, Wikipedia stated that Langdon was born in 1956, but now the date has changed to 1964, so Langdon must have taken the elixir of youth if he keeps getting young all the time! (4) Dan Brown is sticking to the formula of his previous Robert Langdon adventures by having his hero respond to a mysterious summons by phone early in the morning. It's slightly irritating that all of Langdon's adventures thus far begin this way, as it makes it obvious that there is a formula. However, as a device, it's far less irksome than J. K. Rowling starting every Harry Potter novel with her hero staying at the Dursleys'. And at least Robert Langdon's adventures have the good grace to occur within a short time period, rather than the whole of an academic year.

It's interesting to note that the narrator of *The Lost Symbol* equates the Solomons with the Rothschilds, since I believe that the Solomons are based on the Rockefeller family. Like the Solomons, the Rockefellers are extremely wealthy and philanthropic. You will also recall that I thought it significant that Peter's name is derived from the Greek for 'Rock', so there's not much distance between 'Rock' and 'Rockefeller'. According to Wikipedia, the Rockefellers, the Rothschilds, and the Bush family were accused of being "dynastic bloodlines linked to the Illuminati. New World Order conspiracy theories present [them]... as the real rulers or would-be rulers of the world" (5). Such is the accusation in Fritz Springmeier's book *Bloodlines of the Illuminati*. Allegations like these would have become mainstream if Mal'akh had succeeded in disseminating his video. Wikipedia also states that the Rockefeller family has a long association with JP Morgan Chase, the bank founded by Aaron Burr, who was referred to in the Twitter clues as the US Vice President who killed Alexander Hamilton. It's also interesting to see that Peter Solomon is the head of the Smithsonian Institution, as this organisation was mentioned more than once in the Twitter clues.

Harvard, the Ivy League university that Langdon works for, has had a long rivalry with Yale, hence Langdon's long running joke with Peter that Yale is a second rate institution. As Wikipedia relates, "Yale and Harvard have been rivals in academics, athletics, and other activities for most of their history, competing annually in The Game and the Harvard-Yale Regatta" (6). Yale has quite an interesting seal, as it contains Hebrew on it: 'האורים והתומים' or 'ha'Urim vəhaTummim', which is usually taken to mean 'revelation and truth'. Wikipedia states that this phrase is usually associated with the practice of divination (7).

38

However, Yale takes the phrase to mean 'Light and Truth', as they also utilise the Latin 'Lux et Veritas' as a motto. Yale is also the location of the notorious Skull and Bones fraternity (see p. 12), so the narrator could be hinting that Peter Solomon was a member. Since this is a close reading of *The Lost Symbol*, I decided to check out Peter Solomon's phone number - 202-329-5746 – on Google. It turns out that Todd Henry, who runs a website called *Accidental Creative*, actually rang this number, and got through to Peter Solomon's voicemail! I guess people are bound to do this, so it makes sense for the publishers to actually control this phone number. I've found no evidence that any Rockefeller was a member of the Royal Society, an institution that was mentioned in the Twitter clues. Since Katherine works in Noetic Science, she must be a major character in the book, since this area of research was specifically mentioned in the Fact box at the beginning of the novel.

Wikipedia contradicts Langdon's belief that the National Statuary Hall was the original House of Representatives chamber, as they had previously met in a temporary chamber called 'The Oven' (8). This was succeeded by another chamber that was soon burnt down by the British during the War of 1812. The National Statuary Hall, like many other Capitol buildings and monuments is neoclassical in design. It doesn't sound like it's a great place to conduct meetings of any kind, as the acoustics are very bad. Indeed, there's an apocryphal story that John Quincy Adams employed the acoustics to his advantage, as he could eavesdrop on conversations on the other side of the hall. However, the imposition of marble tiles on the floor, and the replacement of the original wooden roof have solved the acoustics problem. There are indeed 38 statues currently in the hall, although the original intention was to have 2 statues from each state. However, this meant that the collection began to outgrow the hall, so now the remaining statues are situated throughout the Capitol building. An 1823 painting by Samuel Morse depicted a night session of the House of Representatives in this chamber. Morse was mentioned obliquely in the Twitter clues, as the American inventor of the telegraph was a Mason. The hall was designed by Charles Bulfinch, who, as Wikipedia notes, is regarded by many as being the first American born man to practice architecture as a profession (9). A Grand Tour of Europe that he embarked upon in 1785 influenced his neoclassical designs, and Thomas Jefferson, who played a great role in the building of the Capitol, was something of a mentor to him. One of Charles Bulfinch's sons was Thomas Bulfinch, of *Bulfinch's Mythology* fame, an anthology that deals with the myths of the Classical World, and those of Britain and France. Amongst these tales is one that will be quite familiar to readers of *The Da Vinci Code*: the story of the Sangreal (the Holy Grail).

It's interesting to see that Langdon has been requested to bring a lecture on the Masonic history of the Capitol building, as many commentators have speculated that this will play a big role in *The Lost Symbol*. Note that Anthony speaks of "the architecture of our nation's capital" (i.e. more that one building), while Langdon talks of "the building" (singular). Bookspan TV only features non-fiction books, mostly histories. Although the flight is only an hour, having a flight at 5pm doesn't seem to leave Langdon with much chance of getting to the lecture on time, although I guess American transportation systems are much better than British ones.

Chapter 4 Pierre L'Enfant did indeed describe Jenkins' Hill as "a pedestal waiting for a monument", as he believed that government buildings should be situated on high ground so that they would have a good panorama (1). However, we have Thomas Jefferson to thank for the distinctive name of the building. As Wikipedia relates, "The word 'Capitol' comes from Latin, meaning city on a hill and is associated with the Roman temple to Jupiter Optimus Maximus on Capitoline Hill" (2). So this is very much in line with the founders' intentions, as stated by the narrator in *The Lost Symbol*, "to echo the grandeur of ancient Rome, whose ideals were the inspiration... in establishing the laws and culture of the new republic". Jefferson arranged a design competition for the building of the Capitol and the President's house, but most entries were rather amateurish, as there weren't that many American practising architects at this time. The best designs were by Frenchman Stephen Hallet, and William Thorton, whose plans were influenced by the Louvre and the Pantheon. Thornton's plans were approved over the more costly Hallet's, although Hallet was hired to overview the amateur Thornton's design.

The new Capitol Visitor Center only opened on the 2nd of December 2008, the 145th anniversary of the placing of Thomas Crawford's Statue of Freedom on the Capitol Dome (3). So the earliest the events in *The Lost Symbol* could have taken place is in January 2009. This could be another reason for the delay in publication for *The Lost Symbol*. When completed, the CVC more than doubled the Capitol Building's footprint. It does indeed include skylights so that visitors can see the Capitol Dome. Building work started in 2000, and was supposed to be complete by 2004, but factors such as the 9/11 attacks and bad weather delayed it. The CVC was built primarily to deal with the ever-increasing numbers of visitors to the Capitol Building. So, one could argue that Dan Brown has been very considerate by delaying publication of *The Lost Symbol*, since fans of the novel will considerably add to the visitor numbers. Indeed, *The Rough Guide to The Lost Symbol* has been specifically written as a guide to the locations mentioned in the novel. The CVC has caused some controversy by running over budget, and Wikipedia relates that, "Senator Jim DeMint of South Carolina said that the CVC fails to 'appropriately honor our religious heritage that has been critical to America's success'" (4). However I would have thought that would have clashed with the ideal of separating church from state.

The Washington Redskins are the local National Football League team, and play in the Eastern division of the National Football Conference (NFC). Their name has attracted some controversy over the years as many critics regard it as a derogatory term for Native Americans. It's good to see that Nunez has been trained to override his natural instinct to give leeway to the handicapped, as Sir Leigh Teabing managed to smuggle a revolver into Westminster Abbey in *The Da Vinci Code* due to the guards' fear of offending a disabled man. Unfortunately, Nunez's human instinct is quite awry, as he doesn't detect that this man, who is wearing concealer just like Mal'akh, could be dangerous. Mal'akh eases past Nunez with a misogynistic joke about a woman that he has supposedly married. Myths of mermaids can be traced back to ancient Assyria, but in British folklore, they are unlucky omens of disaster...

Chapter 5 It looks like Katherine Solomon is at the Smithsonian Museum Support Center in Maryland, as that's at 4210 Silver Hill Road, rather than the home of the Smithsonian Institution. We're told that Katherine's smooth olive complexion is derived from her Mediterranean ancestry, so this is one thing that divides the fictional Solomons from the actual Rockefellers, as this latter family originally came from Germany. Since she's a natural beauty, she could well be an ideal companion for Robert Langdon in this novel. Langdon's previous two female companions, with whom he has enjoyed flirtations, have been much younger than him, so it would be refreshing if this novel's love interest were older than him. Certainly Hollywood's older leading ladies will be vying for this rare role, so hopefully Ron Howard won't cast a younger model. Luckily for Langdon, Katherine has never married, and is presumably single at the time of the novel. Interesting to see that Katherine and Peter's father died while they were young. Since Katherine was 7, that must mean that Peter inherited his father's mantle at the age of 15.

So, Katherine is a leading figure in the field of Noetic science, which has something to do with the power of the human mind. However, Mal'akh, who is just 6 miles away in the Capitol Building, then calls her. This confirms that it must have been Mal'akh who conned his way past Nunez into the building. Mal'akh states that some legendary item that Peter Solomon believes is hidden in Washington DC can be found. Question is though, why is Katherine interacting with Mal'akh, and what this mysterious object got to do with her?

Chapter 6 Security has indeed been stepped up around the Capitol Building in the wake of the 9/11 attacks, especially as it was believed to have been the target of United Airlines Flight 93, which crashed after passengers overpowered the terrorists. Chapter 6 sees the first specific mention in this novel that Langdon's claustrophobia is derived from being trapped in a well overnight. It's no wonder that Langdon's in a hurry, as his 5pm flight really did not give him much scope to get to his lecture on time, so this seems like an oversight on Solomon's part – surely an earlier flight would have been better? The security guard is described as being Hispanic, so it's probably Nunez. I knew it wouldn't be long before Langdon's legendary Mickey Mouse watch would be mentioned!

Jefferson Davis was in charge of the Capitol Construction work in the 1850s, and according to Wikipedia, it was he who came up with the idea for the design of the Statue of Freedom (1). Shortly after, Jefferson Davis became President of the Confederacy, which gives you a great indication of which side he fell on in the great slavery debate. Thomas Crawford, the sculptor of the statue, offended Jefferson Davis by having it wear a 'liberty cap', the Roman symbol for a freed slave. Indeed, many African Americans, both slaves and freemen, were involved in the construction of the Capitol buildings in the 1850s. Due to a labour dispute over wages (not the first time that a labourer claimed they hadn't been paid enough in the construction of the Capitol), the owner of the foundry that cast the statue got one of his slaves, Philip Reid, to complete the work. The liberty cap on the statue was replaced by a military helmet that featured an eagle and feathers, although many commentators think that this now looks like a Native American headdress!

There are indeed many odd items in the Capitol building, such as the bathtub that Vice President Wilson fell asleep in, catching pneumonia when the water cooled.

According to an online article about ghosts in the building (2), there's often a whiff of scented soap in this bathtub. The staircase with the permanent bloodstain is believed to be related to the death of Kentucky congressman William Taulbee, who was murdered by journalist Charles Kincaid in 1890. The staircase is now reported to only trip up journalists as part of Taulbee's ghostly revenge. As mentioned earlier, some of those involved in the construction of the capital city weren't ever really given their full recompense, chief amongst them being the city's designer Pierre L'Enfant. Indeed, "the building got off to a bad start in 1808 when construction superintendent John Lenthall disagreed with architect B. Henry Latrobe over the vaulting in the room now known as the Old Supreme Court Chamber. When Lenthall tried to remove braces from the vaults, the ceiling collapsed and crushed him. In his last breath, legend goes, Lenthall put a curse on the building" (3). The statues in the National Statuary Hall are said to come down and dance whenever a new president is inaugurated. Oh, and the ghost of the Black Cat is supposed to especially appear at times of national crisis, and grows to a huge size... So Langdon had better look out!

I discuss the conspiracy theories regarding Washington DC's layout and Baphomet in more detail on pp. 19-21. However, I must say that it's refreshing to see that Dan Brown has avoided these obvious conspiracy theories, especially since, according to one Masonic website (6), the rumours first appeared in Michael Baigent and Richard Leigh's *The Temple and the Lodge*, the same authors who accused Brown of plagiarism over *The Da Vinci Code*. This scene also employs one of Dan Brown's best devices: that of Robert Langdon as teacher, in which he educates his students (i.e. his readers) about the real nature of symbols. This device is brilliant for providing exposition that would otherwise be unwieldy in the narrator's authoritative tone, and allows for internal debates. You can indeed see similar lines and shapes on the Detroit map, although this could be for the very good reason that the main architect of the city after the great fire of 1805, Augustus Brevoort Woodward, was a Freemason. Indeed, if one were conspiracy crazy, one would think that the Woodward's appointment as the Michigan Territory's first Chief Justice just months before the fire to be a tad suspicious. One could imagine him, like Nero, fiddling while the city burned... Woodward's biographer, the similarly named Arthur M. Woodford, believed that Woodward was probably the archetype for Washington Irving's famous fictional character Ichabod Crane (5). So, Freemasons could well place Masonic symbols into their city plans, but there doesn't have to be anything devilish about it.

'Occult' does indeed mean 'hidden' or 'obscured', from the Latin occultus. Wikipedia quotes Nicholas Goodrick-Clarke's belief that the main aim of today's occult organisations is "a strong desire to reconcile the findings of modern natural science with a religious view that could restore man to a position of centrality and dignity in the universe", a statement that chimes somewhat with the events in *The Lost Symbol* (6). The Sanders Theatre at Harvard was based upon Sir Christopher Wren's Sheldonian Theatre in Oxford, and is renowned for its acoustics, which is why Langdon can hear his students fidgeting in their seats so well (7). The Capitol Building had to be extended in the 1850s due to the rapid expansion of the United States. During these extensions, Bulfinch's original dome appeared to be a bit dwarfed, and since it had always had its critics, it was replaced by the second (current) dome. The second dome was built by Thomas U. Walter, and utilises just under nine million pounds of ironwork. Walter had to revise the plans to incorporate the Statue of Freedom, as the actual statue was taller and heavier than the one originally planned. Although Langdon objects to the use of the word 'awesome', it's been around since the 1590s, so is hardly a modern vulgarity.

The mural of George Washington laying the Capitol Building's cornerstone featured in the Twitter clues. I could find no other reference to the astrological reason for the laying of the Capitol Building cornerstone on the 18th of September 1793. However, I did find a reference to the name 'Capitol' being derived from 'Caput Draconis' (although I think the Capitoline Hill explanation to be far more likely). I found this definition in an online book that made reference to the work of David Ovason (8). Now, David Ovason has written a book called *The Secret Architecture of Our Nation's Capital: The Masons and the Building of Washington*, and according to its listing on Barnes & Noble, one of its main points is that "Washington's founders deliberately aligned the city with the stars, arguing that the capital was, in effect, consecrated to Virgo, the astrological sign, which he also connects with the Egyptian goddess Isis" (9). Ovason's book also starts off in the Foggy Bottom district of Washington, as does *The Lost Symbol*. 'Caput Draconis' is Latin for 'head of the dragon', and is employed in astrological terms to depict the north node of the moon. This is how it is described on Wikipedia (10):

It is (a) neutral figure (good with good, evil with evil) but fortunate with starting or beginning new things. It is favourable for beginnings and profit, and otherwise favourable with other favourable figures, and unfavourable with unfavourable ones. It is associated with the benefic planets Jupiter and Venus, and assigned to the zodiac sign of Sagittarius; its outer element is fire due to its association with Sagittarius while its inner element is earth. Its planetary intelligences are Iophiel and Hagiel and its spirits are Hismael and Kedemel; it is associated with the deities Venus, Iove, and Vulcanus, and the angels Sachiel, Anael, and Zuriel. It is associated with the right arm.

David Ovason has also written a book about *The Secret Symbols on the Dollar Bill*, so one would think that his work was definitely required reading in Dan Brown's research for *The Lost Symbol*.

This chapter sees the first mention of the Order of the Eastern Star in the novel. Eastern Star was set up by the Freemason Rob Morris in 1850, and according to Wikipedia, it's the largest fraternal organisation in the world that both men and women can join (11). The organisation is based upon teachings from the Bible, but Eastern Star is still open to people from other monotheistic faiths. One of the Twitter clues mentioned powerful consorts, which brought Eleanor Roosevelt to mind, as she was the most powerful First Lady Pre Hillary Clinton, so it's interesting to learn that she was a member of Eastern Star.

The Coca-Cola formula is very much a trade secret. I didn't think there was any cocaine to be found in the recipe nowadays, but Wikipedia states that some people believe that there are still trace elements of it in the beverage (12). Discussion of religion is indeed forbidden in Masonic lodges. However, so is the discussion of politics – which sounds like the house rules of any party – don't allow the discussion of anything that could lead to a heated argument! The 'Great Architect of the Universe' is indeed a term that Freemasons employ for the reasons that

Langdon states. Its use within Freemasonry is believed to have been derived from the writings of John Calvin (13). It's also a term utilised by the Rosicrucians, a movement that I discussed in more depth in the Twitter chapter (on pages 15-16, and 24-26).

As I have previously pointed out, the admission of African American men into Masonic lodges was a controversial topic as recently as 1909 in New York, so the Masons haven't always been open to men of all colours. The Order of the Eastern Star website states that some historians believe that it had a French origin in 1703, but I'll take that with a pinch of salt (14). The idea that the Masons control the world is discussed elsewhere on this book, usually in association with Illuminati infiltration. That phrase – "Masonry is a system of morality, veiled in allegory and illustrated by symbols" – is one that is indeed bandied about the brotherhood greatly. For instance, Charles H. Vail employs it on page 203 of *The Ancient Mysteries and Modern Masonry*, in which he goes on to argue further that, "to regard the myths as history is to miss the truth which the symbols were designed to teach. No intelligent Mason will fall into this error".

It was Constantine, the first Christian Roman Emperor, who decreed that the day of rest should be Sunday, as this was the day of the Sun (for worship of the Sun – *dies solis*). Langdon's analogy of the strange practices of Masonry with the more accepted ones of the Church is pretty neat though.

Chapter 7 So, Katherine Solomon does indeed work at the Smithsonian Museum Support Center. Since this is a private installation, it's not too surprising that I was unable to work out what the acronym SMSC stood for in the Fact box at the beginning of the novel. I just hope the SMSC is prepared for all the tourist buses that might visit them in the wake of *The Lost Symbol*! The narrator's description of the SMSC's contents looks to be quite accurate (1). So, Peter Solomon brought his sister here three years ago to create "scientific marvels". The fact that the discoveries Katherine Solomon has made could have multidisciplinary ramifications, across both science and religion, reminds me strongly of the breakthrough that Leonardo Vetra made in *Angels and Demons*. Therefore, *The Lost Symbol* appears to be following the model set by Robert Langdon's first adventure, rather than the breakthrough *The Da Vinci Code*. I thought Langdon was rather mystified by the modern science in *Angels and Demons*, and so did not participate so much in that first novel. Whereas Langdon was very much more to the fore in *The Da Vinci Code*, as that adventure was more focused on art and symbols, and since the science involved was centuries old, Langdon could appreciate it much more fully. So, hopefully Langdon won't be wandering around the pages of *The Lost Symbol* baffled by Katherine Solomon's work, especially if it no longer resembles science.

Security is tight at the SMSC, so strictly speaking, the guard shouldn't be listening to football on the radio. The revelation that Katherine's mother died violently in her arms may well have some bearing on later events in the novel…

Chapter 8 There are indeed pilasters of sandstone in the National Statuary Hall. The breccia is a form of marble quarried close to Washington's Potomac River (1). The Rotunda is adjacent, and is the space below the Capitol Building Dome. It was completed in 1824 under the watch of Capitol Architect Charles Bulfinch, in preparation for the visit that year of the Marquis de Lafayette, who was the first foreigner to address Congress (2). 'Docent' is the term employed in North America and many British museums (such as Westminster Abbey in *The Da Vinci Code*) for the resident tour guides. It's derived from the Latin 'docere', meaning 'to teach'. And it's not long before we learn that 'Anthony' (who is presumably Mal'akh) has invited Langdon to Washington under false pretences!

Chapter 9: the refusal of the call Langdon's abductor claims that his intentions are "purely noble". I doubt that somehow, but there may be a reason for his choice of words. The narrator reports that Langdon's adventures in Europe occurred over the "last several years", giving the impression that the events of *The Da Vinci Code* weren't so long ago. It's strange that the abductor talks of saving Peter Solomon's soul, rather than his life (so presumably Peter is the man who had previously called Mal'akh "a demon" in horror). The abductor states that he is calling from Peter Solomon's private cell phone. However, the number Langdon dialled was the one on the fax, so there's no evidence whatsoever that the kidnapper is ringing from Peter's phone, unless Langdon previously recognised this number as being listed on his own cell phone, and we have no evidence of that either. As Wikipedia relates, "Araf is the Muslim sheol or borderland between heaven and hell for those who are, from incapacity, neither morally bad nor morally good" (1). So it seems that Peter is neither good nor bad, although one would have thought that the Masons' system of morality would have inclined him to the former, and we have definite evidence in the book of his philanthropy. The term 'Hamistagan' derives from Zoroastrianism, the religion of the Magi. Hamistagan looks to have been succeeded by the similar concept of Araf when Islam replaced Zoroastrianism in Persia. However, Wikipedia argues that, "Hamistagan can be compared to Roman Catholic purgatory because it occupies a position between heaven and hell, but hamistagan is a place of waiting, not punishment and purification. As a neutral place, hamistagan is more like the Roman Catholic limbo" (2). 'Purgatorio' is indeed the second canticle of *Dante's Divine Comedy*. On the astrological theme, it's interesting to note that this canticle "is notable for demonstrating the medieval knowledge of a spherical Earth. During the poem, Dante discusses the different stars visible in the southern hemisphere, the altered position of the sun, and the various time zones of the Earth. At this stage it is, Dante says, sunset at Jerusalem, midnight on the River Ganges, and sunrise in Purgatory" (3).

It's very much hinted at the end of *The Da Vinci Code* that the current location of the Holy Grail is in the Louvre. I couldn't find any references online to an ancient portal in Washington DC, beyond reviews of *The Lost Symbol* (a major disadvantage of critiquing such a popular book is that other people are quick to comment about it online!) So this looks to be an element of the plot that Dan Brown has originated himself, rather than based on any of his research. Peter Solomon has stated that only Langdon can unlock the portal, although this information must have been coerced from him under torture. Still, it may be that Peter Solomon is following his own agenda by choosing Langdon.

"As above, so below" is indeed a Hermetical saying. So, I may have been too quick in my discussion of the Twitter clues to dismiss any involvement of the Hermetic Order of the Golden Dawn in *The Lost Symbol* due to their Britishness. It could be quite significant that the kidnapper says "dawned" in this conversation.

For years I've thought that the word 'hermetic' was associated with 'hermits', but it actually derives the Medieval Latin 'hermeticus' from the name of the Greek god Hermes. Wikipedia states that, "The origin of the word Hermes relates to a stone pillar used to communicate with the deities... from at least 600 BCE. The God Hermes is a generic term used by the pre-classical Greeks for any deity, and was only later associated with the God of Knowledge in Athens in the 2nd Century CE" (4). Hermetic beliefs are based on the writings of the apocryphal Hermes Trismegistus, who is a conjunction between the Greek Hermes and the Egyptian God Thoth, who were the deities of magic and writing in these cultures (5). No doubt this combination occurred after Alexander the Great's general Ptolemy and his dynasty became rulers of Egypt. Alexander the Great supposedly found the Emerald Tablet of Hermes Trismegistus in Hermes' tomb, and it's on this tablet that the "As above, so below" ideology comes from. As the narrator succinctly puts it, this is a belief in the "physical connection between heaven and earth". Wikipedia extends this further by relating that "The microcosm is oneself, and the macrocosm is the universe. The macrocosm is as the microcosm, and vice versa; within each lies the other, and through understanding one (usually the microcosm) you can understand the other" (6).

During the Renaissance, Cosimo de'Medici sent envoys out to monasteries to discover ancient texts. One of the texts discovered was the *Corpus Hermeticum*. Hermes Trismegistus is believed to have written over forty books, but most were destroyed along with the Great Library of Alexandria (following an order by the Christian Roman Emperor Theodosius I in 391 to obliterate pagan temples). Wikipedia reports that the Rosicrucian movement adopted Hermeticism, and notes how similar Rosicrucianism was to later Freemasonry, as both are graded systems (7). Hermeticism seems to have a similar concept of God to Freemasonry, as Hermeticists refer to it as simply 'God', 'The One', or 'The All'. Indeed, many Hermeticists throughout the ages have been happy to combine the philosophy of Hermeticism with their own religion (8). 'Trismegistus' means "thrice great", although no one seems really sure why Hermes was called this, so it may not have anything to do with the Christian Trinity (9). More worryingly, Katherine Solomon's field of Noetic Science could be intricately involved in all this, as Wikipedia also relates that, "Hermes explains in Book 9 of the *Corpus Hermeticum* that Nous brings forth both good and evil, depending on if he receives input from God or from the demons. God brings good, while the demons bring evil" (10). 'Nous', as I explained on p. 30, is where Noetic Science derives its name. In the context of the *Corpus Hermeticum*, 'Nous' or 'Poimandres' is the being with whom Hermes is having a dialogue in the book, but yet another name for 'Nous' is 'God'...

In Joseph Campbell's concept of the monomyth, many heroes face a stage where they feel that they have to refuse the call to adventure. Langdon is at this stage now; since he's been brought to the Capitol against his will by Peter's abductor, who quite presumptuously views Langdon as the adept who must be initiated into his mysteries...

Chapter 10 'Handequin' is a term rarely used on the Internet in the manner described by Dan Brown, and most search results come up with pages referring to it as an uncommon surname. I couldn't find any corroboration online as to hands being the most complex human feature, as most results were about the human brain, whereas the narrator is talking about the most complex human feature to draw without performing an autopsy! It's odd that Peter Solomon's severed hand seem to have tattoos on them, just like the tattoos that Nunez noticed on Mal'akh's hand when he entered the Capitol Building...

Chapter 11 Well, if that is Peter Solomon's severed hand on the floor of the Rotunda, then it's no wonder why he's late for his weekly meeting with Katherine. Mal'akh would appear to have told her some secret about Peter...

There is indeed a large corridor in the Smithsonian Museum Support Center connecting all the pods together. It's true that the SMSC contains Sitting Bull's pictographic dictionary, and elephant skulls brought back by President Theodore Roosevelt on safari (well, 'Teddy' shot most things that moved). The ALH-84001 meteorite made the news in 1996 when it was announced that it might contain the fossils of Martian bacteria, and the first evidence of extraterrestrial life. Scientists are still debating whether the 'fossils' are of bacteria, or were formed by other natural phenomenon on Earth. A meteorite featured heavily in one of the Twitter clues, so it may well be that such a rock plays a prominent role later on in the novel. Pod Three is indeed the 'Wet Pod' (1).

So, Peter Solomon has built Katherine her own lab? *The Lost Symbol* is beginning to feel more and more like *Angels and Demons* in tone, rather than *The Da Vinci Code*. Wikipedia seems to have mixed thoughts about the cleanliness of hydrogen fuel cells: "Electrochemical extraction of energy from hydrogen via fuel cells is an especially clean method of meeting power requirements, but not an efficient one, due to the necessity of adding large amounts of energy to either water or hydrocarbon fuels in order to produce the hydrogen. Additionally, during the extraction of hydrogen from hydrocarbons, carbon monoxide is released. Although this gas is artificially converted into carbon dioxide, such a method of extracting hydrogen remains environmentally injurious" (2).

Katherine must be doing some seriously weird science if it can be affected by "brain radiation" or "thought emissions"! The phrase "Leap of faith" is thought to be derived from the 19th Century philosopher Søren Kierkegaard. An example of a leap of faith provided by Wikipedia is the belief that a man who existed (Jesus) who was 100% human and 100% God (3). Like Leonardo Vetra in *Angels and Demons*, Katherine Solomon has made an amazing scientific breakthrough that could change the way that humans see the world, but this is a secret for a moment held by two members of the same family.

Chapter 12 The Capitol police chief Trent Anderson has an unusual first name. Well, unusual for a European, but fairly standard for the more individualistic nomenclature of North America. If there's a reason behind his name, then it could be that he was christened after the Council of Trent, which was the Catholic Church's reaction to the Protestant Reformation. Or it could be a reference to the Trent Affair during the American Civil War, when the arrest of two Confederate ambassadors by Union officials on a British ship could have led to war breaking out between the Union and Great Britain. In any case, Trent seems like the typical security agents that have featured in Langdon's previous adventures, and Dan

Brown doesn't seem to be playing any games with his name. The CCTV is obviously showing Mal'akh depositing Peter Solomon's hand. One would have thought that there would be DNA on the army coat that Mal'akh has abandoned. Then again, no DNA analysis could uncover his identity in time to stop whatever he's planning to do that night. Dan Brown dwells on Mal'akh's change of disguise to ruminate on the powers of transformation...

Chapter 13 The Statue of Liberty could indeed stand inside the Capitol Rotunda, although it would have to leave its pedestal outside. *The Hand of the Mysteries* would appear to be something that Dan Brown has utilised from the Masonic writer Manly P. Hall's *The Secret Teachings of All Ages* (1928). Here's an extract from the book that seems to be applicable to Langdon's current situation –

When the disciple of the Great Art first beholds this hand, it is closed, and he must discover a method of opening it before the mysteries contained therein may be revealed... each of the fingers bears the emblem of a Divine Agent through the combined operations of which the great work is accomplished... To the Qabbalist the figure signifies the operation of the One Power [the crowded thumb] in the four worlds (the fingers with their emblems)... the figure [also] symbolizes the hand of a Master Mason with which he "raises" the martyred Builder of the Divine House... the key represents the Mysteries themselves, without whose aid man cannot unlock the numerous chambers of his own being. The lantern is human knowledge, for it is a spark of the Universal Fire captured in a man-made vessel; it is the light of those who dwell in the inferior universe and with the aid of which they seek to follow in the footsteps of Truth. The sun, which may be termed the "light of the world," represents the luminescence of creation through which man may learn the mystery of all creatures which express through form and number. The star is the Universal Light which reveals cosmic and celestial verities. The crown is Absolute Light-- unknown and unrevealed--whose power shines through all the lesser lights that are but sparks of this Eternal Effulgence. Thus is set forth the right hand... of Deity, whose works are all contained within the hollow of His hand.

This is how Langdon knows that there are other tattoos. As you can see, the extract mentions a "Master Mason", so the Hand of Mysteries is a Masonic symbol. Manly P. Hall goes on to write that such a hand was given to initiates when they entered the 'Temple of Wisdom'. Understanding the symbols on the hand supposedly gave the initiate divine power. There was also a regenerative aspect to it, so that the initiate could be said to have been "born again". That seems to reflect the regenerative powers of the phoenix. So, if Langdon solves the hand of mysteries that Mal'akh has presented to him, could he also bring back Peter Solomon from the dead as well as regenerating himself? One part of the extract from *The Secret Teachings of All Ages* that I omitted was an instruction that initiates should only share the mysteries via parables, and that sounds very much like the veil of allegory that Masons employ. It's somewhat creepy (and presumptuous) that Mal'akh regards himself as the Master, and Langdon the Initiate. So it could be that *The Secret Teachings of All Ages* has been the main text that Dan Brown has most employed in his research for *The Lost Symbol*. Since

Manly P. Hall is deceased, he's never going to complain about the regeneration of his work in Robert Langdon's latest adventure.

Chapter 14 I'm not quite sure what epochal date that Mal'akh is referring to, although I'd take a wild guess that it's 2012, which is the Mayan date for the end of the world that was apparently hinted at on the cover of *The Da Vinci Code*. Oh, and Dan Brown mentioned 2012 in the interview that ran with the serialisation of *The Lost Symbol* in the *Mail on Sunday* on the 13th of September. The end of the Age of Pisces was a similar epoch mentioned in *The Da Vinci Code*. So, Mal'akh very much believes in Katherine Solomon's research. However, the twist is that he wants to stop it for some reason. Again, this is very much like the *Angels and Demons*, as Leonardo Vetra's work was similarly groundbreaking and threatening to other vested interests.

Chapter 15 Electroencephalography is also known as 'EEG', and "is the recording of electrical activity along the scalp produced by the firing of neurons within the brain" (1). All the other instruments in Katherine Solomon's lab are also real, so no science fiction here! PEAR also existed, although it closed down in 2007, and planned to restart its research in a new institution in New Jersey. The idea that human thought could change physical mass is quite frightening – one can only imagine the amount of damage such a force could achieve. Then again, maybe I'm just a 'glass half empty' person.

Dan Brown has indeed cleverly utilised academic reports by scientists working in the paranormal field to spice up *The Lost Symbol*, no doubt with the intention of adding to its verisimilitude. For instance Dr. Roger Nelson has been working with Random Event Generators for decades (2). At first, individual people were asked to try to affect these Random Number Generators, and the success of this experiments encouraged those working at Princeton to expand them further. They then conducted group experiments, with similar spectacular results. Encouraged by this, Dr. Nelson linked a multitude of REGs around the world to his computer, which all seriously deviated from their random patterns on the day of Princess Diana's funeral in 1997. His team then decided to check out the results on the day of any globally reported catastrophe, and discovered that the REGs also seemed to be able to predict these events four hours before they happened! The PEAR website is still running (3), and has the following to say about the spiritual implications of the team's findings –

The evidence of an active role of consciousness in the establishment of physical reality holds profound implications for our view of ourselves, our relationships to others, and to the cosmos in which we exist. These, in turn, must inevitably impact our values, our priorities, our sense of responsibility, and our style of life… Certainly, there is little doubt that integration of these changes in our understanding of ourselves can lead to a substantially superior human ethic, wherein the long-estranged siblings of science and spirit, of analysis and aesthetics, of intellect and intuition, and of many other subjective and objective aspects of human experience can be productively reunited.

Lynne McTaggart and *The Intention Experiment* are also real; the book is currently ranked 470 on Amazon.com, which is probably related to the fact that it's mentioned in *The Lost Symbol*. Indeed, Lynne McTaggart's blog on theintentionexperiment.com mentioned how chuffed she was to be mentioned in Dan Brown's latest magnum opus (4). McTaggart states that Katherine's assistant Trish Dunne, is most likely named after Brenda Dunne of PEAR.

Dan Brown refers to Heisenberg's Uncertainty Principle and Observer Effect: "The measurement of position necessarily disturbs a particle's momentum, and vice versa" (5). However, this is quite a complex concept that very much depended upon Heisenberg's viewpoint of logical positivism, so it may not be an idea that can really be transferred to the theory of the cosmic consciousness.

Katherine's discovery is that the mind's power to affect the physical world is one that can be greatly improved by practice and learning, and that some people have a natural skill for this power that seemingly derives from ancient mysticism.

It's likely that Katherine's book *Quantum Consciousness* is related to the idea "that quantum mechanics is necessary to fully understand the mind and brain, particularly concerning an explanation of consciousness" (6). The subtitle of the *Kybalion* is *Hermetic Philosophy*, and the book was published in 1908 under the pseudonym of 'the Tree Initiates'. So the *Kybalion*, although it's a book on ancient mysticism, is not an old book in itself. Paul Foster Case is thought by some commentators to be one of the authors, and he was a Freemason. The *Zohar* is widely regarded to be the most important book of Jewish mysticism, Kabbalah, and was supposedly written by a second century rabbi, Shimon bar Yochai. However, the *Zohar* only achieved prominence from the 13th Century onwards, and is thought to have been actually written by the man who found it, Moses de Leon. Of interest to readers of *The Lost Symbol* is this description of its content from Wikipedia: "While Maimonides and his followers regarded man as a fragment of the universe whose immortality is dependent upon the degree of development of his active intellect, the *Zohar* declared him to be the lord of the creation, whose immortality is solely dependent upon his morality" (7). So, the contents of Peter's library seem to be of scarce veracity thus far. The next book looks to be more of a bridge with Katherine's concerns, as *The Dancing Wu Li Masters* is all about the connection between ancient mysticism and quantum physics.

Researching Sumerian tablets online leads to some incredible stories with one shared theme: that the whole human race is the result of a genetic experiment carried out by aliens. These stories are far-fetched, but they do mention 2012, the Mayan date for the end of the world, and mention Freemasonry also. The first one I came across was a website called *Paranormal News* that featured a story about the discovery of some ancient Sumerian tablets in a copper box by the US army in 2006 (8). These tablets were then transported to the British Museum and examined under very tight security. Nevertheless, translations of these tablets have made their way online, with seeming references to alien beings, a power source referred to as 'black nectar' (presumably oil), and some kind of blueprint for a new form of power generation far better than fossil fuels or nuclear power. The author of the piece, Jeff Behnke, then discusses an impact crater also found in Iraq, which is possibly the source of the Great Flood experienced by the Sumerian Gilgamesh and the Biblical Noah in the 27th Century BC. Behnke speculates that the crater could have occurred due to a meteor crash, or the landing of an alien space ship.

The other website, *Crystalinks*, has a huge page devoted to 'Sumerian Gods and Goddesses' (9). This page also talks about aliens falling to Earth who later created humanity as a genetic experiment. You may recognise one of their names: the Biblical 'Nephilim' (Hebrew for Fallen Ones). This in itself is suggestive of the fallen angels who rebelled against God with Satan. The Nephilim were supposed to be race of giants that mated with human women, and their offspring were immortals or near-immortals. I always wondered why there are men mentioned in the *Book of Genesis* before the creation of Adam, and why the first people in the Bible often had ridiculously long life spans. So the idea of a race of 'angels' falling to Earth who created humanity is obviously one that has been dreamt up as a possible explanation for this. *Crystalinks* goes on to relate how these Sumerian gods became translated into Egyptian and Israeli culture. It also describes the etymology of symbols mentioned in *The Lost Symbol*, such as the Rod of Hermes and its links with DNA. The site also discusses other themes of the novel, such as 2012, the All Seeing Eye from the US one dollar bill, rebirth, Thoth, and Hermes Trismegistus. So, you get a great idea of the nature and the range of research that Dan Brown has done for this novel just by his subtle reference to "Sumerian tablets".

So, Peter specifically directs Katherine to an understanding of 'Hermetic philosophy' at an early age, so that she can appreciate what he believes are the links between it and modern science. Albert Einstein is, of course, famous for the theory of relativity. Niels Bohr greatly developed our understanding of atomic structure and quantum mechanics, and played a role in the development of the atomic bomb. Stephen Hawking is best known for his work on black holes. The earliest theoretical physicist that Katherine can think of is Isaac Newton, who is most famous for his work on gravity, and the fact that this discovery and his tomb contributed greatly to the climax of *The Da Vinci Code*. The Ptolemy mentioned here is not the general of Alexander the Great who became ruler of Egypt and founded a dynasty that included Cleopatra. No, this Ptolemy came from the Second Century AD, and lived in an Egypt controlled by the Roman Empire after the fall of Cleopatra. However, his cultural heritage was also no doubt derived from the Egypt's previous Greek rulers. In addition to this, Wikipedia states that his work in astronomy was ultimately based on the discoveries made by the ancient Babylonians (i.e. the Sumerians), so that's why he's mentioned here.

According to Wikipedia, Pythagoras was the first man to call himself a 'philosopher' ('a lover of wisdom', 10). Pythagoras is most renowned for his pioneering work in mathematics, and is the author of the famous theorem that states that, in a right-angled triangle, the square of the hypotenuse is equal to the sum of the squares of the other two sides, although some critics argue that this proof must have already been known by the ancient Babylonians. In addition to this, Pythagoras developed an early system of musical ideas, and came up with the idea of the 'harmony of the spheres', believing that planetary bodies moved according to mathematical equations that corresponded to musical notes. Pythagoras' enigmatic and mystical fraternity influenced the set up of both the Rosicrucian and Freemasonry movements. However, the clandestine Pythagoreans aroused suspicions amongst their local community, who turned on them, killing many of their members, and probably Pythagoras himself. However, the main point here would seem to be that these ancient philosophers had links to the even older knowledge of the Babylonians, and possibly back to the Garden of Eden in modern day Iraq.

The practice of alchemy is also believed to have originated in ancient Mesopotamia. The most renowned practice of classic alchemy was the attempt to turn lead into gold, and the manufacture of the elixir of life, which would cure illnesses and lead to long life. According to Wikipedia, "Certain Hermetic schools argue that the transmutation of lead into gold is analogical for the transmutation of the physical body (Saturn or lead) into Solar energy (gold) with the goal of attaining immortality. This is described as Internal Alchemy" (11). To the casual observer, the idea of turning lead into gold is impossible, so this concept does very much make more sense when taken as an analogy. Since this metaphysical and philosophical movement was often seen to be contrary to the teachings of the Church, not least by the Church itself, its practitioners had to veil their writings with elaborate codes that had to be cracked by the reader. So the cryptic alchemists are ideal source materials for Dan Brown's work. Carl Jung regarded alchemical symbols as being very indicative of the more spiritual nature of the alchemist's work. However, alchemy did gradually lead to the modern science of Chemistry, led by such pioneers as the 8th Century Muslim scientist Geber, who came up with a theory that involved 7 elements. Earlier, the ancient Greeks had thought that there were only 4 elements: Earth, Air, Fire, and Water (which were the Illuminati's ambigrams in *Angels and Demons*). Islamic alchemy influenced the work of Roger Bacon and Isaac Newton greatly. However, it was Robert Boyle who laid down the foundations of modern Chemistry in his book *The Skeptical Chymist*.

As Wikipedia states, "Quantum entanglement... is a property of a quantum mechanical state of a system of two or more objects in which the quantum states of the constituting objects are linked together so that one object can no longer be adequately described without full mention of its counterpart—even if the individual objects are spatially separated in a spacelike manner" (12). Wikipedia goes on to relate that (13):

The Dharmakāya (lit. Truth Body or Reality Body) is a central concept in Mahayana Buddhism... composed in the first century BCE. It constitutes the unmanifested, 'inconceivable' aspect of a Buddha out of which Buddhas and indeed all 'phenomena' (Sanskrit: dharmas) arise and to which they return after their dissolution... Unlike ordinary unenlightened persons, Buddhas... do not die (though their physical bodies undergo the cessation of biological functions and subsequent disintegration). In the Lotus Sutra (sixth fascicle) Buddha explains that he has always and will always exist to lead beings to their salvation. This eternal aspect of Buddha is the Dharmakaya. The Dharmakaya may be considered the most sublime or truest reality in the Universe corresponding closely to the post-Vedic conception of Brahman.

Brahman is a concept from Hinduism, and according to Jeffrey Brood's *World Religions*, it's "the unchanging, infinite, immanent, and transcendent reality which is the Divine Ground of all matter, energy, time, space, being, and everything beyond in this Universe" (St. Mary's Press, 2003). Dan Brown is correct that the word 'atonement' was derived from 'at-onement'. This was the name that William

Tyndale created to describe an otherwise untranslatable Hebrew concept in the Bible. Tyndale was one of the first Protestants to translate the Bible into English, and he employed the new invention of the printing press to promulgate his influential work, much of which ended up in the official King James Version of the Bible. Unfortunately, he paid the ultimate price, as did so many others, of upsetting King Henry VIII.

Abhay Charanaravinda Bhaktivedanta Swami Prabhupada, the founder of the Hare Krishna movement, gives this excellent explanation of the concept of the 'dual world' (14):

> We have got in this material world duality. Just like this is now summer season; then again we will have winter season, snowfall... Similarly, happiness and distress... Similarly, honor and dishonor. Because in this world, the world of duality, dual world, everything is to be understood by duality. We cannot understand what is honor if there is no dishonor. If I am not insulted, I cannot understand what is honor... Similarly, I cannot understand what is misery if I have not tasted happiness. Or I cannot understand what is happiness if I have not understood misery... I cannot understand what is cold if I have not tasted hot. This world is... of duality. So one has to transcend. So long this body is there, this duality feeling will continue.

The Upanishads also speak of the Brahman, and the Atman, the soul of a person. As Guhen Kitaoka relates, "The conclusion of *Mandukya Upanishad* is that time, space and causality are all illusion. This conclusion is all the more striking because of the paradigm shift which modern thought has been undergoing for some time, after the modern quantum physicists like Einstein, Heisenberg, Schroedinger, etc. came to the same conclusion as this *Upanishad* which is worth being called '*Philosophia Ultima*'" (15). Vyasa is believed to have been the author of the Mahābhārata, as well as being a major character in the text itself. In Hinduism, he's also considered to be one of the eight 'Chiranjivins' (i.e. immortals still believed to be living). This mention of another long living human reminds me of early humans in the Bible that I mentioned previously, who also had incredibly long life spans. The Philosopher's Stone in alchemy is also supposed to provide its owner with a long lifespan, unless they succumb to drowning or being burnt alive, as Fire and Water were the two major elements required for the formation of the stone. The Twitter clues mentioned a curious long-lived character called Count St. Germain, who I discuss in more detail on pp. 24-26. So it's possible that Mal'akh could be pursuing the literally age-old dream of immortality.

Which brings us nicely back to the concept of immortality that I quoted with regards to the *Zohar* on page 96. While I consider the authorship of the *Zohar* to be questionable, its similarities with superstring theory are indeed of a rather spooky nature. As the kabbalah.com website states, "Both the Kabbalist and the proponents of superstring theory agree that ten dimensions comprise reality, and that six of these dimensions were compacted into one at the moment of creation, or Beresheet" (16). The Sephiroth can be employed as an explanation of the Big Bang, as Wikipedia explains (17):

Lurianic Kabbalah described radical new doctrines of the cosmic origins of Creation. It taught that the first Divine act was a 'withdrawal' ('Tzimtzum') from the 'space' ('Chalal') in which Creation would unfold. This is understood by all interpretations today to be a metaphorical withdrawal, only from the persective (sic) of the Creation. A diminished 'Ray' ('Kav') of new light then shone from the Ein Sof into the Chalal, which became the source of 'light' (Ohr) that created all existence. However, Isaac Luria taught that the first created spiritual 'World/Realm' ('Olam') collapsed. This realm, the 'World of Tohu' ('Chaos', mirroring the phrase at the beginning of *Genesis*), failed because the 10 Sephirot in it had very high lights and weak vessels.... The vessels broke ('Shevirat HaKeilim'-'The Shattering of the Vessels') and their 'Sparks' ('Nitzutzot') fell down into our Four Worlds [dimensions]...

So, Peter Solomon is very persuasive in his belief that the ancients had advanced scientific knowledge that we are only just rediscovering. However, the cynic in me suggests that if you write a philosophy in vague and esoteric terms, then readers will always read their own experience into such works, and read into them concepts that were never there in the first place. The evidence that Peter Solomon provides us with could just be accidental similarities. And yet, plenty of scientific discoveries have been made via serendipity...

Chapter 16 The 'two-headed bird' on Peter Solomon's ring is obviously the phoenix that I have previously discussed in more detail, while the number 33 indicates that Peter has reached the 33rd degree. The CIA does indeed have an Office of Security that 'looks after' its staff. The badge of the CIA would probably be of great interest to a symbologist such as Robert Langdon, as it features the American Eagle from the Great Seal (which we know is derived from the Masonic symbol of the Double-Headed Phoenix), and also contains an image analogous to a Rose Cross (see pp. 15-16). I think Dan Brown may be playing linguistic names with the Director the Office of Security, as 'Inoue Sato' is a fairly close fit to 'Country's welfare' or 'Homeland Security'. Remember that Bishop Aringarosa's name in *The Da Vinci Code* meant 'Red Herring'. It's interesting to see that Sato was born into confinement at Manzanar, a form of concentration camp that is still quite controversial, as the rights of these Americans of Japanese descent were clearly violated. They were relocated from their homes under duress after the attack on Pearl Harbor. When the war ended, some of them had to be forcibly removed from Manzanar because they had nowhere else to go. Although their predicament was considerably less complex than the current Guantanamo Bay detainees. Sato has a physical ailment in the form of the scar left over from her throat cancer surgery. In a Hollywood spy thriller, she'd be a villain (why does the image of Rosa Klebb in *From Russia with Love* spring into my mind?) This slight, but very noticeable affliction, could indeed place her within that stereotypical pantheon that is the disabled man who, angered by his affliction, wants to take it out on the rest of the world (I'm thinking here of Dr. Strangelove and his atomic bomb, but no doubt you come up with your own examples). Not that I can think of any historical disabled people who have acted in this manner. However, in Dan Brown's own work, we have the examples of Max Kohler (who was eventually discovered not to be a villain, turning the usual stereotype on its head), and Sir

Leigh Teabing, who had committed the sin of being English as well as being a disabled genius (in Hollywood thriller terms, that akin to sprouting horns, hoofs, and a forked tail). Sato's internment as a child could have made her harbour a grudge against the land of her birth. There were certainly several Twitter clues that referred to treacherous double agents. However, one would have thought that she would have had ample scope for mischief during the Cold War, and since she would have been a toddler when she was released from Manzanar, it's doubtful that she would have remembered anything about the experience. Although how did she know that Langdon was in the Capitol Building?

Fyodor Dostoevsky is, of course, the Russian writer best known for the novels *Crime and Punishment* and *The Brothers Karamazov*. Like Sato, he was imprisoned unjustly by his own country in an inhospitable landscape (Siberia). Sato states that the nation is facing a crisis, but how does the dismemberment of Peter Solomon's hand constitute a national crisis? And how did she get to the Capitol Building so fast from the CIA headquarters in Langley, Virginia?

Chapter 17 Hmmm... So, not only does Sato have an unsightly scar on her neck, but she also suffers from the same skin condition that Michael Jackson said accounted for his loss of skin pigmentation, vitiligo. She also has a moustache, and her throat surgery has made her voice so much deeper that she now sounds like a man. For some reason, Dan Brown keeps mentioning the intensity of her "jet-black" eyes. So, in Hollywood terms, she'd definitely be a villain. Sato must be quite formidable even when interviewing other CIA agents. The FAA is, of course, the Federal Aviation Administration. Chief Anderson is right to question Sato's presence, as the CIA is prohibited from dealing with domestic law enforcement. However, Sato again insists for some reason that this is a national security incident.

Chapter 18 So, Katherine Solomon has no off-site backup for her data? That may not be such a great idea. Then again, I'm sure the Solomons are rich enough to afford both the time and money to repeat her experiments if anything went wrong. Besides, if they're recovering the lost knowledge of the ancients, then that knowledge will still exist, albeit still in its rather opaque form. This chapter introduces a new character in the form of Trish Dunne. At the age of 26, she's probably a bit too young to be Langdon's love interest in this novel, and she's obviously not as athletic as Vittoria Vetra in *Angels and Demons* (not that this should count against her). Peter Solomon's apparent difficulties with his iPhone give an indication that he may be more comfortable with old technology rather than new. Trish's search has indeed been made more easier with the increasing online digitisation of old texts, and this certainly would have made Langdon's life a hell of a lot easier if these developments had been around at the time of *The Da Vinci Code*.

In the Middle Ages, Old Frisian was spoken from Bruges to the river Weser in Germany. There must have been a great deal of interaction between this region and England then, as according to Rolf H. Bremmer Jr.'s *An Introduction to Old Frisian* (2009), Old Frisian is the language closest to English apart from Scots. However, since then, the Dutch language has had a great influence on Frisian, and English has been transformed by the introduction of French words. Although the spelling of the words is quite different, many English and Frisian phrases are pronounced in the same way. Most of the Old Frisian texts that have been preserved and translated have been legal documents. Maek is regarded as an extinct language from the Korean region, and the only evidence of its existence today seems to be from place names. Although the website linguist.org states that "the existence of the language is questionable" (1). Under these circumstances, it's not surprising that Trish Dunne would be the only person who built OCR translation modules for this language. Akkadian is another extinct language that goes back to the cradle of civilisation, Mesopotamia. By Alexander the Great's time, only priests in temples and scholars would have known of the language. These three languages give you some indication that Katherine has truly incorporated Peter's faith in the ancient mysteries into her research.

It seems that Trish's skills with metasystems allow Katherine to analyse large amounts of data in a very quick time. Her software's ability to determine the mood of the nation seems benign, but it is akin to the kind of surveillance issues that prompted Dan Brown to write *Digital Fortress*, and indeed, Katherine does raise the ethical issues involved. Still, the results do go hand in hand with the data produced by the random event generators beloved of Noetic scientists. There is again another reference to America's heightened security following the 9/11 attacks. However, I don't think Katherine's analogy with the grain of sand is quite exact, as Trish isn't trying to detect the mood of the grain of sand, rather the overwhelming mood of the whole beach, although she can probably do stats on how many grains of sand are feeling which emotion. Somehow, I don't think a trillion grains of sand are enough to exert a gravitational force on another body (when you're living in these times of extreme national debts, a trillion doesn't seem like all that much any more). And then Katherine goes completely far out by suggesting that thoughts have mass. This is the kind of crazy idea that leads to Noetic science being dismissed as a serious intellectual pursuit.

Chapter 19 Sato's still not sharing her leads with anyone at the beginning of this chapter, and it's suspicious that she wants to cooperate with Mal'akh. Sato is also firmly on the side of torture when it comes down to extracting information, as were many other CIA agents and the executive following 9/11.

There have been tales of a Fountain of Youth throughout history, such as one that Herodotus wrote of in Ethiopia, which he said explained why Ethiopians lived so long. Probably the most famous story is of the Spanish explorer Juan Ponce de León's attempts to find it in the New World, which were fruitless, although he did discover Florida in the process. However, many historians believe that this tale is actually apocryphal. Shangri-la is a much more modern invention, as it's an earthly paradise that first featured in the 1933 novel *Lost Horizon* by James Hilton. Interestingly enough with regards to my theory that Mal'akh may be seeking immortality, the inhabitants of Shangri-la have extremely long life spans. There is, of course, no historical evidence that Moses parted the Red Sea. Joseph Smith did indeed claim to have translated the *Book of Mormon* from a series of gold plates with a set of magic glasses that, conveniently, he was forbidden by angels from showing to anyone else. Smith had employed 'seer stones' in his youth to assist him in treasure hunting. Unfortunately, these seer stones neglected to warn him that he would be murdered by an angry mob in 1844.

Tarot started out as playing cards on continental Europe, and only later developed their occult reputation in Britain and North America, mostly in the 18th and 19th Centuries. The Swiss Freemason Antoine Court de Gébelin proposed that the Marseilles Tarot represented the Egyptian mysteries of Isis and Thoth (1). He also argued that Gypsies had brought the cards into Europe from Egypt. Gébelin's theories are probably apocryphal, but they caught the imagination of later figures in the Hermetic movement. For instance, Aleister Crowley produced a Thoth Tarot deck. The *I Ching* is said to have originated with the apocryphal Fu Xi, who, like Joseph Smith, had esoteric symbols revealed to him in a supernatural manner (2). Spookily enough, Fu Xi and his sister were the only survivors of a great flood (echoes of Noah and Gilgamesh here). Fu Xi and his sister prayed to the Emperor of Heaven, who allowed them to procreate, and also showed them a way of creating humans from clay (possibly the utilising the same method that the Greek legend Prometheus employed). Fu Xi then went on to live for close to two hundred years, like many early humans in the Bible... Another possible spooky coincidence is that the modern South Korean flag features the *I Ching* symbols for Heaven, Water, Earth, and Fire, which must surely be related to the four elements of the Classical World: Earth, Water, Air, and Fire. The Ancients also referred to an fifth element, which they called the 'Void': the black empty space around Katherine's lab is undoubtedly named after this. It was also called 'Aether' or 'quintessence' (as 'quint' means 'fifth'). According to Wikipedia, "In Greek thought the philosopher Aristotle added aether as the quintessence, reasoning that whereas fire, earth, air, and water were earthly and corruptible, since no changes had been perceived in the heavenly regions, the stars cannot be made out of any of the four elements but must be made of a different, unchangeable, heavenly substance" (3). There have been several cosmogonies (creation stories) hinted at throughout *The Lost Symbol*; so much so, that I'm beginning to think that Katherine Solomon's lab may be a metaphor for the Big Bang itself.

The current practice of Wicca has surprisingly modern origins. In 1954, the British civil servant Gerald Brousseau Gardner published a book called *Witchcraft Today* that recounted his own personal knowledge of the subject. In 1939, he attended a theatrical performance about the life of Pythagoras held by the Corona Fellowship of Rosicrucians (although some websites refer to them as the Rosicrucian Order 'Crotona' Fellowship). According to Wikipedia, Gardner was quite sceptical about some aspects of the group, including the fact that their leader, Aurelius, claimed to be the reincarnation of Pythagoras, Roger Bacon, and the real author of Shakespeare's plays (4). However, Gardner was on much friendlier terms with other members of the group who he felt had more of a genuine interest in witchcraft, and who turned out to be members of the New Forest Coven. Gardner was initiated into the coven later that year, and during the ceremony, he heard the word 'Wicca' called out, which he recognised as being the Old English for 'witchcraft'. Gardner was convinced that this coven had survived through the centuries. However, he also believed that witchcraft was in danger of dying out, and thought it best to disregard his vows of secrecy to write about the movement, just as Aleister Crowley had broken rank with the Golden Order of the Hermetic Dawn to write about their practices. Gardner believed that a couple of his ancestors had practised the craft, which is probably why he was so predisposed towards it. There's speculation that Gardner may have joined the Co-Freemasonry

57

movement (i.e. a Masonic branch that allowed women members), as several Co-Freemasons were also members of the Corona Fellowship of Rosicrucians. Gardner also had a great interest in Nudism, which he practised during occult ceremonies. In addition to this, Gardner had several Wiccan tattoos on his body, which I'm sure must have influenced Mal'akh's body adornment and his earlier nude scene.

Langdon believes that Mal'akh has been taking the symbolism of the Ancient Mysteries too seriously, as they are only metaphorical. Indeed, as mentioned previously, alchemists weren't literally trying to turn lead into gold; they were just trying to enhance their own learning and understanding of the universe. There are indeed many people who believe that the US Capitol Building is a temple. Take, for instance, an article on William Henry's website called *The US Capitol and the Temple in Man* (5). Henry quotes several historical figures that referred to the Capitol Building as a temple. For instance, Thomas Jefferson called it "The first temple dedicated to the sovereignty of the people". And President John Adams, while addressing Congress in 1800, stated that "It would be unbecoming the representatives of this Nation to assemble for the first time in this solemn Temple without looking up to the Supreme Ruler of the Universe and imploring His blessing".

Chapter 20 I can't find any evidence online that Washington DC was originally going to be called Rome, although a tributary of the Potomac River was indeed called 'Tiber Creek'. After some more research though, I discovered that the land that the Capitol was built on was originally called Rome. However, this name for the region dates back to 1663, and the owner of this land was one Francis Pope... What better name to give your land if you're a Pope? So, America's Founding Father's had no intention of keeping the name of their capital as 'Rome', as this might have been a tad confusing with the old Rome still very much around, so I think this is a mistake on Dan Brown's part (1). The obelisk referred to is, of course, the previously mentioned Washington Monument. 'Pantheon' is derived from the Greek for 'every god'. I can also find no evidence online that the Capitol Rotunda was designed as a tribute to the Temple of Vesta, although the Temple of Vesta did have a circular structure. The Vestal Virgins did indeed guard the Sacred Fire of Vesta (although how Sato knows this particular nugget of history, beyond helping out Langdon's argument, is uncertain). Rome was said to be in peril if the Sacred Fire ever went out. However, in 394, the Christian Emperor Theodosius I extinguished the Sacred Fire and disbanded the Vestal Virgins. Perhaps he should have listened to the ancient prophecy, as he was the last emperor of both the Eastern and Western Roman Empire, and the Western Roman Empire fell within a hundred years. According to the website Visit Washington DC Online.com (2), there was an eternal flame, but the office of the Keeper of the crypt was abolished after the American Civil War, probably because this sacred flame hadn't prevented America's bloodiest war. William Henry's site shows a picture of the four-pointed star compass that sits in the centre of the crypt in place of the eternal flame.

Sato also assists Langdon's argument by mentioning "knowledge that lets men acquire godlike powers": it seems that there is a great deal that Sato is not telling us.

Chapter 21 The figures on the *Apotheosis of Washington* are fifteen feet tall. They have to be this height, as the fresco is 55 metres above the ground. The fresco is visible through the oculus of the dome of the rotunda. As their name would suggest, Brumidi designed the Brumidi Corridors, which was part of the extension of the Capitol Building during the 1850s. The paintings of the Corridors feature many animals, copied from specimens provided by the Smithsonian Institution. According to William Henry's article, Washington is sitting "enthroned on a rainbow in front of a Sun gate", which is similar to historical images of godlike figures, such as Christ and Buddha, sitting on rainbows. William Henry also states that the goddess Liberty, who is next to Washington, is holding fasces, "a goddess symbol of transformation". The thirteen maidens attending Washington in the picture are thought to represent the thirteen states then present in the Union, and the maidens with their back to Washington are possibly that states that seceded prior to the American Civil War.

Minerva is the Roman goddess of crafts and wisdom. Benjamin Franklin and Samuel Morse were mentioned in the Twitter clues, but not Robert Fulton, who was commissioned in 1800 by Napoleon Bonaparte to build the first serviceable submarine, the Nautilus (which ultimately inspired Jules Verne to write *20,000 Leagues Under the Sea*). Vulcan, appropriately enough, is the god of fire, and Neptune is the sea god. The transatlantic cable was for the telegraph, the Victorian version of the Internet. "Any sufficiently advanced technology is indistinguishable from magic", is the third of Arthur C. Clarke's three laws of prediction from his book *Profiles of the Future*.

Again, it is Sato who first makes it explicit that Mal'akh wants to become a god, although this has not previously been stated elsewhere in the novel. However, Langdon does not challenge her assertion. Thus it seems that Sato has hidden knowledge that she's not willing to share. We learn for the first time in this chapter that Langdon is somewhat nervous of heights as well as confined spaces, as he definitely did not enjoy a previous visit to the Capitol Dome's catwalk.

Da Vinci's *St. John the Baptist* does indeed point heavenwards with both his index finger and thumb. Some critics have argued that Da Vinci's St. John appears to be a rather androgynous figure with his long flowing flocks of hair. Having written that, the figure does have a hairy chest, although this was possibly added later on by another artist along with the cross and the wool that also feature in the picture. Thomas is the disciple who appears to be making the same gesture in *The Last Supper*. I can't see the same gesture being made in *Adoration of the Magi*, so this painting is probably included here as an allusion to Zoroastrianism, the ancient Iranian religion. From 'Magi' we derive both 'magic' and 'magicians', since the Greeks regarded the prophet Zoroaster as being the inventor of both magic and astrology. Dan Brown has obviously mentioned these paintings as a direct nod back to *The Da Vinci Code*. ESPN is, of course, a famous American sports channel. Usain Bolt is one of those athletes who elaborately points to the heavens after he's won a race.

Hmm... Langdon makes a bit of a boo-boo here, as the sculpture of Zeus that the statue of George Washington was based upon stood in the Temple of Zeus at Olympia, not the Pantheon. I mean, why would Romans erect a statue of the Greek Zeus rather than say, Apollo, in the Pantheon? Due to the secrecy surrounding *The Lost Symbol*, only a few people would have read it prior to publication, so it's inevitable that a few mistakes like this would have crept in, such as describing the whole of the Washington area as 'Foggy Bottom'. Langdon does tend to make crucial mistakes in the early part of his adventures, so this may be one of them!

It's rather cheeky for Sato to accuse Langdon of not being forthcoming, as she's hardly been explicit herself. Sato's staff may well have found the same answers as Langdon, but probably a lot more slowly. The hand has obviously been freshly dismembered, as Sato doesn't have any great difficulty extending the fingers.

Chapter 22 Katherine obviously hasn't been asking Trish to do OCR on ancient Hebrew texts. If she had, then she might have realised that 'Abaddon' is another name for Hell, and is related to the Hebrew word for 'to perish'. In the later *Book of Revelation*, 'Abaddon' came to represent an evil entity in hell, and later on, it became another name for Satan or the Antichrist. According to Wikipedia, Abaddon was also the Angel of Death in the view of the Egyptian Coptic Church (1). However, in Gustav Davidson's *A Dictionary of Angels, Including the Fallen Angels* (1964), "In *Revelation* 20:1 he 'laid hold of the dragon, that old serpent, which is the Devil, and Satan, and bound him a thousand years'. According to the foregoing, Apollion is a holy (good) angel, servant, and messenger of God; but in occult and, generally, in noncanonical writings, he is evil" (with Apollion here derived from the Greek name for Abaddon). In this manner, some Jehovah's Witnesses believe that Abaddon is another name for Jesus. This reminds me of the thought ascribed to Mal'akh in Chapter 2: "the guardian angel who conquered your enemy in battle was perceived by your enemy as a demon destroyer". St. Christopher is the patron saint of travellers, so I guess that you could translate 'Christopher Abaddon' as meaning 'Traveller to Hell', or 'Traveller from Hell', or perhaps it's a subtle reference to the Antichrist. Which is a bit more sophisticated than the etymology that originally occurred to me: 'A Bad One'! Given this guy's name, it's amazing how quickly he secured Katherine's trust.

'Kalorama' is the Greek for 'fine view', a name that was first used for a house in this upmarket area by the poet Joel Barlow in the early 19th Century. Remember that in Chapter 2, Mal'akh's house had a great view of the Capitol, presumably the same view that Barlow was referencing. One of Barlow's claims to fame is that he helped Thomas Paine with the publication of *The Age of Reason* while Paine was imprisoned in Paris during the Reign of Terror. Katherine soon notices that Abaddon appears to be wearing make-up, so this is the most obvious clue that she is unwittingly visiting Mal'akh's mansion. There's also classical music playing in the background, and we know that this is another of Mal'akh's preferences from Chapter 2, along with the antiques. Although it's stated that earlier that Katherine instinctively trusts Abaddon, his home does make her skin crawl. The Three Graces were daughters of Zeus: Aglaia, Euphrosyne and Thalia, who are said to represent Chastity, Beauty, and Love. They have been the subject of many famous artists, such as Raphael and Canova. According to Wikipedia, many of Michael Parkes' works have "Strange beasts encounter mysterious winged women, good and evil fight out their eternal conflict" (1). Although the narrator states that the three graces are nude in Parkes' picture, only one is fully nude in the actual picture, and one of them bears a halo.

Abaddon claims that he is Peter's therapist. There's quite an awkward bit where he refers to the Solomons' love of tea, which is more of a British habit, although the family like theirs' black. So, Peter's son and their mother died within a space of five years. Abaddon states out that he is a 33rd degree Mason by pointing to a certificate bearing the double-headed phoenix, and we know that Mal'akh has recently attained this degree.   Since Abaddon regularly donates his family's inheritance, and has an interest in mythology, he obviously has a very similar mindset to Peter, as Katherine observes. 'Psychiatrist' is derived from the Greek for 'mind' or 'soul' doctor. Abaddon reveals that Peter has been discussing Katherine's research with him, as there are obvious psychological implications, although this is something of a shock to Katherine, as Peter had previously insisted on the utmost secrecy. Abaddon then claims that Peter has suffered some form of breakdown. Katherine then makes it explicit that Peter is the only family she has left following the death of their mother almost ten years ago on Christmas Eve. However, Abaddon states that Peter is in deep anxiety, as he knew exactly what the intruder was looking for, but said nothing. Abaddon then claims that Peter has told him a fantastic story about hidden treasure in Washington DC.

Chapter 23 Our modern number system is indeed Arabic in origin, although Arabia had derived them from Indian numerals. Thus it was the Indians who invented the number '0'. Performing mathematics in Roman numerals is a long and laborious process, not less due to the length of the numbers themselves; so Arabic numerals had a great advantage due to this. It's surprising that the original word for alcohol could derive from the temperate Islamic culture, but 'Al-kuhl' in Arabic actually means 'fine powder', relating to the eyeliner 'kohl'. It was only later that it was employed in a metaphorical sense to connote the distillation of a liquid also (1).

Runes have long been associated with divination, which is probably why Langdon thinks of them here. According to Wikipedia, knowledge of the meaning of runes was restricted in the elite in ancient Germanic cultures (2), and indeed, 'rune' means 'something hidden, secret'. This chimes with the theme in this novel that there is some knowledge that is too powerful for ordinary folk. Or could be that the elite were the only ones that could read or write, which would indeed give them power, albeit not in a magical form. There's no real substantial evidence that runes were ever used to tell the future.

Google is certainly not a synonym for research, as Google itself would probably point out. But it's an invaluable tool if you're delving into a novel as esoteric as *The Lost Symbol* in a very limited amount of time. Besides, Dan Brown admitted in his plagiarism trial that he used the Internet for research, so what's good for the goose… And according to Wikipedia, and some naughty people who have posted the entirety of *The Lost Symbol* online, Dan Brown is the first person to have ever used the word 'Alumbradian'. This is a reference to the Alumbrados, which according to Wikipedia "were practitioners of a mystical form of Christianity in Spain during the 15th-16th centuries" (3). Their name means 'Illuminated' in English; although there is no evidence that they were related to the Illuminati. The Alumbrados were mostly Jewish or Islamic converts to Christianity who became suspect during the Inquisition because they retained some of their old practices. It didn't help that the property of those convicted of heresy during the Inquisition had their property confiscated, as this led to bishops accusing their rich Jewish and Moorish neighbours, with greed as the main motive.

Dan Brown seems to be bending over backwards not to be offensive to the Masons, and it may be that *The Lost Symbol* will help recruit more people to the fraternity. However, why does Sato say that she has evidence that Masons are not so trustworthy? The Mason Edward L. King provides a whole variety of reasons of why it's unwise to engage an anti-Mason in an argument (4). It's interesting to learn that Peter's ring also has the Masonic symbol of the Double-headed Phoenix upon it.

So, it seems that Peter has actually mastered his iPhone enough to place Katherine's photo upon it. It's confirmed that Mal'akh is indeed Abaddon. If Mal'akh does indeed desire to become a god, as Sato maintains, then this would be the best explanation as to why he wants to destroy Katherine Solomon's research, as there's little point in becoming a god if loads of other people suddenly develop godlike powers around you. Mal'akh wants the world to remain adrift in ignorant darkness, so he could seem to be performing the opposite function of Lucifer, the light bearer. Although I guess that could also mean that he's keeping the light of knowledge to himself.

Chapter 24: supernatural aid Crimson is the official colour of Harvard, and Langdon's joke is about the rivalry between the two academic institutions. Hercules is, of course, the Romanised name of the Greek hero Heracles, who was sent to complete a number of labours. His twelfth labour was to capture the monstrous three-headed dog Cerberus from the gates of Hades (the Greek Hell), so Hercules' name is probably sly witticism on Peter's part. Vellum is actually made from animal skin, so you can kind of see why Hercules thought this rare Bible might have been tasty.

So, Peter Solomon has given Langdon something even more valuable than this Bible to safeguard. The box, although fairly small, is quite heavy, and Peter thinks it might contain some kind of rock. Langdon is amazed to discover that no one has opened the box since Peter's great-grandfather sealed it with his Masonic ring. Langdon is even more intrigued that the box is due to remain sealed until the 'right time'. Langdon suspects that this is a ploy to get him to join the Masons. Peter is right, the Masons do not recruit, and you do have to petition to join them. Langdon will never join the Masons, as if he did, he would take the vows of secrecy seriously, meaning that he could never discuss Freemasonry with his students. I can find no evidence that Socrates refused to participate in the Eleusinian Mysteries. Wikipedia reports that in the Eleusinian Mysteries, "The rites, ceremonies, and beliefs were kept secret, as initiation was believed to unite the worshipper with the gods and included promises of divine power and rewards in the afterlife" (1). However, according to Plato's *Dialogues*, "In the Meno, he [Socrates] refers to the Eleusinian Mysteries, telling Meno he would understand Socrates' answers better if only he could stay for the initiations next week" (2). In the *Dialogues*, Socrates also apparently discussed such esoteric topics as reincarnation and the mystery religions.

'Talisman' is derived from the Greek 'telesma' or 'telein' which means 'to initiate into the mysteries' (3), so maybe Peter is trying to get Langdon to join the Masons after all! Talismans are still in vogue today, as there's no handier tool than a crucifix to ward off demons! According to Joseph Campbell, such talismans are often given to heroes by their older mentors, as a kind of supernatural aid. Peter states that Langdon is a very sceptical person in his view, although Langdon does get to state some very crazy things from time to time. 'Ordo ab chao' is indeed Latin for 'Order out of Chaos'. One of the most prominent websites featuring this motto is unfortunately a conspiracy one that alleges that the Illuminati infiltrated Masons organised 9/11, so that they could create a demonic New World Order out of chaos. This website is on Geocities, so it will soon no longer exist, but it's a good example of the accusations that are hurled at Freemasons (4).

Peter believes that powerful people want to steal this amulet, rather suggesting that he considers himself somewhat impotent compared to his unknown adversaries. So, Mal'akh has tricked Langdon into bringing the talisman with him to Washington...

Chapter 25 Trish is excited at the number of results that her search spider has gathered, but is not too surprised due to the expansion of the web in the last few years. Although the web would probably get a lot bigger much sooner if Google's digitisation project wasn't so controversial! In literary terms, redaction is the practice of pulling texts together from multiple sources so they are transformed into a single work, such as the *Old Testament*. When I searched for the same keywords as Trish, I came to a page by Tom Horn, author of *Apollyon Rising 2012: The Lost Symbol Found and the Final Mystery of the Great Seal* (1). This is an edited transcript of the blurb, which will give you a great idea of what the book is about –

> Best selling author Thomas Horn was awoke by the Lord at 2 AM one year ago... He had been wrestling with certain images and enigmatic information for years having to do with the beliefs of an Occult Elite pertaining to the return of a pagan deity, which they believe will rule a final earthly empire... the Antichrist. But now things were making sense to Thomas world affairs, changes to U.S. domestic and foreign policy, a renewed focus on the Middle East, Israel, Iran, Iraq, Babylon and he found it astonishing. The words, deeds, gestures and coded language of the worlds most powerful men were clearly pointing to an ancient, prophetic, cryptic and even terrifying reality. What even the best researchers of... the Freemasons were never able to fully decipher is spelled out herein for the first time. The power at work behind global affairs and why current planetary powers are hurriedly aligning for a New Order from Chaos is exposed. Perhaps most incredibly, one learns how ancient prophets actually foresaw and forewarned of this time.

Which gives a great indication of the kind of theories that are currently spreading with respect to the proximity of the Mayan date for the end of the world, especially as this was written prior to the publication of *The Lost Symbol*. Maybe Mal'akh sees himself as the Antichrist, especially as we know that 'Apollyon' is the Greek version of 'Abaddon'?

'Symbolon' is Greek for 'to throw together' or 'coincidence', and it's from where we derive the word 'symbol'. So, it should be a word that Langdon would be very much familiar with! According to Wikipedia, "the earliest attestation of the term is in the Homeric Hymn to Hermes where Hermes on seeing the tortoise exclaims συμβολον ηδη μοι 'symbolon [symbol/sign/portent/encounter/chance find?] of joy to me!' before turning it into a lyre" (2). So the website containing all the keywords that Katherine gave to Trish is in the Washington DC area, but finding its owner seems more tricky than usual. However, Katherine is distracted by the fact that Peter seems to have finally learnt how to text from his iPhone.

There's another mention of the House of the Temple's oculus in this chapter, an architectural feature that Dan Brown seems inordinately fond of. Katherine relates that Peter has invited Abaddon to visit the lab, but unfortunately for her, she has no idea that Mal'akh sent the text from Peter's iPhone. With this accomplished, Mal'akh destroys the iPhone. The narrator makes clear that Mal'akh intends to destroy both Katherine and her research…

Chapter 26: the crossing of the first threshold Langdon suspects that it may be the CIA that wants the talisman, as they surely fit Peter's description of being powerful. So Langdon has to confabulate to avoid being taken to Langley. It helps that he has an eidetic (photographic) memory. 'Eidetic' is derived from the Greek 'eidos' meaning 'form'. Since most messages are communicated in one language, he knows that his previous attempt to decipher the tattoo on Peter's palm was wrong. However, it's his experience of dealing with ambigrams in *Angels and Demons* that enables him to recognise that messages can be viewed differently from other angles. So all he has to do is to turn the hand upside down to produce a more coherent message. Although I'm sure that other readers will have spotted this solution first, just as I was shouting at Langdon when he failed to recognise elementary mirrored writing in *The Da Vinci Code*! Even though "SBB XIII" means nothing to Langdon, it does relate to Sato and Anderson. Although Mal'akh's remarkably sloppy tattooing hasn't helped translate his message at all! One can only hope that his artistry has been much better on his own body, or else he'll look even more like a freak.

Sato orders that Anderson sends her the X-ray of whatever is in Langdon's bag, and that Peter's hand be sent to Langley. She also appropriates Peter's Masonic ring. The account of Tad Lincoln being lost in the Capitol basement is derived from Julia Taft Bayne's book *Tad Lincoln's Father*, as Tad got lost with her brother Holly. As Julia wrote, "they got the idea of seeing how far down they could go in the Capitol. They knew the way around the ordinary places but had never been in the sub-basement. 'We went down steps pretty near to China,' Holly explained, 'and when there weren't any more steps to go down, Tad dared me to explore around and we did and got lost.' Tad said, 'We knew there couldn't be any bears there, but there were rats and it was awful dark" (1). A workman finally heard their calls for help, and led them out. Yet the two boys only spent a day down there, so they weren't really that close to perishing. This journey into the depths of the Capitol Building represents the crossing of the first threshold for Langdon in his hero's journey. For, although he knows the Capitol Building very well from above the ground, he knows nothing of what inhabits it below the ground…

Chapter 27 Hmmm… I'm not sure about the etymology of Mark Zoubianis's name. This is definitely a name that Dan Brown has made up, since there are no other references to this surname online apart from to *The Lost Symbol*. 'Mark Zoubianis' sounds Greek, but doesn't appear to have any meaning in Greek.

'Ianis' looks to be the Greek version of 'John', which comes from the Hebrew for 'God is Gracious'. However, 'Zoub' is much more problematic, as it's an Arabic slang word for 'penis'… 'Ianis' is also the Latin for 'inane'. So, Zoubianis could mean 'Gracious knob', or 'Silly Knob' and 'Inane Penis'. Which, if true, is really quite rude on Dan Brown's part. Then again, we do know that Trish has previously been exasperated by Zoubianis giving her unwelcome advances, so this nomenclature could very well reflect Trish's feelings for this hacker. On the other hand, Mark is derived from the Latin 'Marcus', which means 'dedicated to the Roman God Mars', which could reflect that Mark has previously been too strenuous in his efforts to woo her. Although a Symbologist would quite rightly point out that since my interpretation of Zoubianis's surname involves more than one language, and therefore no "consistent symbolic system", it may well be wrong.

Trish is apparently afflicted with the same social ineptitude that affects most geeks, as Mark isn't happy to have been disturbed on the night of the play-off. Since Mark hasn't had much joy in his search so far, he suspects that the source of the website might be government intelligence or military. It seems that Mark has always suspected that Trish was lesbian, just because she's not interested in him.

Chapter 28 The forty Doric columns in the Capitol Crypt do indeed support the floor of the Rotunda above, and are more evidence of the architects' neoclassical influences. A 'catalfaque' is a raised, moveable platform designed for moving coffins, and the term is derived from the Italian word for 'scaffolding'. The original plan, following the death of George Washington in 1799, was for this to be his final resting place. However, delays were caused by the War of 1812, in which the British set fire to the Capitol building, so the crypt was not completed until nearly thirty years after Washington's death. The then owner of Mount Vernon, the president's resting place, refused to allow the body to be moved, and so the crypt never got to fulfil its function. Langdon even feels claustrophobic in this place, although this may also be due to its near association with death. He's not too happy to find out that they have to go further underground, as the 'SB' in the tattoo stands for 'Senate Basement'.

Chapter 29 The 'DMV' is the Department of Motor Vehicles, and the guard at the SMSC is amazed that someone has dressed up so much just for their driving licence photo. The narrator reveals that Peter had once pulled a gun on Mal'akh, and yet, for some reason, he doesn't recognise Mal'akh in this flashback. Again, the Solomon custom of serving tea to their guests is mentioned, and Mal'akh impresses Peter by asking for black tea. Mal'akh suspects that Peter voted against raising him to the 33rd degree, but Mal'akh's very generous donation to charity in the name of the lodge swayed the votes of the rest of the inner circle his way, even if they were still not prepared to share their secrets with him. However, the narrator again states that something unique happened within the Temple Room during Mal'akh's initiation that has somehow given him power over them.

Mal'akh then makes it explicit that he and Peter have met before, and then incapacitates Peter. The narrator then makes it clear that Mal'akh has come for wisdom rather than wealth. He also wants to know more about a secret hidden in Washington. Mal'akh then reveals that it was he who had killed Peter's mother, and that Peter had shot him. Mal'akh had warned Peter that if he pulled the trigger, then he would haunt Peter forever, and I think that this confirms my belief that Dan Brown had intended part of Mal'akh's name to connote 'ghost'... Mal'akh wants to know all of Peter's secrets, including why he had left him for dead.

Chapter 30 According to the accounts of the Egyptian Mystery Schools that I have found online, some believe that the Schools were founded by survivors of Atlantis, or from some civilisation that was more advanced than ancient Egypt was at the time (1). There also some commentators that go beyond this to say that the Schools' founder was an extraterrestrial from Pleiades, who became known as Osiris. The first pupil was Thoth (Hermes to the Greeks), and it was this godlike being that became known as Hermes Trismegistus (see p. 46). The most popular website on the Egyptian Mystery Schools states that:

According to the credo of the mysteries, only by developing one's faculties of will, intuition, and reason to an extraordinary degree could one ever gain access to the hidden forces in the universe. Only through complete mastery of body, soul, and spirit could one see beyond death and perceive the pathways to be taken in the afterlife. Only when one has conquered fate and acquired divine freedom could he or she, the initiate, become a seer, a magician, an initiator.

The next most popular website on the schools claims that "they taught the mystery of the immortality of the human soul" (2). Pythagoras and Jesus are claimed by such websites to have attended the Mystery Schools.

I have previously mentioned the Invisible College, the Royal Society, and Sir Francis Bacon in my discussion of the Twitter clues. Einstein, Hawking, and Bohr, the modern scientists that Peter and Katherine had previously mentioned in Chapter 15, were all indeed members of the Royal Society. Anders Celsius was the Secretary of the Royal Society of Sciences in Uppsala in Sweden, but I can find no evidence that he was a member of the British Royal Society, so this may be a mistake by Dan Brown, although no doubt he was part of the wider, international 'Invisible College'. Langdon doubts that these scientific revolutionaries were ever exposed to the Ancient Mysteries via the Invisible College, so this is evidence of his scepticism.

Newton's letter to Boyle has been slightly misquoted in *The Lost Symbol* – there's no "cannot". Here is an extended version of this extract: "Because the way by the Mercurial principle may be impregnated has been thought fit to be concealed by others that have know it, and therefore may possibly be an inlet to something more noble that is not to be communicated without immense damage to the world if there be any verity in Hermetic writers. There are other things besides the transmutation of metals which none but they understand", which sounds very much like the secrecy exhibited by the Freemasons. However, the website that I took this quote from, www.alchemylab.com, suggests that Newton may have been made Master of the Royal Mint because he did discover how to turn base metal into gold! So, one can very much understands Langdon's scepticism when dealing with such issues. Since Peter's Masonic ring bears the motto 'Ordo ab Chao', this is probably a good time to quote Newton's translation of Hermes Trismegistus' *Emerald Tablet*, as this is surely its original source:

It is true without lying, certain and most true. That which is Below is like that which is Above and that which is Above is like that which is Below to do the miracles of the Only Thing. And as all things have been and arose from One by the mediation of One, so all things have their birth from this One Thing by adaptation. The Sun is its father; the Moon its mother; the Wind hath carried it in its belly; the Earth is its nurse. The father of all perfection in the whole world is here. Its force or power is entire if it be converted into Earth. Separate the Earth from the Fire, the subtle from the gross, sweetly with great industry. It ascends from the Earth to the Heavens and again it descends to the Earth and receives the force of things superior and inferior. By this means you shall have the glory of the whole world and thereby all obscurity shall fly from you. Its force is above all force, for it vanquishes every subtle thing and penetrates every solid thing. So was the world created. From this are and do come admirable adaptations, whereof the process is here in this. Hence am I called Hermes Trismegistus, having the three parts of the philosophy of the whole world. That which I have said of the operation of the Sun is accomplished and ended.

Albert Pike, one of the two men buried in the House of the Temple, was the most influential promulgator of the Scottish Rite of Freemasonry. Langdon's well placed to compare the House of the Temple with Rosslyn Chapel, as he famously visited the latter at the climax of *The Da Vinci Code*. After he has helped Sato decipher the meaning of Peter's ring, Langdon is most grateful when Sato complies with his request that he looks after it. There are about 1600 pages online referring to 'thirty-third degree', 'portal', and 'pyramid', although this number has somewhat increased since the publication of *The Lost Symbol*! Having now read to the end of *The Lost Symbol*, I realise now that Langdon's view of the pyramid's symbolism is quite important: "The pyramid essentially represents enlightenment. It's an architectural symbol emblematic of ancient man's ability to break free from his earthly plane and ascend upward toward heaven, toward the golden sun, and ultimately, toward the supreme source of illumination".

An example of the conspiracy theories that Langdon refers to is the online article *The New World Order and the History of the United States of America* by H. O. Summers (3). Referring to the pyramid on the Great Seal of the United States, he states –

This Masonic symbol consists of a pyramid with the all-seeing eye of Osiris... above it. Underneath the pyramid is written 'Novus Ordo Seclorum,' which means The New Order of the Ages (or The New World Order) in Latin. This symbol was designed by Masonic interests and became the official reverse side of the Great Seal of the United States in 1782... although not a secret, remained largely unknown to the American people for more than 150 years, until it was placed on our one dollar [bill]... At the time the seal was designed, the New World Order was still in the early stages of being built and was not yet complete. This is symbolized by the capstone being separated from the rest of the pyramid. However, once the New World Order has been built and the one world government is in place, the capstone will be joined to the rest of the pyramid, symbolizing the completion of the task. The hierarchy of Freemasonry and the occult societies, resembling a multi-level pyramid structure, will now be complete, with the Antichrist taking his seat of power atop the pyramid.

I've already discussed how much damage could be done if Katherine's research fell into the wrong hands, and Langdon explains that previous guardians of the Ancient Mysteries held the same fears. According to Langdon, the Freemasons feared their fraternity would also collapse as others protecting the Ancient Mysteries had before them. So they transported their knowledge from the Old World of Europe to the New World of America, which they hoped would be free of religious tyranny. In the New World, they built a hidden pyramid to protect the Ancient Mysteries until the whole of mankind was mature enough to handle them and to reach their full potential. Langdon's not sure what's supposed to be inside the hidden pyramid, but according to the legend, it could only be deciphered by the most enlightened. I can't find any other reference to the legend of a hidden pyramid online, so I think this is one of Dan Brown's own 'fictional constructs'.

You're most likely to find discussion of 'Archetypal hybrid' within the study of English literature. Indeed, probably the best argument for what Langdon's beliefs here is Joseph Campbell's book *The Hero with a Thousand Faces* (1949), in which Campbell expounded upon James Joyce's concept of the 'monomyth', the idea that almost all fables follow the same pattern. *Star Wars: A New Hope* is a great example of the monomyth, as many of these tales begin with the hero being initiated into ancients arts by a wise old man or woman, and thus it was with Luke Skywalker and Obi Wan Kenobi. Interestingly enough, one of the stages that Campbell says the hero must go through is called 'Apotheosis', which is Mal'akh's supposed goal. According to Wikipedia, Campbell's Apotheosis involves "When someone dies a physical death, or dies to the self to live in spirit, he or she moves beyond the pairs of opposites to a state of divine knowledge, love, compassion and bliss" (4). Campbell himself wrote of this stage "Those who know, not only that the Everlasting lies in them, but that what they, and all things, really are is the Everlasting, dwell in the groves of the wish fulfilling trees, drink the brew of immortality, and listen everywhere to the unheard music of eternal concord". Which to me means sounds a lot like the death of Obi Wan, and his subsequent return as a voice inside Luke's head reminding him of the invisible but universal power of the Force. One could apply the same model to *The Lost Symbol*: although Mal'akh claims to be the wise one that calls for Langdon to be initiated, it's actually Langdon's older mentor, Peter Solomon, who requested that he be the one to fulfil this particular hero's journey... And it is to his memory of what Peter has previously taught him that Langdon keeps returning to, now that his mentor is effectively dead...

Sato is correct that there is a common belief that the Egyptian pyramids were designed as 'Resurrection Machines'. As Wikipedia relates, "The Egyptians believed the dark area of the night sky around which the stars appear to revolve was the physical gateway into the heavens. One of the narrow shafts that extends from the main burial chamber through the entire body of the Great Pyramid points directly towards the center of this part of the sky. This suggests the pyramid may have been designed to serve as a means to magically launch the deceased pharaoh's soul directly into the abode of the gods" (5).

Chapter 31 Trish goes off to meet Abaddon; curious to see whom else the Solomons could have trusted to their work with. On her way, she relives her first experience of visiting the Cube via the Void, when Peter had reassured her that her other senses would compensate for her lack of vision in the complete blackness.

Chapter 32 Anderson's anecdote about the basement previously containing a dirt floor and rats looks to have come directly from Julia Taft Bayne's book *Tad Lincoln's Father*. To Langdon's amazement, it's revealed that the room SBB Thirteen is a private room set aside for the use of Peter Solomon. Anderson reveals that 'SBB' is an acronym for 'subbasement'. I'm not sure why Dan Brown includes the plan of the basement and the terrace of the Capitol Building; it's probably just there to add some verisimilitude to the story.

Chapter 33 Zoubianis is somewhat surprised when he gets a call from the CIA asking why he's trying to hack into one of their databases. So, his hunch about the source of the IP being government intelligence turns out to have been correct.
The Architect of the Capitol has an interesting name, as 'Bellamy' is derived from the French and Latin for 'fine friend'. 'Warren' is also an appropriate name for the supervisor of the mazelike Capitol subbasement. Incidentally, the office of the Architect of the Capitol is currently vacant, so Warren Bellamy is not a depiction of the current office holder. Bellamy's arrived at the Capitol as he's heard about the incident, and security officer Nunez lets him in. Nunez is feeling guilty about having let Mal'akh in, so he's uneasy about obeying Bellamy's order not to alert Anderson to his presence. The narrator explicitly points out that Nunez has spotted a gold ring on Bellamy's finger, although Nunez has previously met Bellamy before, so this piece of jewellery shouldn't be so new to him.

Chapter 34 Trish notices that Abaddon seems disappointed to have been met by her and not Katherine, so she suspects that Abaddon and Katherine may be secret lovers, although their liaison might be awkward with Peter tagging along too. Trish notices that Abaddon seems to have a strange fake tan. The SMSC does indeed refrigerate its trash, and does have a "dead zone" (1). Dan Brown's reference to the latter might be an oblique mention of the Stephen King novel *The Dead Zone*, in which the hero wakes up from a coma with psychic visions of the future. Trish is notably talking a lot about dead things on her mini tour...

Chapter 35 The death theme continues with the fact that Langdon visited the Vatican's Necropolis in *Angels and Demons*. Sato subtly suggests that Langdon should leave the bag containing the talisman behind. Langdon is astonished to discover that the subbasement floor still has dirt on it. He then cryptically thinks *"Journey to the center of the Earth"*. This could be just a casual observance on Langdon's part, but I think that it is more of a direct reference to the famous Jules Verne novel, which starts of with Professor Lidenbrock rushing home to decipher a book of runes that he's just purchased. He and his nephew find a coded note in the book written in runes, which they translate into Latin. However, the note stills seems meaningless, and Lidenbrock suspects that a transposition cipher has been employed, but he still can't crack the code. So, he takes the unusual step of locking everyone in his house with no food until they can decipher it. Axel accidentally cracks the code when he realises that it does make sense when read backwards. It turns out to be a note from the alchemist Arne Saknussemm claiming that he has travelled to the centre of the Earth. Professor Lidenbrock then impulsively decides that he must make the same journey, and he and Axel proceed to discover strange peoples and animals at their appropriate geological strata as they journey into the Earth. As Wikipedia states, Jules Verne was a great fan of cryptology, and would often employ codes in his novels (1). So, it would appear that Dan Brown is doffing his hat at one of his literary predecessors, making it clear that Langdon is embarking on a similar kind of fantastic journey. He is also acknowledging that there is great drama to be had from the solving of such mind-bending puzzles.

ACME is, of course, the legendary company that featured in the Looney Tunes cartoons. The name was an acronym for 'A Company That Makes Everything'. 'Acme' also means 'prime' or 'best' in Greek, so this name is considered to be quite ironic, as ACME products usually failed spectacularly in the cartoons. The Catacombs of Domatilla also don't exist, but the Catacombs of Domitilla do. One can't be too hard on Dan Brown for typos, as this strictly embargoed book will not have been proofread by many (if any) people, and it's very common to find such errors in novels nowadays anyway. These are the oldest underground catacombs in Rome and the only ones to still contain bones…

The 'Thirteen' conspiracy is indeed quite widespread on the Internet, as some people do find it suspicious that there are so many representations of the number 13 on the Great Seal. The most obvious explanation, if indeed this was deliberate in the first place, is that this represents the original thirteen colonies of the United States. According to Wikipedia, "The number 13 has been considered bad luck since around the time of Ancient Mesopotamia, proof of this can be seen in the missing 13th law of King Hammurabi of Babylon. It is stated that law number 13 is missing since the number is considered evil and unlucky" (2). However 13 is most associated with the Masons since it was on Friday the 13th of October 1307 that the Templars were effectively wiped out, so it's hardly a day of celebration for them.

Interesting that Dan Brown should use the phrase "phalanx of doorways", as the original 'phalanx' was an infantry formation first developed by Alexander the Great's father. According to the Columbia Encyclopedia, "Because it lacked tactical flexibility, the phalanx was a better defensive than offensive formation" (3). So, these doors guard secrets… Since the door to SBB XIII is sealed, Sato orders Anderson to shoot the lock, since she half-suspects that it may be the secret portal. The door is blasted open to reveal a room that looks like a prison cell with an unholy smell…

Chapter 36 SBB XIII contains a skull and cross bones surrounded by arcane objects. As I have previously mentioned, one of the most notorious fraternities at Peter Solomon's university, Yale, is the Skull and Bones club, so Sato may be alleging Peter is a member. The skull and cross bones are also a Masonic symbol. The addition of a scythe is a grim touch though… The strong smell originates from a saucer containing sulphur, rather than from the bones. Anderson and Sato are taken aback by the contents of this room, but Langdon claims there are rooms like this all over the world.

Chapter 37 Trish gives Mal'akh a tour of Pod 3, the Wet Pod. Mal'akh barely listens while Trish talks about the Coelacanth, a fish that was thought to have died out with the dinosaurs, only to have been rediscovered alive and well off the coast of South Africa in 1938. The technical term for such a species that disappears from one or more periods of the fossil record, only to be discovered later, is a 'Lazarus taxon' (1), named after the man that Jesus famously brought back to life. So, this mention of the Coelacanth is just one of the many references to 'rebirth' running throughout *The Lost Symbol*. The appearance of the giant squid could be another nod back to Jules Vernes, as such a beast featured in a set piece battle in *Twenty Thousand Leagues* under the Sea, with Verne believed by some to have employed the monster as a metaphor for the crushing of the French revolution of 1848 (2). Mal'akh may have revolutionary ideas against his state. However, the Architeuthis is a famous resident of the SMSC Wet Pod, so it merits inclusion in *The Lost Symbol* for this reason alone. The giant squid is preserved in ethanol, so its tentacles shouldn't be decaying as much as Dan Brown states, and no doubt he's employing the word 'decaying' here to emphasise the atmosphere of death in this room. Then again, the majority of giant squids carcasses are recovered from the stomachs of sperm whales, where they are in poor condition. This, in itself, gives an indication that Trish is very much overstating the cases for a giant squid's chances against a sperm whale. Although giant squid sucker marks have been found on the hides of sperm whales, giant squid are still very much the whale's prey, rather than vice versa.

Mal'akh attacks Trish and demands her PIN. Despite the fact that he has been on a fast, the narrator states that Mal'akh has "seemingly supernatural strength". Once Trish has compiled, Mal'akh drowns her in the giant squid's ethanol tank. So, Trish is not going to be Langdon's love interest in *The Lost Symbol* – not unless he suddenly develops a taste for necrophilia! The narrator then reveals that the only other woman that Mal'akh has killed was Isabel Solomon. Mal'akh now has the key to Katherine's lab…

Chapter 38 Langdon relates that SSB XIII is a Masonic Chamber of Reflection. He also states that the items in this room are symbols of mortality. It's obviously no accident that the discovery of this room is interspersed with the first murder of the novel, another rather obvious symbol of mortality. *Symbols of Freemasonry* is indeed an actual book by Daniel Beresniak. Ganesha is one of Hinduism's main gods, and he is worshipped as the Remover of Obstacles (although he may place obstacles in the way of the unworthy), and he is also regarded as the Lord of Beginnings. Many fables relate that Ganesha started with a human head, as Wikipedia relates: "when Ganesha was born, his mother, Parvati, showed off her new baby to the other gods. Unfortunately, the god Shani (Saturn), who is said to have the evil eye, looked at him, causing the baby's head to be burned to ashes. The god Vishnu came to the rescue and replaced the missing head with that of an elephant" (1). Thus Ganesha can also be seen as a symbol for renewal. In addition to this, Ganesha is often depicted with a third eye, which may be of some relevance to the finale of *The Lost Symbol*.

'Caput Mortuum' derives from the Latin for 'dead head' or 'useless remains' (2). This term is also employed in alchemy to describe the left over waste material from experiments, and as Langdon states, the salt and sulphur in the chamber also refer to alchemy. Caput Mortuum was also the name given to a pigment in the Sixteenth Century, although artists stopped using it when they found out it came from ground-up Egyptian mummies! Langdon goes on to state that the candle represents primordial fire, and since man's ability to make fire played a pivotal role in his development, it represents "transformation through illumination". Langdon then goes on to say that scythe is not a death symbol, contradicting himself from earlier in this chapter when he included it in the list of death symbols in the chamber. Instead, the scythe represents the reaping of nature's gifts, as does the McCormick reaper in the *Apotheosis of Washington*. A lot of Masonic lodges do indeed maintain Chambers of Reflection. In South American and Continental Europe lodges, a visit to the Chamber of Reflection is part of the Masonic initiation ceremony. So, Mal'akh's instructions to Langdon to visit this room are part of his manoeuvre to initiate Langdon, who he obviously regards as an inferior. However, it seems that Peter could be undertaking what Langdon has always suspected him of doing, and that is to initiate him into Freemasonry, albeit via proxy. However, since this tradition doesn't derive from the House of the Temple, this could be another hint that Peter Solomon could be of the Yale Skull and Bones fraternity.

Sato seems to be disgusted with the room, saying that a lot of Americans would have problems with the image of "their leaders praying in closets with scythes and skulls". Langdon, as per usual when it comes to the Masons, puts a more positive spin on this, thinking that it would be much better if world leaders did ponder on mortality before rushing off to war, which is doubtlessly a reflection on the less than successful invasion of Iraq in 2003. However, there seems to be nothing in the Chamber to explain why Langdon was invited to Washington. After Sato lights the candle, they find the word "VITRIOL" on the wall, which, as Langdon explains, is often to be found in Chambers of Reflection. 'Vitriol' is another substance used in alchemy, and since it's quite caustic, it has been employed as an idiom for 'unpleasant remarks'. Langdon is quite right that the acronym of VITRIOL stands for the Latin 'Visita interiora terrae, rectificandoque, invenies occultum lapidem', which means "visit the interior of the earth, and rectifying it, you will find the hidden stone". This could be another reason why Langdon referenced Jules Vernes' *Journey to the Centre of the Earth* in Chapter 35. Sato takes this to be a reference to the hidden Masonic pyramid, although, since Peter's name is the Greek for 'rock', this 'stone' could be a subtle allusion to him. Indeed, Langdon does specifically mention, "St. Peter – the Rock", after whom Langdon's mentor was named. However, the conclusion of the novel points to another more infamous stone entirely... This is an indication of how clever Dan Brown can be, to adapt ancient symbols so that they nestle very nicely into the fabric of his fiction. I previously mentioned the Holy of Holies, as one of the Twitter clues referred to the Dome of the Rock, the Muslim temple that now stands where King Solomon's Temple was supposedly built. The Holy of Holies is the inner sanctuary of the Temple that could only be entered by the High Priest on Yom Kippur.

The most popular article online about Chambers of Reflection provides further insight into the purpose on this room. As W. Bro. Helio L. Da Costa Jr. writes –

The chamber reminds one's self of the caves where primitive men lived... It is also a symbol of the maternal womb. The profane is regressing to a time of innocence and to a state in his mother's womb. When he emerges from the chamber, it shall be as if being born as a new man. Contrariwise, the cave can also be the symbol of a [tomb]... Thus, the chamber indicates, at the same time, a beginning and an end: the end of one's life as a profane, and the beginning of a new life as an initiate in search of light, truth and wisdom. This can also be interpreted as a form of resurrection. This motif of death and resurrection is mentioned in Plutarch's *Immortality of the Soul* thus:

The soul at the moment of death, goes through the same experiences as those who are initiated into the great mysteries. The word and the act are similar: we say *telentai* (to die) and *telestai* (to be initiated)

So, the Chamber of Reflection here is a representation of rebirth as well as death, and this is a Masonic metaphor that Dan Brown will use throughout *The Lost Symbol*.

The candlelight flickers from a draught of air, and Anderson suspects that someone may have closed the door upstairs. The draught also moves a sheet of canvas at the back of the chamber that Langdon draws aside to reveal a pyramid...

Chapter 39 The stone pyramid is only nine inches tall, so Langdon dismisses it from being the Masonic pyramid, since it also doesn't have a golden peak. However, such an artefact is not usually to be found in a Chamber of Reflection. The Unfinished Pyramid is famously present on the US one dollar bill, and could indeed be said to represent, as Dan Brown writes, "a reminder of America's yet-unfulfilled destiny and the work yet to be done, both as a country and individuals". However, the Eye of Providence also features in the hovering capstone above the Unfinished Pyramid, which is often taken to mean that God is overlooking humanity's undertakings. The Eye of Providence is derived from the Egyptian Eye of Horus, and this striking image has been adapted throughout the ages, with Christianity adopting it as a representation of the Trinity, since the Eye of Providence is often depicted within a triangle, with each side of the triangle conveying an aspect of the Trinity. The Eye of Providence is a symbol that has been much employed by Freemasonry, so much so that many conspiracy theorists have thought that its presence on the Great Seal is evidence of a Masonic plan for a New World Order. However, Benjamin Franklin was the only Mason present on the design committee for the Great Seal, and none of his ideas were accepted (1).

Anderson removes the pyramid from its alcove, and Langdon thinks that they've become little more than grave robbers, so this may be an oblique reference to the extract from Howard Carter's diary that features on the Kryptos sculpture. Sato reiterates that, according to the legend, the Masonic pyramid was created to protect secret information. However, Langdon points out that such artefacts will only ever reveal their secrets to the most 'worthy', which would seem to preclude Peter's mysterious kidnapper. The secrets are supposed to be hidden in "a mystical tongue of lost words". Sato postulates that this may be exactly the reason why Langdon was brought here, as she turns the other side of the pyramid around to face him...

Chapter 40 Katherine is getting worried, as Trish and Abaddon have yet to reach the Cube, so she checks on their movement with a security guard, and discovers that they have stopped in on Pod 3 along the way. Katherine is feeling anxious, but dismisses her intuition, as it was wrong in Abaddon's house…

Chapter 41 Langdon is faced by a series of seemingly undecipherable symbols and geometric shapes, which the narrator likens to an alien keypad. Sato asks Langdon if he can read them, as this is obviously why he's been called to this room.

The Phaistos Disc was found in a the remains of Minoan palace in Crete in 1908, and is a clay disc featuring a whole variety of symbols that have only ever been found elsewhere on the island on an axe. Since there is not enough of the text to provide a coherent context, its meaning has puzzled archaeologists for years. The most prominent symbol on both the axe and the disc is of a man's head with what appears to be a Mohican style haircut, although these artefacts are well over a thousand years older than the first native Americans! The writer Jared Diamond has postulated that the Phaistos Disc could be an early form of movable type, such as that employed in the first printing presses. The Dorabella Cipher was created by Edward Elgar, and was utilised by him in a letter to Miss Dorabella Penny in 1897. Dorabella must have been unworthy, as she could never make sense of it. Then again, no one else has ever been able to either, but I doubt that it contains any world shattering revelations. Dorabella was famously the focus for the tenth of Elgar's *Enigma Variations*, so named as each variation was a veiled portrait of one of his close friends. Beyond this, there was supposed to be a hidden enigmatic theme to the variations, a "dark saying", with the most probable explanation being that it drew from the First Epistle to the Corinthians by St. Paul: "For now we see through a glass, **darkly**; but then face to face: now I know in part; but then shall I know even as also I am known", for in the Latin Catholic mass the 'darkly' is written as 'enigmate' (1). Note that this very much chimes with Langdon's mention of the "dark sayings" from the Bible, which I discuss on pp. 134-135. There was also a reference to the Nazis' cipher machine, the Enigma, in the Twitter clues. Since Elgar and Dorabella were never lovers, and since Elgar became a fan of Wolverhampton Warriors following his first visit to the Penny family (who lived in Wolverhampton), it's likely that the Dorabella Cipher contains a soccer chant, as Dorabella kept him up to date with what was happening with the team (2).

The Voynich Manuscript is an illustrated book full of a text that nobody has ever been able to decipher. It's thought that it could possibly date back to the Fifteenth century. The illustrations haven't really helped in the deciphering of the text, as the pictures of plants in the herbal section of the book seem to combine, say, the aspects of three different plants into one image. The book is named after Wilfrid M. Voynich, who owned it in the early part of the Twentieth Century. However, it now resides at Yale (did Peter ask Langdon to decipher it?) Of most interest to readers of *The Lost Symbol* however, is the assertion that it could have been the work of Roger Bacon, the Franciscan Friar who was one of the first to propound modern scientific methods, and who also dabbled in alchemy. The book is also said to have been sold to the Holy Roman Emperor Rudolf II by John Dee, the famed British alchemist and Hermeticist. According to Wikipedia, John Dee "devoted much time and effort in the last thirty years or so of his life to attempting to commune with angels in order to learn the universal language of creation and bring about the pre-apocalyptic unity of mankind" (3). John Dee had an extensive library that included many arcane books, and had acquired a reputation for being something of a magician from the elaborate effects he had created for a stage play in his youth. In addition to this, he was a pioneer in the field of Mathematics, and an expert in navigation: so much so, that he trained many of the famed explorers of the Elizabethan age. John Dee is also believed to have coined the phrase "the British Empire". Some decades after his death, the Rosicrucians claimed him as a member, as he shared many of their beliefs. In short, John Dee is one of the most fascinating and enigmatic characters from British history.

Although the symbols on the pyramid appear strange to Sato, Langdon has recognised them as an encrypted cipher language from the Seventeenth Century. Yet he is reluctant to violate the trust placed upon him by Peter, so is still reticent. Sato pulls Anderson aside to reveal the image of the X-ray of Langdon's bag. Sato then confronts Langdon with the image of the small pyramid that he has been carrying; which is, of course, a revelation to him, as he has never opened its box. Langdon immediately realises that this is the capstone to the unfinished pyramid, as do Sato and Anderson. So, the capstone, once placed upon the top of the unfinished pyramid, will turn it into a 'true pyramid' (i.e. one with smooth sides rather than stepped). Langdon now realises that Peter was being literal when he called the capstone a 'talisman', as another meaning of the Greek word from which it is derived, 'telesma', means 'completion'. Langdon now begins to suspect that the capstone and the unfinished pyramid combined would indeed become the famed Masonic pyramid of legend. From the brightness of the X-ray image, Langdon deduces that the capstone could well be made of gold.

Sato, not realising that Langdon was unaware of the box's contents, then threatens to take him to the CIA HQ in Langley, Virginia. Sato reveals that her analysts are already working at deciphering the symbols on the pyramid. Before Sato can arrest Langdon however, Bellamy rushes in and overpowers Anderson and Sato, commanding Langdon to seize the pyramid…

Chapter 42 Langdon instantly trusts the African American man who has saved him, as he obviously has the keys to the Capitol Building, he has put himself at great risk to safeguard Peter's pyramid, and he also wears a ring that declares he is a 33rd degree Mason just like Peter. They encounter Officer Nunez in the visitor centre, and Bellamy instructs him to cover up their escape in a dark passageway that reminds Langdon of the tunnel he'd utilised between the Vatican and the Castel Sant'Angelo in *Angels and Demons*.

Meanwhile, Mal'akh heads off to the Cube. The narrator reveals that Mal'akh has a contact in the Capitol Building who has just run into 'unforeseen difficulties'. The sinister Sato, forever tapping away on her Blackberry, is the obvious suspect in the reader's mind.

Chapter 43 Mal'akh calls Langdon on his cell phone and orders him to decipher the symbols on the pyramid in exchange for Peter's life. Mal'akh then reveals that the pyramid does not contain the Ancient Mysteries as it is obviously too small, but instead points to where the Ancient Mysteries are hidden. In addition to this,

Mal'akh states that the pyramid is the portal. Mal'akh also somehow knows that Peter has the capstone. 'Tempus fugit' is, of course, the Latin for 'Time flies'.

Chapter 44 Langdon's editor, Jonas Faukman, seems a very diligent publisher indeed to be working at his offices on a Sunday night. Faukman is based upon Dan Brown's own editor, Jason Kaufman. Langdon is apparently late in delivering his latest book, just as Dan Brown was. Like Dan Brown, Katherine apparently wanted to publish her research on some magical date in the future (probably 2012, the Mayan date for the end of the world). Faukman suspects that Langdon may have a romantic reason to call Katherine, as he seems very urgent in asking for her number, although he's quite bewildered when Langdon reveals that he's in a tunnel under the US Capitol Building. Faukman then thinks what publishers throughout the ages have thought: "Book publishing would be so much easier without the authors"!

Chapter 45 Katherine is somewhat surprised to get a call from Langdon, especially as he never called her back after their meeting at one of Peter's parties the previous summer. She makes a romantic joke about a bookish bachelor seeking a single Noetic Scientist. However, Langdon quickly warns her that Peter has been kidnapped, and that her brother couldn't have sent the text she got from Peter's iPhone. Katherine consults the security guard watching the SMSC's CCTV, and discovers that Abaddon left the Wet Pod without Trish, but carrying her key card. Katherine's in the void when she discovers that Abaddon is already in there...

Chapter 46 The Library Room was declared "the most beautiful room in the world" by the leading British geologist Sir Charles Lyell when the Library of Congress was reopened in 1853 following a fire two years previously. The Library of Congress is the national copyright library in the US, which is why it receives so many items a day. Bellamy and Langdon are in a tunnel connecting the Capitol Building to the Library of Congress. Langdon has arranged a rendezvous with Katherine, but is worried for her, as he has no idea what he wants at her lab. Minerva is the Roman goddess of wisdom, so it's very appropriate that she adorns the library. Aluminium is actually the most abundant metal in the Earth's crust, although it's rare in its free form, so it was very expensive before the development of modern manufacturing processes (1). As Wikipedia so ably puts it, "The Enlightenment, is a term used to describe a time in Western philosophy and cultural life, centered upon the eighteenth century, in which *reason* was advocated as the primary source and legitimacy for authority" (2). This was the era in which Freemasonry first flourished. The growth in capital and improvement in printing processes meant that the works of philosophers such as John Locke were much more widely available, and were evidently discussed within the lodges. The successful resolution of the American War of Independence for the colonists encouraged the spread of Enlightenment theory. So much so, that many commentators believe that the French lodges played a great contribution to their own later revolution.

The mention of Gian Lorenzo Bernini is an allusion to the Italian architect who created the Path of Illumination for the Illuminati that Langdon endeavoured to follow in *Angels and Demons*. Bernini's sculptures literally pointed the way for the skilled Illuminati initiates to find their fellows. Dan Brown is doubtlessly suggesting that Langdon is following a similar path here, employing similar methods, as Langdon did much of his research for that novel in the Vatican library, which is analogous to the Library of Congress.

It is thought that Johannes Gutenberg utilized the Giant Bible of Mainz for his edition of the Bible, which famously involved his new practical invention of movable type. Gutenberg employed a new form of ink derived from oil, as this stuck better to the metal types than traditional water based inks. The Gutenberg Bible started off with 40 lines per page, which was gradually increased to 42 lines later on, presumably to save paper. I've just reduced the font size of the text of this book for much the same reason! Only about 45 copies of the Gutenberg Bible were ever printed on vellum, so surviving complete copies are very rare. Many Christian churches are cruciform in shape so the narrator's analogy – "Hiding in here was like breaking into a cathedral and hiding on the altar" is quite apt.

The Library of Congress Reading Room seems like a strange place to hide, because it is so public, but Bellamy reassures Langdon that he has good reason to choose this place. He then suggests that they take another look at the pyramid. Langdon identifies the strange symbols on the pyramid as the Freemason's Cipher. Since the code is so easy to break, Langdon is astounded that anyone would think that he alone could read it. The Freemason's Cipher, also known as the Pigpen Cipher, is so simple that it often appears in children's puzzled books. Indeed, it's probably called the 'Pigpen Cipher' because you can imagine the dots in the square as being little pigs in an enclosure. Bellamy suggests that the reason why Sato wants him to decipher the code may be because she's discovered its secret potential.

Chapter 47 *The Lost Symbol* is Dan Brown's first book after the success of *The Da Vinci Code*, and is therefore the first that he knew would be filmed. So, this scene in the void, although challenging for Ron Howard to film, will doubtlessly make a thrilling set piece in the movie, an excellent contrast to the beautiful expanse of the Library of Congress Reading Room. However, unless every cinema has 'smellovision', the ethanol left on Mal'akh's clothes from his murder of Trish won't be so much of a factor. Katherine escapes from the void via the bay doors, although Mal'akh is still in hot pursuit. She disorientates him by activating some very powerful security lighting, which allows her enough time to get to her car. Mal'akh tries to break into the car, and shouts that he should have killed Katherine along with her mother ten years ago. However, Mal'akh is unable to break into the car, and Katherine escapes.

Chapter 48 Officer Nunez sees that both Anderson and Sato have been injured in Bellamy's attack, and the arrival of a heavily armed CIA team is enough to persuade him to disregard Bellamy's instructions not to reveal his and Langdon's escape route.

Chapter 49 Langdon's worried because Katherine's not answering her phone any more. Bellamy is also not having much luck trying to contact someone who can provide them with sanctuary. Langdon is incredulous at Bellamy's insistence that the pyramid is the legendary Masonic Pyramid, since it was supposed to be tall enough to be touched by God. However, Bellamy points out the most important guideposts in history have always been carved in stone, such as the Ten Commandments. Bellamy then refers to images of the 'Horned Moses', which occurred due to a mistranslation by St. Jerome. After meeting with God, Moses' face became radiant. However, the Hebrew word for 'radiant' also meant 'horned'. Indeed, throughout the rest of the Bible, this word did mean 'horned', so one can understand St. Jerome's mistake. The narrator relates how Langdon was haunted as child when he first saw Michelangelo's 'horned Moses' in the Basilica of St. Peter in Chains. It should be noted that this is also a subtle allusion to Peter Solomon's captivity on Dan Brown's part. Langdon apparently hates being lectured too. St. Jerome's mistranslation reminds Langdon of the *SanGreal: Holy Grail* and *SangReal: Holy Blood* dichotomy that he encountered in *The Da Vinci Code*. Bellamy goes on to say that the 'Legend' of the Masonic Pyramid is not some long lost story, but that the capstone is the 'Legend' to the map to the Ancient Mysteries, it is the guide that tells you how to read the map. The pyramid is high enough to be touched by God, as the enlightened man, who realises that God is within him, can indeed touch the pyramid's peak. Although Langdon believes that he has successfully deciphered the symbols, the resulting letters are meaningless…

Chapter 50 A CIA analyst is also working on an image of the symbols, since Sato has emailed her a photo of them. Like many Dan Brown characters, Nola Kay has an interesting name. 'Nola' is derived from the Latin for 'Of Noble Birth', and 'Kaye' is derived from an Old English word for 'Key'. So, Dan Brown could be implying that Nola Kaye is an 'important key', judging from her name. Still, it's a good name for a cryptanalyst. The Vigenere cipher was wrongly attributed to Blaise de Vignere in the Nineteenth Century, since it was actually created by Giovan Battista Bellaso in the Sixteenth Century. Although the Vigenere Cipher appears unbreakable to novices, it can be broken by experienced cryptanalysts, as the Confederacy discovered to their cost during the American Civil War (1).

Sato has apparently revealed the secrets of some powerful men to Nola. Nola's analysis of the X-ray of the capstone leads her to believe that it's solid gold, although she still hasn't been able to read its markings. Sato then sends her heavily armed squad to retrieve the pyramid and capstone, with the implication that they can kill Langdon and Bellamy if they get in their way… Sato's close call with lung cancer hasn't stopped her from smoking.

Chapter 51 Katherine's narrow escape from Mal'akh has got her thinking of the night that she heard Peter shooting her assailant on Christmas Day ten years before. This was the night that she first told Peter about her interest in Noetic Science. Such family gatherings were always painful reminders for Peter regarding the absence of his son, Zachary, who had died at the age of 21. Incidentally, 'Zachary' means 'remembered by God', so is an appropriate name for a lost son. Zachary had been a rebellious child, so there had been family discussions over whether he should receive the Solomon inheritance at the age of 18, as was the family tradition. Peter had insisted that the tradition continue, but once Zachary had his hands on the money, he ran off and partied. Soon enough, Zachary ended up in a

Turkish prison in Soganlik after carrying drugs across the border. Since the conditions in the prison were supposed to be quite dire, Peter flew out to retrieve his son, but failed, and was devastated when Zachary was murdered two days later, something that also cost him his marriage.

Mal'akh had interrupted the family gathering with the aid of a key that Zachary had told of just before he killed him. Mal'akh then demanded a pyramid that the Solomons denied all knowledge of. Alerted by the shouting, Katherine's mother had come out with a shotgun and shot Mal'akh. Peter pursued the wounded assailant, and Katherine heard his shot. And then Peter screamed in agony when he returned to find his dead mother...

Chapter 52 Mal'akh is troubled by Katherine's escape, as she knows where he lives and his true identity as the Solomon's previous assailant. Mal'akh has found out from Peter that Katherine's research has allowed her to answers such as whether there is life after death, and whether people have souls. However, Mal'akh is determined that humanity as a whole should not have access to the Ancient Mysteries, so he wants to destroy the holographic memory drives on which she has stored her research. Unable to gain access to the Cube, Mal'akh opens up some liquid hydrogen tanks, since this gas is very combustible, as the passengers of the German airship the Hindenburg found to their cost when the hydrogen that made the craft buoyant caught fire in New Jersey in 1937.

Meanwhile Katherine rings the police to get them to check Mal'akh's mansion, as Peter may well be there, although the police operator thinks she may well be a lunatic.

Chapter 53 Although Langdon is bemused by the apparently meaningless collection of letters that he has deciphered, the narrator hints that Langdon will eventually solve it, as the word *Chaos* is italicised. Remember that when Peter gave Langdon the pyramid in Chapter 24, he stated that, "it can imbue its possessor with the ability to bring order from chaos". Bellamy relates that the pyramid hides its meaning behind a variety of veils, and that the capstone is key to deciphering it. However, Bellamy warns that the Ancient Mysteries must be protected at all costs, and that the pyramid must not be completed.

Chapter 54 An SMSC security guard investigates what is happening in Pod 5. However, Mal'akh surprises him and drags him inside, before making his getaway. The security guard only has a few moments to comprehend what is happening before he and the Cube are blown sky high. This security guard is the second innocent person to be murdered by Mal'akh during the night's events. Since matter explodes into the void from the Cube, this explosion could be read as a metaphor for the original Big Bang itself, albeit Mal'akh's act of Creation is more destructive than most.

Having called the police from a gas station pay phone, Katherine tries to call Langdon's cell phone, but it's unlisted. So Katherine heads to the Library of Congress, Langdon's last reported location. Katherine is still puzzled as to why Abaddon didn't attack her earlier when she was in his home, but then she sees her lab explode in the distance...

Chapter 55 Bellamy tells Langdon that the pyramid leads to the entrance of a spiral staircase that goes hundreds of feet into the earth, the entrance of which is supposedly covered by a massive stone, like Jesus' tomb. However, neither Langdon nor Bellamy know of such a structure in Washington, so Bellamy keeps attempting to contact one of the older Masons who have more knowledge of it. Bellamy insists again that Langdon must not decipher the pyramid, even at the cost of Peter's life. It's then that Katherine reaches the Library of Congress and starts banging on the door.

Chapter 56: the meeting with the goddess Katherine is the goddess to Langdon's hero in *The Lost Symbol*. In the typical hero's journey, the goddess is the perfect woman with whom the hero falls in love. However, since this is Langdon's third adventure, we know that he will love her and leave her, as the lure of the next adventure will be too strong. It's also not a good omen that her name is 'Katherine', as this means 'pure' and 'virginal'. And so, sadly enough for Langdon, the amount of physical contact he has with his heroines diminishes with each passing novel. Oh, how he must long for the early days of tantric sex with Vittoria Vetra! In *The Da Vinci Code*, he had to make do with a snog and Sophie's eyes being "full of promise". Yet, Sophie, unlike Vittoria, doesn't get a mention in Langdon's subsequent adventure, so it looks like that promise was not long fulfilled, if at all...

The narrator emphasises greatly that Katherine is really relieved to see Langdon, and that the feeling is mutual, as he gathers her into her arms. Obviously the reunion is very emotional due to the traumatic events of the night, but there is a subtle hint of romance here. Katherine is also immensely grateful for Langdon's warning to her. However, they then hear another loud crash due to Bellamy's improvised alarm system, and know that the CIA is bearing down upon them. As they make their escape, Katherine sees Bellamy gather up the pyramid, and she instantly recognises it as the object that her mother's murderer demanded. Before she can ask any questions, Bellamy urges her and Langdon to hide in the octagonal circulation desk of the Library of Congress.

Chapter 57: Mal'akh – homosexual villain or bisexual god? Mal'akh has only just escaped the explosion of the Cube. As he heads back to his mansion, he reflects back upon his time in Soganlik Prison just outside Istanbul. Like Zachary Solomon, he was there due to drugs, and while there only had the title of 'Inmate 37', as 'Mal'akh', despite sounding Turkish, was not his name. The narrator then mentions that Mal'akh had a new cellmate. In his flashback, Mal'akh recalls overhearing a conversation from the grill in his cell between the prison administrator and the father of an American inmate. Mal'akh is amazed to hear that the father would not attain his son's immediate release and the clearing of his name just by bribing the administrator, as the father declares that he doesn't want his son to learn that having money solves everything. This gets Mal'akh to think of a plan to exploit the fact that Zachary Solomon himself was well known to have access to plenty of money, but the plan that he suggests to the administrator involves killing Zachary. So, two days later, the US State Department informed the Solomons that Zachary had been viciously murdered, and that before he died, he had authorised his vast fortune to be moved to a private account that had now also been emptied. The main suspect was the prison administrator, whom Mal'akh had murdered, so that there would be no trail leading to him. The blue manna crabs are probably named after the 'Manna' from Heaven that sustained the Israelites in the *Book of Exodus*. Technically speaking, 'Manna' is believed to be derived from the Arabic for 'plant lice' (1), although the crabs were probably so named as their flesh is very sweet, and Manna was supposed to taste like honey.

Mal'akh then names himself 'Andros Dareois', from the Greek for 'Wealthy Warrior', and we obviously get the word 'dare' from the same root as Andros' surname. 'Arni Souvlakia' is the Greek for 'Lamb on skewers'. Dan Brown places the phrase *I am reborn* in italics as this is a very important theme throughout the novel. It's interesting to learn that Mal'akh settles on Syros, as its main city is Ermoupoli, which means 'Hermes Town' in Greek. This city used to be Greece's main port, so is possibly far too hectic a location for Mal'akh's rejuvenation. 'Possidonia' seems to be derived from the name of the Greek God of the Sea, Poseidon. 'Bella gente' is, of course, the Italian for 'beautiful people'. Mal'akh is inspired to start doing body building after reading Homer's *Odyssey*, although I would have thought that Homer's *The Iliad* would provide more images of "powerful bronze men doing battle" during the Trojan War. Then again, Mal'akh, like Odysseus, is about to embark on a long quest... Mal'akh's new strictures against using recreational drugs don't stop him from utilising hormones and steroids to pump up his muscles. As well as changing his body size, the drugs also change the timbre of his voice.

It's interesting to note that Mal'akh sleeps with the occasional young man as well as women. This sexual 'deviancy' (as it would be regarded from a typical conservative point of view), is often a sign of villainy in Hollywood movies. Take, for instance, the Roman dictator Crassus, the nemesis of Kirk Douglas' Spartacus. In one notorious scene that was cut from the original release due to its homosexual overtones, Crassus (Lawrence Oliver) plies Antoninus (Tony Curtis) with snails and oysters in a Roman bath. There is also the example of the homosexual hit men Mr. Wint and Mr. Kidd in James Bond's *Diamonds Are Forever*. Perhaps the most monstrous homosexual villain in the movies was Baron Harkonnen from David Lynch's *Dune*, who glories in spilling the blood of flower-bearing youths. Incidentally, Frank Herbert's novel also had hints of Homer's oeuvre, as the hero's family was named after the Greek Atreides in *The Iliad*. In 1954, Norman Mailer wrote an article for the magazine *One* called *The Homosexual Villain* in which he admitted:

> I have been as guilty as any contemporary novelist in attributing unpleasant, ridiculous, or sinister connotations of the homosexual (or more accurately, bisexual) characters in my novels... I did believe - as so many heterosexuals believe - that there was an intrinsic relation between homosexuality and 'evil,' and it seemed perfectly natural to me, as well as symbolically just, to treat the subject in such a way.

So, this one line in *The Lost Symbol* harks back to a time when villainy was associated with homosexuality. Now that we live in a more secular society where the Church is less influential, and following the repeal of laws against homosexuality, we see less of these gay villains on our movie screens, probably because homosexuality is no longer regarded as a threat, as was the case during more conservative eras. However, Dan Brown grew up in an era when homosexual villains were still common in popular culture, so this shorthand for depicting evilness probably did influence him in some way, much as 'Englishness' used to be connected with villainy in the movies (such as Sir Leigh Teabing in *The Da Vinci Code*). However, Mal'akh is not satisfied with reaching the pinnacle of male beauty, and the desire that he arouses in others, and so looks elsewhere for fulfilment.

Yet Mal'akh's sexuality is extrapolated further in later chapters, so I now believe that Dan Brown was doing something else here, rather just lazily resurrecting the stereotype of the homosexual villain. No, I've now come to the conclusion that Dan Brown was utilising Joseph Campbell's concept of the bisexual god from *The Hero with a Thousand Faces* (see p. 104)

The P2 or 'Propaganda Due' lodge in Italy was mentioned in the Twitter clues, so is discussed in more detail on p.28. While watching TV, Mal'akh came across a documentary about the mysteries of Freemasonry that mentioned the Masonic Pyramid, which he immediately connects with a mysterious pyramid that Zachary's father had told his son about. Soon enough, he set plans in motion to steal the pyramid. However, his plan goes awry when Isabel Solomon peppers him with birdshot. During his escape, he comes across a boulder with the legend *Zach's Bridge* upon it, but no bridge is there. Doubling back on himself, Mal'akh is confronted with Peter. Mal'akh accuses Peter of effectively killing Zachary in his bid to escape, but Peter shoots him.

One of the reasons why Mal'akh now wears tattoos is to hide these wounds. Mal'akh believes that it was not his destiny to succeed that night. As the narrator states, "He had walked through fire, been reduced to ashes, then emerged again…" This is the masculine image of rebirth as symbolised by the Masonic Phoenix.

Chapter 58 Key4 is indeed an amusing bastardisation of the name of the C-4 explosive, as it can very forcefully open doors. 'Turner' is a name that could apply to a fast runner, and 'Simkins' means 'gracious hearing'. I haven't found any evidence online that thermal imagery can now look into the past, but then I suppose that the security services like to keep this to themselves. Thus technology here demonstrably provides humans with superhuman powers, which is what Katherine believes that her research will achieve. The reason why Bellamy headed for the octagonal circulation desk was because it led to the library's vast underground storage space. No doubt Bellamy and Langdon would be smarting as they heard the CIA's explosives carelessly destroying the archives' temperature controlled environment. The phrase "You can run, but you can't hide" is a staple from thriller movies, but it's believed to have originated from the American boxer Joe Louis before his bout with the lighter and faster Billy Conn.

The Library of Congress employs motion-activated lights to save energy, so Simkins and his team have an easy path to follow in their pursuit. The Sandia National Laboratories have been involved in the production of more lethal weapons than Silly String, such as the atom bomb. Simkins is somewhat puzzled to discover that there have been no lights activated ahead of Bellamy, so he must have been fleeing on his own.

Chapter 59 Langdon's impressed by Bellamy's idea to hide in the labyrinth that is the Library of Congress stacks. As I have noted before, Bellamy's first name is 'Warren', so it's entirely appropriate that he should be in charge of a labyrinth. Bellamy gets Katherine and Langdon to lie on the conveyor belts that form part of the Library of Congress's circulation system. Bellamy gives Langdon his key card so that they can exit from another library building, and tells him to expect a call from someone who can help them. This is a timely reminder of Langdon's fear of confined spaces, as the tunnels the conveyors go through are very narrow.

Chapter 60 The 911 operator calls Mal'akh's alarm company to investigate Katherine's call regarding his house. As the female security guard makes her checks, she notices a black limousine slowing outside the house before resuming its journey, to which she ascribes the term 'Rubbernecking neighbors'. 'Rubbernecking' is an American term used to describe people slowly down in their cars to see what has happened in an accident. Seeing a chink of light from a window, she investigates. Horrified by what she sees, she moves to radio for help, but is tasered before she can do so. Mal'akh was presumably in the black limousine...

Chapter 61 Bellamy is bound and blindfolded by the CIA men. However, he still has the wits to lie about Katherine and Langdon's escape route, as he is accustomed to such restrictions during Masonic initiations. Bellamy finally got through to the man who could help them further while they were escaping through the reading room.

   Bellamy then has a flashback to another time the pyramid and the capstone were together, the night of Zachary's eighteenth birthday at the Solomons' Potomac estate (where Isabel Solomon was later killed). The narrator makes a point of mentioning that Peter Solomon's private study smells of 'loose-leaf tea" amongst other things. Since Zachary is Peter's firstborn, he is given the traditional choice of 'wealth or wisdom', and Peter places the Masonic Pyramid before him. However, Zachary is not impressed that it leads to the treasure of the Ancient Mysteries. Peter states that if Zachary joins him in the fraternity of Freemasons, then he will receive the education that will enable him to learn of the importance of his choice. Yet Zachary states that he is the first Solomon who has no desire to join the Masons. Peter reassures him that the door of the fraternity will always be open to him. Peter also gives Zachary the opportunity to consider his choice over several days, and also promises to hold Zachary's inheritance until he proceeds up the ranks of Masons so that he can then acquire both wealth and wisdom. Perhaps if he'd studied his Bible better, Zachary would have realised that King Solomon, builder of the Temple, prospered quite well when he asked God for wisdom rather than riches or a long life in *1 Kings 3*:

> And God said unto him, Because thou hast asked this thing, and hast not asked for thyself long life; neither hast asked riches for thyself, nor hast asked the life of thine enemies; but hast asked for thyself understanding to discern judgment; Behold, I have done according to thy words: lo, I have given thee a wise and an understanding heart; so that there was none like thee before thee, neither after thee shall any arise like unto thee. And I have also given thee that which thou

hast not asked, both riches, and honour: so that there shall not be any among the kings like unto thee all thy days. And if thou wilt walk in my ways, to keep my statutes and my commandments, as thy father David did walk, then I will lengthen thy days.

Zachary is too impatient to wait, and snatches the portfolio that contains his inheritance. Before he walks away, Peter pleads that he never shares the secret of the pyramid with anyone. The narrator then reveals Bellamy is the guardian of the capstone. Concerned about Zachary's unreliability, Bellamy suggests that Peter find a new warden for the capstone, as anyone that Zachary told about the pyramid would come after him, as he was present on the night of his inheritance. Peter only agrees six years later after the murder of his mother, taking up Bellamy's idea to hide the pyramid in the Capitol Building.

Chapter 62 As they are conveyed between the library buildings, Katherine fills Langdon in with the details concerning the night her mother was murdered, a murder that she now knows was linked to the pyramid in Langdon's possession. Langdon informs her of what has happened to Peter, and that his kidnapper has promised to return him alive if Langdon deciphers the pyramid. Katherine and Langdon then arrive in the John Adams Building, named after the president who approved the founding of the Library of Congress.

It's significant that Dan Brown returns to the motif of *rebirth* again here. However, this is not the masculine violence of the Phoenix's rebirth. No, this is more feminine, as "Langdon felt like he had just emerged from some kind of subterranean birth canal".

Since the Masonic Pyramid has caused so much damage to her family, Katherine is determined that they should decipher it, despite Bellamy's warnings. Note that Dan Brown has chosen to employ the rather melodramatic word 'exploded' to depict the breaking of the seal, to emphasise Katherine's momentous decision.

Chapter 63 Dan Brown introduces a dramatic change of scene in the form of a medieval style walled garden. A young acolyte tells a mysterious elderly man that he has just received a message for him from Bellamy. Despite his advanced years, the old man leaps into action upon hearing the message.

Dan Brown has given us enough clues here, especially the Carderock gazebo known as the Shadow House, for us to Google and to work out the location of the old man. So, it turns out that he's in the Bishop's Garden of the Washington National Cathedral (1). However, the Washington National Cathedral is of the Episcopal Church, which was founded after the American Revolution, as Anglican clergy had to vow loyalty to the British king. So, Bellamy's friend, although he appears to be some sort of clergyman, is not a Catholic, which may come of some relief to Langdon after his run-ins with Rome in *Angels and Demons* and *The Da Vinci Code*.

Chapter 64 Having broken the seal, Katherine and Langdon are bemused to find themselves confronted with a stone box with no apparent hinges. However, Katherine soon finds the hidden opening. They're both amazed as, "the interior of the box seemed to be glowing. The inside was shining with an almost supernatural

84

effulgence". However, they shouldn't be surprised, as containers full of gold always glow this way in Hollywood movies. Gold doesn't oxidise in either air or water, which is why it lasts so long. It also doesn't dissolve in nitric acid as other metals do, and this is the 'acid test' of yore. Of more relevance to *The Lost Symbol*, the transition of base metal into gold was a metaphor employed by alchemists as a metaphor for enlightenment, so it's very appropriate that the capstone is made from gold. Unfortunately for would-be alchemists, the only way possible to currently synthesise gold is via a nuclear reactor, which is kind of expensive.

The CIA are prepared to employ tear gas to flush Langdon out of the library, so it's obvious that they care little about their national heritage. Sato notices that Bellamy has the key to a building with the acronym USBG, and so, in violation of the strict CIA interrogation protocols, she instructs that Bellamy be taken there. Eager Googlers will have noted that this is the acronym for the United States Botanic Garden, that was previously one of the Twitter clues, and is very close to the Capitol Building, judging from the photos on the USBG website.

Katherine and Langdon are both baffled by the text on the capstone: "The secret hides within The Order".

Chapter 65 In which Mal'akh potters around at home, cleansing himself after his recent trials, having 'dealt' with the female security guard. The narrator employs this brief respite to remind the reader that, as per tradition, Langdon has until midnight to perform his task.

Chapter 66 Katherine asks Langdon if the year 1514 means anything to him, as she has just found this date written on the stone box, along with an oddly stylised rendition of 'AD'. Katherine's suggestion of a building dating from 1514 is somewhat ridiculous, as the first Europeans didn't reach the DC area until the Seventeenth Century. Langdon states that the 'AD' doesn't stand for 'Anno Domini', but that it is a 'symbature': a symbol used in the place of a signature, historically employed by artists to add mystique to their work and to prevent them from being persecuted if they offended the establishment. So, 'AD' stands for a person...

According to my online research, Dan Brown is the first writer to have ever employed the word 'symbature', so like the Masonic Pyramid, this may be something that he's made up.

Chapter 67 The blind old man at Washington National Cathedral is very anxious to return Bellamy's phone call. Dan Brown seems to be actively encourage readers to Google the phrase "Is there no help for the widow's son?" However, the most popular results point back to *The Da Vinci Code*, as this phrase was highlighted on the inside cover of the American edition of Dan Brown's previous novel (with the appropriate letters in bold). This phrase is indeed a Masonic cry for help that relates back to the murder of the architect of King Solomon's Temple, Huram (or Hiram) Abiff, who was the son of a Tyrian widow. I mentioned this murder on p. 32. These words were also believed to have been uttered by Huram Abiff as he was murdered, as well as by King Solomon. Remember, Peter Solomon's father died when he was still a boy, so since Peter Solomon is himself a 'widow's son', this Masonic cry for help is more specific than usual.

Chapter 68 Renaissance artist Albrecht Dürer was mentioned twice in the Twitter clues. His 'AD' symbature features on the cover of his *Vier Bücher von menschlicher Proportion* (*Four Books on Human Proportion*). And indeed, as I suspected, 'symbature' is not a word, since such symbols employed by craftsmen are usually called 'monograms'. Yet Dürer's monogram is not a typical one, in that the 'A' and the 'D' are not overlapping. Dürer is one of Peter Solomon's favourite artists, and was, according to Langdon, an alchemist and student of the Ancient Mysteries. As well as being a supremely talented artist, Dürer was fortunate that his godfather was the most successful printer in Germany at that time, and since Dürer's engravings were printed, this gave him far more popular fame than many other artists of the time whose paintings could only be seen in private collections.

Langdon states that the clue on the box refers to *Melencolia I*, an engraving that Dürer completed in 1514, and which features the number 1514. Langdon also says that, "As you may know… *Melencolia I* depicts mankind's struggles to depict the Ancient Mysteries". However, I could only find one book that connected *Melencholia I* with a discussion of the Ancient Mysteries, and that's Ernesto Frers' *Secret Societies and the Hermetic Code: The Rosicrucian, Masonic, and Esoteric Transmission in the Arts*, which must have been on Dan Brown's reading list. The most common interpretation of *Melencolia I* is that it's an expression of Cornelius Agrippa's concept of "*Melencholia Imaginativa*, which he held artists to be subject to, 'imagination' predominates over 'mind' or 'reason'" (1). Cornelius Agrippa, a German contemporary of Dürer's seems to be worth a mention in a Dan Brown novel, as he had a great interest in the occult arts, and upon his death, his familiar, a black dog, was said to have been released from his body! *Melencolia I* has indeed been the subject of many treatises, including a two-volume study by Peter-Klaus Schuster. However, perhaps Erwin Panofsky, who suggested that *Melencolia I* was a kind of "spiritual self-portrait" of Dürer, provides the most persuasive interpretation. No doubt Dan Brown emphasised greatly with this image of the frustrated author as he wrestled with *The Lost Symbol*. If *Melencolia I* was Dan Brown's self-portrait, it would undoubtedly feature the pair of gravity boots that he uses whenever he's stuck for inspiration!

Katherine points out that *Melencolia I* is actually in the Washington National Gallery of Art. Langdon's eager to head off there, but Katherine vetoes this as she knows what happens when Robert goes to museums; which is presumably a jocular reference to the murder of Jacques Sauniere in the Louvre in *The Da Vinci Code*. Katherine prefers to do her research the 'easy way' via the Internet. Via the Internet, I can find very little evidence at all that Dürer practised 'Mystic Christianity', with the main source for this term being a chapter of Manly P. Hall's *Secret Teachings of All Ages*, which we know from the epigraph of *The Lost Symbol* to be a major source for this novel. Hall's *Mystic Christianity* chapter starts off stating that Jesus didn't die at 33, but lived on in to old age. However, if anything, Dürer seems to have been influenced by Lutheranism towards the end of his life, but he never left Roman Catholicism.

Langdon says something about Dürer's *The Last Supper*, but Katherine's not listening, so this is probably another jovial reference to *The Da Vinci Code* that famously featured Leonardo Da Vinci's *The Last Supper*. According to Langdon, *Melencolia I* represents "mankind's failed attempts to transform *human* intellect into *god*like powers". Langdon then opens up his solution to the Freemason's Cipher and states that *Melencolia I* will create order from its chaos, via the magic square of numbers that Dürer created...

Chapter 69 In which Bellamy is taken to the United States Botanic Garden and Sato begins her interrogation of him.

Chapter 70 Dürer is most likely to have been further influenced by Heinrich Cornelius Agrippa's *De Occulta Philosophia*, which contained magic squares, and was distributed in manuscript form after he completed it in 1510. So although *Melencolia I* was the first piece of Western art to incorporate a magic square, I still believe that Agrippa was the 'occultist' rather than Dürer, and it's doubtful that he intended it to be read as meaning that the Ancient Mysteries were being guarded by European fraternities, having passed from Egypt. I was perplexed by the fact that Dürer's monogram seemed to be missing from *Melencolia I*, but apparently those two letters are represented by the 4 and the 1 on the bottom row, next to 1514, albeit it the wrong way round. Wikipedia presents a closer look at Dürer's magic square in which you can clearly see that the 5 was originally a 6, and I'm not convinced that the 9 was supposed to be in its original place either, so it looks like Dürer realised that he had made a mistake during the engraving (1). Perhaps the best account that I found online about Kubera Kolam was written by someone called Karthik who was so inspired by the symbols in *The Da Vinci Code* that they began to explore all the symbols around them, including the Kubera Kolam, and to describe them via an online blog (2). It would be nice to think that Dan Brown came across this blog article, *Mathemagic*, and decided to include Kubera Kolam in *The Lost Symbol* because of this.

As Fr. Dennis Mercieri points out in his review of *The Lost Symbol*, 'Jeova Sanctus Unus' doesn't mean 'One True God' (3), as this surely means 'One Holy God'. I couldn't find any evidence that Roman translations of the Old Testament used 'Jeova Sanctus Unus', as one would have thought that 'deus', the Latin word for 'god', would have sufficed. However, it's clearly evident from Internet searches that Isaac Newton employed 'Jeova Sanctus Unus' as a pseudonym for his secret alchemical work (4). It's hard to say whether such websites were ranked so highly prior to the publication of *The Lost Symbol*, but if they were, then close readers of the novel, such as myself, may well have had a jumpstart on Katherine and Langdon in solving another part of the puzzle. Langdon may well eschew the Internet, but as Katherine proves, it's invaluable in solving a puzzle such as *The Lost Symbol*!

Since 'One True God' doesn't mean anything to them at this moment, Langdon suggests that it could point to a metaphorical location – enlightenment via the 'One True God'. At that moment, the mysterious old man from Washington National Cathedral rings Langdon, and informs him that the Pyramid points to a real location. He then gives Langdon a riddle about his location, which does indeed fit entirely with his locality. However, we'll discuss this later on, when Langdon explains his solving of this riddle.

Chapter 71 Mal'akh goes a bit too far in his depilation, as according to Diodorus Siculus' *Library of History*, the Heliades (Greek for 'Children of the Sun') had "absolutely no hair on any part of their bodies except on the head, eyebrows and eyelids, and on the chin" (1). The seven islands of Heliades were a kind of utopia, as the inhabitants on these equatorial islands could live to the age of one hundred and fifty, at which point they voluntarily killed themselves. There also seems to be some form of eugenics involved, as the disabled were either murdered or killed themselves. Apart from this unpalatable aspect, the Heliades were also distinct in having tongues that were split in two, which enabled them to conduct more than one conversation at a time, although Siculus provides us with no evidence as to whether the women were still better at this than the men. However, the most likely reason why the Heliades get a mention here is that they're children of the sun, and the sun is a very important motif that runs throughout *The Lost Symbol*.

Abramelin oil is so named because it was described in the medieval grimoire (magical book) *The Book of Abramelin*, written by Abraham of Worms (this sounds like a weird name, but is inescapable, due to the fact that this particular Abraham came from the German city called Worms). In the book, Abraham tells of how he was inducted into the knowledge of magical and Kabbalistic secrets by an Egyptian mage called Abramelin. S.L. MacGregor Mathers translated the grimoire into English under the name of *The Book of the Sacred Magic of Abramelin the Mage*. Mathers was, of course, the head of the Golden Order of the Hermetic Dawn. The most famous member of the Golden Dawn was Aleister Crowley, who later adapted Mathers recipe for Abramelin oil, by including much more cinnamon, so Mal'akh can't be using Crowley's recipe, as his "receptive flesh" would develop in rashes (not that this would be too noticeable under the tattoos!) Thus Mal'akh is more likely to be using Mathers' recipe. Abramelin oil contains myrrh, so this is probably why Mal'akh associates it with the Magi, as one of this was one of the gifts they gave to Christ. Incidentally, *The Book of Abramelin* contains Magic Word Squares, which are related to the more traditionally numeric Magic Squares depicted in the previous chapter, so this could be a deliberate bridge between the two by Dan Brown.

Another interesting development in Dan Brown's depiction of Mal'akh's masculinity is the revelation that he has a large penis. Yet, at the same time, he has been castrated, so he is symbolically (if not symbollockly) both potent and impotent at the same time. The eunuch Narses, who had commanded armies under the rule of the Eastern Roman Emperor Justinian I, and nearly recovered the whole of Italy, founded the Katharoi monastery. 'Ouranos' is the original Greek name for the sky god 'Uranus', who was castrated by his son Cronus, at the urging of his mother Gaia. According to legend, Ouranos came down every night to mate with Gaia, but hated the children she bore him, and it would appear that he had good reason to do so! Attis was the unfaithful lover of the goddess Cybele, who like Gaia, was a goddess of the earth. To complicate matters somewhat, Attis was her son as well as her lover. Jealous of his infidelities, she drove him so mad that he ended up castrating himself. Sporus was a slave in Nero's household who bore an unfortunate resemblance to the Emperor's wife, Poppaea Sabina. After a fierce

88

row, Nero is purported to have kicked his pregnant wife in the stomach, causing her death. He then had Sporus castrated, and then married him. When Nero died, the emperor's successor, Vitellius ordered that gladiators rape Sporus on stage. Rather than face this fate, Sporus killed himself. One does wonder why Mal'akh would willingly follow the example of these wretched men.

I don't think there are that many castrati magicians in Arthurian legend, and I can only find one: Clinchsor. He features in Wolfram Von Eschenbach's account of the grail quest in *Parzival* (Percival). Clinchsor, having been castrated by a jealous husband, builds a magical fortress and imprisons beautiful women in his bitterness. Osiris' brother Set tore his body into many pieces. Isis, Osiris' wife, gathered up the pieces of his body, except his penis, which had been swallowed by a fish. This act of devotion impressed the gods, who resurrected Osiris as the god of the underworld. Again, it must be noted that rebirth is a prevailing theme of *The Lost Symbol*. The tale of Tammuz and Ishtar from Sumerian myth is similar to that of Osiris and Isis. What's going on here is perhaps best summed up by *The Encyclopedia of Love in World Religions* (Volume 1, 2008, pp. 298-299):

> Common to the mythology of these deities is the theme of the self-castration of the male god and his subsequent death and sojourn in the underworld, from which the goddess rescues him and restores him to life. The death of the god often corresponds in the myth to the barrenness of nature - the Earth, whose fertility is restored by the goddesses's sexual reunion with her consort.

One of the many aspects of the Hindu god Shiva is Ardhanarishvara, the depiction of him as half-woman, in the form of his consort Shakti. This androgynous symbol is meant to represent the masculine and feminine forces of nature. Another representation of Shiva is the Lingam, which many Western commentators have regarded as being a phallic symbol. There is also a story of Shiva being castrated, as Devdutt Pattanaik relates in *The Man who was a Woman and other Queer Tales of Hindu Lore* (2002, p. 104):

> Naked with penis erect, Shiva wandered into a forest in a state of inebriation, oblivious of his surroundings. In the forest lived sages whose wives were so besotted by his body that they chased him like mad women, begging him to embrace them. The sages blamed him for arousing adulterous thoughts in his wives and cursed him to lose his penis. Instantly, Shiva's manhood dropped to the ground. It transformed into a fiery missile and threatened to destroy the whole world. Terrified, the sages invoked the mother-goddess, who... caught the fiery missile in her womb and contained its destructive power.

Note here the same conjunction of the penis with potency, literally as a weapon of mass destruction. Dan Brown also has Mal'akh appear to be potent despite his castration by pointing out that he has a large penis.

I've never heard any stories of Buddha being castrated, but there is a discourse in psychoanalysis that regards images of Buddha as being 'castrated', as Kazushige Shingu explains in his essay *Freud and Lacan on Japan* (2):

Castration symbolises the final vanishing of desire. From beyond castration, something rare returns to appear as an object of desire; thus did Lacan introduce the Buddha image. This explanation is congruent with the everyday beliefs of the Japanese people in regard to Buddha, and may even expand our understanding of our individual relationships with the Buddha. That most Buddha images are made with an ambiguous sexuality must be related to castration.

Thus it would appear that by castrating himself, Mal'akh wanted to abolish his sexual desire, as he had previously found carnal pleasures to be as narcotic as drugs. The *Jewish Virtual Library*'s entry on Castration gives the best indication of why Mal'akh has undergone this procedure, to become spiritually pure: "The explicit disqualification of priestly castrates strikingly indicates how repulsive to Judaism is the notion of emasculating ecclesiastics or temple servants in order to promote their spirituality, let alone for so slight a motive as to preserve the soprano voices of religious choristers" (3). Remember that way back in Chapter 2, Dan Brown presented Mal'akh in his home listening to a castrato singing *Dies Irae* from Verdi's *Requiem*. In this sequence, Dan Brown not only symbolised Mal'akh's own forthcoming *Day of Judgement*, but the fact that Mal'akh himself is castrated, as listening to the castrato was a "reminder of a previous life" before castration. The multiple levels of meanings that Brown conveys here is evidence that his prose is not as dumb and thoughtless as his critics would often have us believe.

Tucker Lieberman's excellent essay *When I Stop Naming Eunuchs* states that, "Jesus, by a few maverick interpretations, was part of the expansive brotherhood" (4). I can find no other tales to suggest that Jesus was ever castrated, an operation that would have certainly threatened his ability to have a child with Mary Magdalene if it had been performed early on in his life, and would have thus spoiled the plot of *The Da Vinci Code*. So the mention of Jesus here is probably due to his following injunction in *The Gospel of St. Matthew* that his followers should "make themselves eunuchs for the sake of the kingdom of heaven". Jesus spoke in parables, so he probably did not mean for this to be taken literally. Unfortunately, some sects throughout the centuries, such as the Heaven's Gate cult, did take this too literally. The Skoptsy sect in Russia believed that by removing their sexual organs, their members (both men and women) could return to the innocent state of Adam and Eve prior to their expulsion from Eden, because they thought that the primal couple had had the halves of the forbidden fruit grafted onto their bodies to make testes and breasts (5). Mathew Kuefler has written of his book *The Manly Eunuch: Masculinity, Gender Ambiguity, and Christian Ideology in Late Antiquity* (2001) that –

Every one of the Church fathers who spoke on self-castration spoke to condemn it... they were working hard to demonstrate the manliness of Christianity within a traditional Roman framework, for the purpose of attracting converts from the male aristocracy, and self-castration did not support that agenda. Nonetheless, most betray a begrudging admiration for the goals of self-made eunuchs: after all, virtually all of the Church fathers were also encouraging men to renounce sex, even while they preferred that it was done,

90

as Ambrose said, "by will" rather than "by necessity." Tertullian, in the same treatise, could both ridicule self-castration by saying: "Can anyone ... be called abstinent when deprived of that which he is called to abstain from?" but also praise those persons, "both men and women, whom nature has made sterile, with a structure which cannot procreate," seeing them as a foretaste of the absence of sexual desire in Heaven. Jerome, while discounting the "girding of the loins" as support for castration, also wrote that "all the Devil's strength is in the loins." In each, an awkward support for the end of castration is joined to a condemnation of the means (6).

Tucker Lieberman's essay *When I Stop Naming Eunuchs* also states that –

I can start with... the thousands of monks who massed on the Nile after Constantine gave Christians the right to associate in 315. Many were castrated despite the Nicaean Council's prohibition. Their leader Pachomius was a fanatical believer in celibacy, and his initial devotion to cult of the castrated Egyptian god Osiris before converting to Christianity is reason to think he personally may have been castrated. Osiris was known in Rome but the castrated Greek god Attis had a greater influence there. Standing out with their crimped, bleached hair and loud public displays, the Attis-worshippers called gallae immigrated to Rome from modern-day Turkey in the second century BCE. Their castration ritual occurred on the spring equinox when they celebrated the death and resurrection of their god and decorated a pine tree to symbolize his body. Comparing celibate Christians to gallae was used as an insult for a thousand years, even by other Christians.

The fact that Mal'akh has chosen a blond wig for his disguise might be a casual reference to the bleached hair of the gallae. Mal'akh's belief that "Every spiritual metamorphosis is preceded by a physical one" could just be a reflection of the fact that Christ was crucified and resurrected, rather than that he was castrated. Yet, as shown above, many Christian sects have practised castration, and stories of gods being castrated have often been linked to the concept of rebirth, which is a very important theme in *The Lost Symbol*.

'Fontanel' is Old French for 'fountain', and is indeed used to depict the 'hollow' in a baby's skull. Unfortunately for Mal'akh, there is more than one fontanel on a baby's skull, so it looks as though the source of this idea is likely to be the concept of the 'Brahman's Crevice' from Hinduism (7). So, along with the castration, this misunderstanding of anatomy gives an indication that Mal'akh has been taking his mystical readings far too literally. Mal'akh's approach is also in opposition to Katherine's, as he ignores modern scientific evidence. The area on the top of Mal'akh's skull is most likely to correspond to that of the frontal fontanel. Note that the reference to the *oculus* is italicised. Remember, 'oculus', the Latin for 'eye', has been already been mentioned in the novel, as the House of the Temple has a circular skylight that is also known as an 'oculus'. Again, the oculus of the Pantheon played a significant role in *Angels and Demons*, a movie that was released on DVD simultaneously with the publication of *The Lost Symbol*, so this term should resonate with Dan Brown fans. Beyond this, the oculus on the top of Mal'akh's head could represent the third eye displayed in images of Hindu gods such as Shiva. The skin here is described as 'virginal' in the sense of 'unblemished', and gives another indication of how pure Mal'akh now regards his body to be.

'Ouroboros' is derived from the Greek for 'tail-eater'. This symbol is believed to have derived from Ancient Egypt. According to Plato, this mystical snake devouring its own tail was immortal and the first living thing in the universe. However, it's Carl Jung's analysis of the alchemical employment of this symbol that is probably of most relevance to readers (8):

> The alchemists, who in their own way knew more about the nature of the individuation process than we moderns do, expressed this paradox through the symbol of the Ouroboros, the snake that eats its own tail. The Ouroboros has been said to have a meaning of infinity or wholeness. In the age-old image of the Ouroboros lies the thought of devouring oneself and turning oneself into a circulatory process, for it was clear to the more astute alchemists that the prima materia of the art was man himself. The Ouroboros is a dramatic symbol for the integration and assimilation of the opposite, i.e. of the shadow. This 'feed-back' process is at the same time a symbol of immortality, since it is said of the Ouroboros that he slays himself and brings himself to life, fertilizes himself and gives birth to himself. He symbolizes the One, who proceeds from the clash of opposites, and he therefore constitutes the secret of the prima materia which [...] unquestionably stems from man's unconscious.

So again, Mal'akh is referring to powerful symbols of regeneration, and thus of immortality. Since Ouroboros is a snake, it could be regarded as a phallic symbol. However, since Ouroboros is also circular, it could also be regarded as a vaginal symbol, and therefore the combination is quite androgynous. So it appears that Mal'akh is attempting to create an androgynous image of himself, although he hasn't gone all the way, as his penis still remains.

Mal'akh's frontal fontanel is described as a void waiting to be filled with the mysterious lost symbol of the title. However, the last time a void was filled in this novel was when Mal'akh blew up Katherine's lab, so that's not a good omen. The loincloth is now regarded in Western society as a primitive garment, so by wearing one Mal'akh is probably reflecting his pre-Christian beliefs. It's also the garment that Christ is depicted on the cross as wearing, so this could be yet another symbol of death and resurrection that Mal'akh is employing. Yet Mal'akh is very much an Antichrist, as he's not intending for anyone but him to have salvation.

Mal'akh gets an email from his contact saying that everything is running to plan. Since Sato's been typing away into her Blackberry all night, the reader naturally assumes that she and Mal'akh are working in cahoots.

Chapter 72 In which the CIA discover that Langdon and Katherine rode the conveyor belt into the Adams building.

Chapter 73: the road of trials Langdon believes the cryptic location provided by the aged Mason is a very apt place to find the 'One True God'. The Folger Shakespeare Library, as its name would suggest, has the largest collection of Shakespeare's printed works in the world, and the third largest collection of

English books printed before 1641. I discuss Sir Francis Bacon's *New Atlantis* in more detail on pp. 25-27.

Langdon and Katherine get into a cab to head for their cryptic destination. However, there is a buzz of activity around the Library of Congress, so Katherine is determined that the pyramid does not fall into CIA hands. Referring to Langdon's eidetic memory, his ability to remember every phone number, she throws Langdon's phone out of the cab window. The cab driver, Omar, gets a message from his company's dispatcher telling him that the CIA are looking for two fugitives. Omar informs his dispatcher that he is carrying them, so the CIA get on the radio to give him further instructions...

So, Katherine and Langdon have literally hit the road of trials in his *hero's journey*. Not that it was easy before this stage, but now they will have to traverse even more challenges.

Chapter 74 The narrator confirms that Bellamy is indeed being held captive in the US Botanic Garden's Jungle. Bellamy isn't comfortable to be amidst the strangler figs. Bellamy suspects that Sato is behind the whole of the night's events. Sato wants Bellamy to ring Langdon to tell him to hand himself into the CIA, and to go along with the kidnapper's demands to avoid a catastrophe, but Bellamy refuses to break his Masonic vows. Sato gets a call from one of her agents about Langdon's cab, and tells them to direct it to the Botanic Garden. She then warns Bellamy that he's outliving his usefulness... This seems to be a reference to the CIA's recent reputation for adopting an approach of dubious morality in the battle against Al Qaeda.

Chapter 75 As I discussed on p. 58, the Washington area was already called Rome prior to the building of DC, so there was never any plan to call the capital 'New Rome'. However, the city's planners did fill DC's streets with buildings in the neoclassical style that was all the rage at the end of the Eighteenth Century. Langdon had asked the cab driver to go to Northwest on Massachusetts Avenue, as this was the location of the place described in the Masonic caller's cryptic message. This address is crying out to be Googled by interested readers, but we already know form his previous clues that this is Washington National Cathedral. Dan Brown may be taking advantage of the fact that the Internet, with the recent advances in cell phones like Peter's iPhone, is now far more mobile than ever before, and so it wouldn't interrupt his readers too much to Google such things, giving them pleasure when their solution of this riddle is confirmed. Still, if Langdon had already explained this to Katherine, why didn't he just ask the cab driver to go to Washington National Cathedral in the first place? Langdon's somewhat perplexed when Katherine exclaims that they're going the wrong way, and that they should go to Freedom Plaza instead.

Langdon's even more amazed when Katherine starts drawing the Seal of Solomon on a dollar bill, and refers to the common conspiracy theory that since the points of the star spell out 'Mason', this is evidence of Masonry's hidden power over the nation. Now the CIA move in for the kill...

Chapter 76 The reverse of the Great Seal is indeed present in Freedom Plaza, not far from the Capitol Building. Omar watches on as Langdon and Katherine walk around on L'Enfant's original street plan for DC. Langdon comes back to the cab, and asks what direction Alexandria, Virginia is. Katherine then states that they need King Street Station on the Metro. As they rush off, Omar informs the CIA where they're headed. The CIA's chopper lands and Simkins consults with Omar, and comes to the conclusion that their quarry is headed to the George Washington Masonic Memorial.

Chapter 77 Starts off with a flashback to how Mal'akh survived his fall into the icy water after being shot by Peter Solomon a decade before. A couple of days later, Mal'akh hears on the radio that Isabel Solomon was murdered, something that disorientates him. After the incident, he lives in New York, but depressed by his mutilated body, he starts taking hard drugs again. One day he buys drugs from a dealer who has a distinctive lightning bolt tattoo, and finds out that the dealer got it to hide the scars from a car wreck. Mal'akh goes to a tattoo parlour and asks them to conceal his scars with anything they'd like, but the artist refuses, and tells Mal'akh to come back after he has some more idea of what he'd like. Researching tattoos leads Mal'akh to read more books, with esoteric texts increasingly becoming his favourites.

De Praestigiis Daemonum et Incantationibus ac Venificiis ('On the Illusions of the Demons and on Spells and Poisons') was written by Heinrich Cornelius Agrippa's student Johannes Wier. He was a Dutch doctor who campaigned against the persecution of witches that was prevalent in the Sixteenth Century, and he is believed to have been the first to employ the phrase "mentally ill" when the depicting the actions of witches. *De Praestigiis Daemonum* is believed to have influenced the anonymous of author of the *Lemegeton* (which is also known as *The Goetia, The Lesser Key of Solomon*) (1). As I've previously mentioned, Aleister Crowley edited the most famous English translation of this grimoire. The author of *The Goetia* claims that he is King Solomon, although the actual contents date from the Medieval era. As the original title of *The Lost Symbol* was *The Solomon Key*, this book itself could be key to Dan Brown's intentions in this narrative. As noted previously, *The Goetia* is the best-known list of sigils, so this undoubtedly where Mal'akh gets the inspiration for the majority of his tattoos. *Ars Almadel* is part of *The Goetia*, as is *Ars Notoria*. *Ars Almadel* "tells how to make the almadel, which is a wax tablet with protective symbols drawn on it" (2). *Ars Notoria* contains revelations to the author given by King Solomon of knowledge disseminated to him by an angel, and includes prayers that can invoke angels. '*Grimorium Verum*', which is Latin for 'True Grimoire', states that it was written by Alibeck the Egyptian in Memphis in 1517 (3), although this is blatantly false. Like most grimoires, it claims to have originated with King Solomon, who, has we know, plays a great role in Masonic mythology. Having read these books, Mal'akh believes that there is knowledge out there that transcends human understanding.

The narrator states that Mal'akh then discovered the writings of Aleister Crowley. However, since Crowley edited the most famous English translation of *The Goetia*, Mal'akh must have already discovered his work. If you've read the Twitter clues, you'll know that I dismissed the involvement of the Hermetic Order of the Golden Dawn in *The Lost Symbol*, since I thought this movement would be too English to affect the American based events of this novel, and because I thought it no longer existed. What I hadn't counted upon was someone taking the writings of one of the order's leading lights, Aleister Crowley, seriously. Abramelin oil was utilised by both Crowley and the Golden Dawn. It appears that Mal'akh wants a 'greater mind' so that he will be feared by 'lesser minds'. I don't think, "Become something holy" and "Make yourself sacred" are actual Crowley quotes, as I haven't been able to find them online. There were a couple of Twitter clues about German spy rings, so it's interesting to note that in his book *Secret Agent 666: Aleister Crowley, British Intelligence and the Occult*, Richard Spence argues that Crowley's time in America during the First World War was spent writing for German propaganda magazines and infiltrating Irish republican groups. Spence even goes on to argue that Crowley may have played a role in the sinking of the Lusitania, which brought America into the war, as part of his duties as a secret British intelligence officer.

'Sacrifice' is indeed derived from the Latin for 'making sacred', from 'sacra' for 'sacred', and 'facere', which means 'to make'. Sacrifices were the 'law of the land' in the days of the Temple in Jerusalem, and the rules were laid down in the *Book of Leviticus* in the Bible. When the Romans destroyed the Second Temple in 70 AD, prayer replaced sacrifice (4). Chichen Itza was mentioned in the Twitter clues. The spell that Mal'akh uses on the crow is the *Exorcism of the Bat* from *The Book of Solomon*, although it doesn't appear to be from the S.L. MacGregor Mathers edited version, which reads like so:

CAMIACH, CANTAC, EMIAL, MIAL, EMORE, BARCA, MARBAT, CACRAT, ZANDAC, VALAMACH; by these most holy names, and the other names of angels which are written in the book ASSAMAIAN, I conjure thee O bat (or whatever animal it may be) that thou assist me in this operation, by God the true, God the holy, the God who hath created thee, and by Adam, who hath imposed thy true name upon thee and upon all other animated beings.

This spell applies to any winged animal, so Mal'akh is applying it correctly. As a funny aside, it must be noted that there's a note from the editor with this spell (presumably Mathers himself) that reads, "I cannot too strongly impress on the readers of this volume that the use of blood is more or less connected with black magic; and that it should be avoided as much as possible" (5). Although Crowley did sacrifice at least one living animal, this was something that he was not comfortable doing (6). Note that if Dan Brown was utilising the S.L. MacGregor Mathers edition of *The Book of Solomon*, then he has adapted it to include the "One True God" mentioned in the latest deciphering of the Masonic Pyramid. Dan Brown has quoted the rest of the exorcism more or less in full, only missing out some of the divine names to include them further on in the text:

Almighty ADONAI, ARATHRON, ASHAI, ELOHIM, ELOHI, ELION, ASHER EHEIEH, SHADDAI, O God the Lord, immaculate, immutable, EMANUEL, MESSIACH, YOD, HE, VAU, HE, be my aid, so that this blood may have power and efficacy in all wherein I shall wish, and in all that I shall demand.

Mal'akh associates this sacrifice, and the energy that it supposedly gives him, with the phoenix. Again, it must be noted that this metaphor of the phoenix renewing itself by fire is quite a violent, combustible one. Mal'akh then starts trapping other animals, such as rats and squirrels, for sacrifice. He begins to get physically stronger again, but regards his body as just being a vessel for his potent mind. Mal'akh begins to justify his evil nature by regarding it as indeed *natural*, since destruction and entropy are inevitable in any closed system.

This chapter reveals that Mal'akh named himself after the chief of Satan's Angels in John Milton's *Paradise Lost*, however I think that the etymology of his name that I've previously discussed is still valid. When you read *Paradise Lost*, you can immediately begin to see why Mal'akh has chosen this name:

First MOLOCH, horrid King besmear'd with blood / Of human sacrifice, and parents tears, / Though for the noyse of Drums and Timbrels loud / Their childrens cries unheard, that past through fire / To his grim Idol. Him the AMMONITE / Worshipt in RABBA and her watry Plain, / In ARGOB and in BASAN, to the stream / Of utmost ARNON. Nor content with such / Audacious neighbourhood, the wisest heart / Of SOLOMON he led by fraud to build / His Temple right against the Temple of God / On that opprobrious Hill, and made his Grove / The pleasant Vally of HINNOM, TOPHET thence / And black GEHENNA call'd, the Type of Hell.

So, according to Milton, it was Moloch who fraudulently persuaded King Solomon to build the Temple in such an inauspicious place, since both Jewish Temples on this site were fated to be destroyed. Mal'akh has chosen this name because it's an allusion to his surname. Since Solomon's Temple is so beloved by Masons to the point of wanting to rebuild it, 'Moloch' is also a metaphor for Mal'akh nefarious intentions against the fraternity. Note also that Moloch is a figure that has been traditionally associated with the practice of child sacrifice through fire, which is also referred to in this extract from *Paradise Lost*.

Bertrand Russell's 1903 essay *A Free Man's Worship* gives an indication of the kind of god that Mal'akh wants to be (7):

The savage, like ourselves, feels the oppression of his impotence before the powers of Nature; but having in himself nothing that he respects more than Power, he is willing to prostrate himself before his gods, without inquiring whether they are worthy of his worship. Pathetic and very terrible is the long history of cruelty and torture, of degradation and human sacrifice, endured in the hope of placating the jealous gods: surely, the trembling believer thinks, when what is most precious has been freely given, their lust for blood must be appeased, and more will not be required. The religion of Moloch — as such creeds may be generically called — is in essence the cringing submission of the slave, who dare not, even in his heart, allow the thought that his master deserves no adulation. Since the independence of ideals is not yet acknowledged, Power may be freely worshipped, and receive an unlimited respect, despite its wanton infliction of pain.

However, it was probably H. G. Wells who first employed the term 'Moloch' to depict the downtrodden working classes. In his novella *The Time Machine*, the working class have devolved into subterranean monsters, 'Morlocks', which eat the remnants of the indolent rich, the Eloi. In the 1960 movie adaptation by George Pal, the Eloi are shown mindlessly responding to the air raid siren that is the signal for them to be culled by the Morlocks in their lair, which is presided over by the monstrous statue of a sphinx. In contrast, a similar sphinx-like creature swallows the downtrodden workers in Fritz Lang's *Metropolis*, which is called "Moloch" by the protagonist in horror. H. R. Giger utilised the same metaphor in his depiction of Geidi Prime in David Lynch's *Dune*: "Harkonnen is a gigantic Moloch, which functions by converting living beings into energy…" (8). So, the rest of humanity is doomed to face an unenlightened everlasting darkness with Mal'akh in charge.

Thus Mal'akh becomes determined to perform a *true* sacrifice; note that Dan Brown highlighted the word *true* here. With his vision complete, Mal'akh is finally able to instruct the tattoo artist.

Chapter 78 The George Washington Masonic Memorial is indeed modelled on the famous Pharos lighthouse of Alexandria, in Egypt, one of the Seven Wonders of the World. After serving as president, George Washington became Charter Master for the Alexandria Lodge. By a happy coincidence, this city in Virginia was named after its founders, John and Philip Alexander. It's interesting to see that the George Washington Masonic Memorial describes the inaugural president thus: "Washington was, in Masonic terms, a *living stone* who became the cornerstone of American civilization" (1). The Ark of the Covenant is, of course, the famous receptacle for the Ten Commandments that was kept in the Holy of Holies in King Solomon's Temple, but which was later stolen and is now lost to history. Along with the replica of King Solomon's throne room, and the Knight Templar Chapel, this seems like an ideal place for Langdon to visit, and the CIA are lying in wait for him.

Katherine wonders why the CIA would be interested in the Masonic Pyramid, but reminds herself of the Stargate/Scannate program that the CIA had run from the 1970s to the 1990s, to investigate whether it was possible to spy on the Communist bloc countries via ESP, which was partly funded by the Institute of Noetic Sciences. This programme was set up as a response to similar programmes in the Communist states.

The CIA are very surprised when they discover that Langdon and Katherine aren't on the Metro train…

Chapter 79 Which isn't too surprising, as Langdon and Katherine have actually left a train 8 miles north of Alexandria. Langdon commends Katherine on her acting skills when she drew his attention to the fact that the CIA were listening to them in Omar's cab. Langdon explains the riddle set by their mysterious benefactor as they arrive at Washington National Cathedral. It's a common mistake for people to think that 'Darth Vader' means 'Dark Father' in some Nordic language, and one I shared myself until I researched it some years ago, and found out it wasn't true. Despite this misconception however, the reference to 'Luke's dark father' is still valid in the clue, as it's pretty obvious that this is Darth Vader. Luke Skywalker is the epitome of Joseph Campbell's *The Hero with a Thousand Faces*, so it's interesting to see him mentioned here.

Chapter 80 Bellamy is relieved to hear that Langdon and Katherine have escaped the CIA's clutches. However, Sato begins to detail the evidence that she has acquired of Bellamy's contact with Mal'akh, including a text that the reader had previously assumed had been sent by Sato. She then reveals that as she saw Peter Solomon as a threat to national security, she had his phone tapped. This explains how Sato had got to the Capitol Building so quickly, as she had intercepted Langdon's confused call to Peter to ask where the lecture was being held. Sato says that the Masons have been careless, and their most 'dangerous secret' is about to be unveiled. Bellamy thinks she's referring to the Ancient Mysteries, and that she may be a member of the Eastern Star (pp. 43-44). Sato orders one of her agents to bring in a briefcase, and Bellamy fears that he's about to be tortured…

Chapter 81 Mal'akh visits his basement, where he performs the dark arts. 'Cerulean' is believed to be derived from the Latin for 'Heaven/sky' (1). With diabolical cheek, Mal'akh names this secret place 'Sanctum Sanctorum', Latin for the 'Holy of Holies', the inner sanctuary of the Jewish Temple in Jerusalem that could only be entered by the High Priest on Yom Kippur. The seven gates of Heaven were mentioned in the *Book of Revelation*: "The twelve gates were twelve pearls, each gate being made from a single pearl". *The Book of Revelation* is referred to again with the mention of the seven seals of revelation. *The Table of Planetary Hours* is from *The Greater Key of Solomon*, with Yanor, Nasnia, and Salam being some of the magical names of the hours. *The Table of Planetary Hours* involves the seven 'naked eye' planets, i.e. those celestial bodies that could be seen by the ancients without telescopes, such as the Moon, Mars, Mercury, Jupiter, Venus, Saturn, and the Sun, which correspond with the days of the week (starting with Monday) (2). Since the hour is Caerra, this must mean that it is now 11pm, and that Langdon hasn't got long to accede to Mal'akh's demands.

Mal'akh then opens a box that supposedly contains the most famous knife in history (according to Google, the most famous knife in history is… the Bowie knife, but this blade is most assuredly not as commonplace as that). Mal'akh believes the Black Magic that he is dabbling with to be as powerful as nuclear physics, although the use of the phrase 'reflux current' is seems a bit clumsy. As noted with regards to the destruction of Langdon's vellum bible in chapter 24, this 'paper' is indeed made from animal skin, although Mal'akh has gone to extreme lengths by making this vellum himself. Peter Solomon has provided the blood for this living sacrifice. Mal'akh refers to the five symbols that are found on the Hand of Mysteries, reinforcing the message that the *key* is the missing piece. By intoning the "blood *eukharistos* of the ancients", Mal'akh is acknowledging the Christian Eucharist's origins in pagan practices (3). Mal'akh intends to use this blood as the ink to which to tattoo the missing symbol on his head…

Chapter 82 Washington National Cathedral is indeed the sixth largest cathedral in the world, and is the fourth tallest structure in Washington DC. 'Colin' is derived from the Gaelic for 'young child' or 'peaceful dove', although the latter seems more likely in this context. 'Galloway' could be taken to mean 'strange road'. According to Wikipedia (1),

The cathedral was built with many intentional "flaws" in keeping with an apocryphal medieval custom that sought to illustrate that only God can be perfect. Artistically speaking, these flaws (which often come in the form of intentional asymmetries) draw the observer's focus to the sacred geometry as well as compensating for visual distortions, a practice that has been used since the Pyramids and the Parthenon. Architecturally, it is thought that if the main aisle of the cathedral where it meets the cross section were not tilted slightly off its axis, a person who looked straight down the aisle would have a slight feeling of disorientation, like looking down railroad tracks

This is no doubt what Dan Brown means when he mentions the "softening optical illusion". Rood screens are very much a feature in medieval churches, and usually depict the crucifixion, since the name is derived from the Saxon for 'cross' ('rood'). Frankincense was, of course, one of the gifts that the Magi gave to Christ, so is another pagan practice adopted by Christianity. Strictly speaking, a reredos image is usually behind the altar. The armoire is a writing desk.

Galloway reveals that he is also a Mason as they fill each other in on the night's events. Since he is blind, Galloway uses his hands to get an impression of the Masonic Pyramid's meaning. Galloway states that the pyramid has "miraculous transformative power" and that it can change its shape, like King Arthur's sword from the stone (another example of a stereotypical *Hero with a Thousand Faces*). However, everyone knew what the sword would look like when released from the stone, so this isn't the best analogy. Galloway then makes an oblique mention of the concept of gravity, first coined by Sir Isaac Newton, as an example of an enlightened mind sweeping away archaic beliefs, as he claims that he can transform the pyramid with the touch of his finger. Langdon is very sceptical of such claims, and so in the monomyth of the *Hero's Journey* that Joseph Campbell presented in *The Hero with a Thousand Faces*, Galloway is the wizened old man who provides the hero with supernatural aid, like Merlin.

"Know ye not that ye are gods?" comes from the *Book of Psalms* (82:6), which Dan Brown acknowledges at the end of this paragraph. This phrase is indeed utilised greatly within the circles of Hermeticism, as shown by Sarah Belle Dougherty's online article *The Infinity Within* (2). Albert Einstein did indeed make such statements about a 'cosmic religion'. According to Brian Dennis in his book *Einstein: A Life* (1996, p. 127), in 1929 Einstein told a rabbi that, "I believe in Spinoza's God, who reveals Himself in the lawful harmony of the world, not in a God Who concerns Himself with the fate and the doings of mankind". According to Greek mythology, Pandora was the first woman. She was created by the gods after Prometheus had stolen the secret of fire, and given it to mortal men. Thus Pandora was intended to be a "beautiful evil" gift on the part of the gods. Pandora opened the box that was given her out of curiosity, and unwittingly unleashed all the evil in the world, leaving only hope inside. From this story, and that of Eve in the Garden of Eden, one gets an indication of the astounding degree of misogyny present in ancient patriarchal cultures. The Seven Seals of Revelation were also mentioned in the previous chapter, so this probably serves as a foreshadowing of an apocalyptic event. When Galloway states that Langdon does not yet "have eyes to see", he couldn't sound more like Yoda if he tried.

Chapter 83 Sato shows Bellamy a computer file that horrifies him…

Chapter 84 Galloway begins to think that it's appropriate that the Ancient Mysteries have started to emerge from the inner circles of the Masons, and into the light. He also reveals that he used to be the Worshipful Master at the House of the Temple, and that Peter Solomon consulted him in this role when he became concerned about a 'dark force' in his life. Katherine reveals that she has photographic proof of fields of energy disseminating from a faith healer's hands, which Galloway likens to Jesus' healing of the sick, and miraculous cures effected within his own cathedral. CCD cameras are very useful tools in astronomy. Langdon refers to the *Book of Revelation* again, but Galloway dismisses this biblical tome "because no one knows how to read that". Instead, when he talks of a 'transformative enlightenment', he is referring to the works of St. Augustine, Sir Francis Bacon, and Newton etc.

It's debateable whether St. Augustine really was a progenitor of the Enlightenment, a way of thinking that really sparked off in the Eighteenth Century, and as I have previously discussed, led to the foundation of the United States. In an article by Peter Mullen, *Augustine, Antidote to the Enlightenment* (1), he states that, according to the current Pope, Benedict XVI -

the history of Western psychological understanding and insight comes directly from Augustine. If Descartes had properly understood the relationship between the "I" and the God who created it and who is eternally present within it, he would not have made the mistake of starting where he did: with his Cogito ergo sum which makes individual consciousness the centre of philosophical reference. Pope Benedict, like John Paul before him, is fascinated by Augustine not least because he recognises in him the antidote to the Enlightenment which made man the measure of all things.

On the other hand, there are many others who do regard St. Augustine as having been pivotal to the Enlightenment. For instance, Paul Alois' article *What was the Western Enlightenment?* (2), states that -

In his early adulthood, St. Augustine belonged to a sect of Christians called Manicheans, who believed that the universe was split into Good and Evil. These forces manifested themselves through man, who could only passively accept the evil done through him and pray that the forces of good would prevail. Manicheans had no concept of free will or an individuated soul, and clearly expressed their 2D consciousness in their belief that the individual is completely subsumed by two poles... After a decade as a Manichean, St. Augustine became dissatisfied, saying, "I could make no progress in it." He turned to Plato (the original 3D thinker) and integrated Plato's ideas of the separate soul, free will, and reason into Christianity. As St. Augustine's writings spread through the Christian world, the seeds were sown for 3D consciousness to eventually emerge.

The mention of Sir Francis Bacon here is probably a reference to his utopian work *The New Atlantis*, which I previously discussed on pp. 25-27. Chapter 30 of *The*

Lost Symbol did mention Newton's anxiety that the rest of humanity were not ready for the dissemination of the Ancient Mysteries in his day. According to Wikipedia, Newton tried to decode scientific data that he believed to be present in the Bible, and predicted that the Apocalypse would come no sooner than 2060 (3). He also went on to predict that the Apocalypse would see "the ruin of the wicked nations, the end of weeping and of all troubles, the return of the Jews captivity and their setting up a flourishing and everlasting Kingdom" (4). The Christian quote is from the synoptic gospels (i.e. those gospels not composed by St. John, who supposedly wrote the *Book of Revelation*); in Matthew, it's 10:26, in Luke 8:17, and in Mark 4:22. So, this was a very important message that Jesus imparted to his disciples: "Nothing is hidden that will not be made known, nor secret that will not come to light". Langdon takes this as a reference to the current exponential growth of scientific knowledge.

Galloway realises that since Katherine has broken the seal to the capstone, he is no longer a gatekeeper to the Masonic Pyramid and its mysteries, but its guide. He takes Langdon's finger, and guides it inside the box that contained the capstone. Indented on Langdon's fingertip is a small dot enclosed within a circle that Katherine recognises as the alchemical symbol for gold. Galloway then makes what Langdon thinks is a throwaway remark about transforming a worthless substance into gold. Langdon relates that this symbol, the circumpunct, has a whole variety of meanings, such as being the symbol for the Egyptian sun god Ra, the third eye, the eye of God, and the All-Seeing Eye. 'Kether' means 'crown' in Hebrew, referring both to a monarchical crown, and the head or consciousness of a person. Wikipedia states that, "Monad (from Greek μονάς monas, "unit"; monos, 'alone'), according to the Pythagoreans, was a term for God or the first being, or the totality of all beings, Monad being the source or the One meaning without division" (5). Wikipedia also provides perhaps the best example of the concept of 'Divine Truth' with regards to the works of C. S. Lewis and J. R. R. Tolkien (6):

> Christian mythologists such as C. S. Lewis and J. R. R. Tolkien understood the narrative of Christ's sacrificial death of atonement for humanity as a "true myth" with the special property that it had been enacted historically in time and space. Lewis wrote, "The story of Christ is simply a true myth: a myth working on us in the same way as the others, but with this tremendous difference that it really happened." In this view, mythological predecessors of the "drama" of Christ were inspired glimpses of divine truth that would only become fully manifest at an appointed moment and place, viz. in Roman Judea. For these authors, the mythological elements in the story of the Christ do not undermine but rather enhance the transcendental truth of the gospel... Lewis and Tolkien did not intend to demythologize the gospel, understanding myth as an intrinsic component of its truth. Instead, they felt a challenge to make use of their "subcreative" powers to rework these mythemes into mythologies of their own in their works of fiction.

'Prisca Sapientia' is Latin for 'Ancient Wisdom', and also refers to the practice of Renaissance scholars, such as Newton, of scouring texts such as the Bible for this hidden knowledge (7). Therefore the circumpunct is indeed the symbol utilised to represent the Ancient Mysteries. Galloway then reminds them that the capstone's box was sealed using Peter's ring a few generations previously, and states that he believes that this unique ring is part of the symbolon. Sure enough, there's a small circular incision on the ring that Langdon proceeds to connect the ring with the circumpunct. He then realises that he has to turn the ring 33 degrees, mindful of the Masonic saying that 'all is revealed at the thirty-third degree'.

Chapter 85 According to Wikipedia (1), the ashlar is a symbol of progress within freemasonry:

> The rough ashlar represents a rough, unprepared or undressed stone, and is an allegory of the uninitiated Freemason prior to his discovering enlightenment; the smooth ashlar represents the dressed stone as used by the experienced stonemason, and is an allegory of the Freemason who, through education and diligence, has achieved enlightenment and who lives an upstanding life.

Langdon is certainly enlightened when he sees that the stone capstone box has transformed itself into a Rose Cross. Thus it has the ability to transform its shape, much as the cryptex did in *The Da Vinci Code*. 'Symbolic Alchemy' is a phrase that is mostly associated online with Joseph Lewis Henderson and Dyane N. Sherwood's book *Transformation of the psyche: the symbolic alchemy of the Splendor solis*. The *Splendor Solis* (i.e. 'The Splendors of the Sun') is a Sixteenth Century illustrated vellum alchemical text. As Wikipedia states "The symbolic process [in the book] shows the classical alchemical death and rebirth of the king, and incorporates a series of seven flasks, each associated with one of the planets. Within the flasks a process is shown involving the transformation of bird and animal symbols into the Queen and King" (2).

Although the box now looks like a Christian crucifix, this doesn't make sense to Langdon, as Masons derive from all faiths. Langdon then identifies it as the 'Rose Cross'. One man who wrote a great deal on the symbology of the Rose Cross was Albert Pike, one of the men who are buried in the House of the Temple. You can read what Pike wrote about the Rose Cross on pp. 15-16, as this symbol was mentioned in the Twitter clues. Indeed, you can read more about the Rosicrucians on pp. 15-16, and 24-26. Elias Ashmole was one of the founders of the Royal Society, and this Freemason also instituted the famous Ashmolean Museum. Wikipedia states that Robert Fludd "was not a member of the Rosicrucians, as often alleged, but he defended their thoughts in the Apologia Compendiaria of 1616" (3). I previously discussed John Dee on p. 75. The Rosicrucians claimed that Paracelsus was really the founder of their order, Christian Rosencreutz. According to Gary L. Stewart's book *Awakened Attitude*, it's hard to to tell if polymaths such as Rene Descartes were Rosicrucians, as it was dangerous for them to admit affiliation to such a mystical fraternity in a time of religious upheaval (4), although Descartes is believed to have been a Deist (see pp. 17-18). Blaise Pascal was a pioneer in the field of Mathematics, and developed one of the first mechanical calculators, dubbed the Pascaline. Pascal's Triangle is a mathematical piece of trickery that is worth comparing to the Magic Square employed by Dürer in *Melencholia I*. Pascal was a member of the Jansenist movement that very much propounded the ideas of St. Augustine. The great philosopher Spinoza did employ the rose symbol on his seal, but some commentators have suggested that this was due to similarity of his name to the Latin for 'rose with sharp thorns', 'espinosa' (5). Leibniz, along with Descartes and Spinoza, is regarded as being one of the most important philosophers and rationalists of the Seventeenth Century. Both he and Newton independently developed Infinitesimal Calculus, and had a bitter argument regarding it. Leibniz also invented binary notation, which is of great use in the development of computers (6). Again, there's no real evidence that he was a Rosicrucian.

Dan Brown then quotes from Professor Carl Edwin Lindgren's seminal article *The way of the Rose Cross; A Historical Perception*, 1614-1620 (*Journal of Religion and Psychical Research*, Volume18, Number 3:141-48. 1995). Another part of this same article has struck me as being quite pertinent to *The Lost Symbol*:

> The Fraternity, created in the early 17th Century, has for centuries intrigued and baffled students of Christian mysticism, esoteric philosophy and occultism. Professing an interest and mastery of Spiritual or Mental Alchemy, not to be confused with Physical Alchemy, these esoteric scholars and scientists attempted to transmute the evil in man into that which was divine or, in alchemic jargon, the transmuting of base metals into finest gold. "As above, so below..."

As Galloway discusses Rosicrucianism further with Katherine, Langdon finally remembers that 'Jeova Sanctus Unus' was the pseudonym that Isaac Newton employed for his alchemical writings, and according to Galloway, he had obviously read the Rosicrucian manifestoes. Galloway also states that Newton used this pseudonym because he understood himself to be divine. Langdon demonstrates that 'Jeova Sanctus Unus' is an anagram of 'Isaacus Neutonnus' in Latin. Note that Galloway employs the word 'Adept'; this was a term that Nineteenth Century Hermeticists used for their initiates. According to Wikipedia, Aleister Crowley included an 'Order of the Rose Cross' for his three forms of adept (7), which may be an indication that Mal'akh is on the right track also. Langdon has a flashback to the resolution of *The Da Vinci Code*, as Newton's tomb in Westminster Abbey played a large role in Langdon's previous adventure, and Langdon comes to the conclusion that Newton will always be seen as a guidepost for those seeking secret knowledge. Katherine then exclaims that she can transform the pyramid employing traditional alchemical and Newtonian science.

Galloway's acute sense of hearing warns him that they may soon be interrupted, so he urges Langdon and Katherine to leave. Meanwhile, Bellamy tries to ring Langdon with a warning...

Chapter 86 Mal'akh's belief is that "Transformation requires sacrifice", although this mantra is more usually associated with the works of modern day management gurus. However, Mal'akh is referring to the sacrifice of his gonads. It's possible that Mal'akh paid for his orchiectomy rather than performing it himself, although one would have though he would have been given anaesthetic, so the operation would not have been painful. In the UK, patients are required to attend psychoanalysis before committing to major cosmetic surgery, and if the same is routine in America, then I would have liked to have sat in on that conversation! This is the first time that it's specifically mentioned that Mal'akh is seeking immortality. It would appear then that Mal'akh is seeking to become a god in the manner of the Hermetic Order of the Golden Dawn (1):

In the Hermetic Tradition, each and every person has the potential to become God, this idea or concept of God is perceived as internal rather than external. The Great Architect is also an allusion to the observer created universe. We create our own reality; hence we are the architect. Another way would to be to say that the mind is the builder.

Mal'akh describes himself as an androgyne, and the androgynous look today was perhaps most popularised by David Bowie in some of his 1970s incarnations. Mal'akh then uses the words of Jesus to justify his castration, although Jesus would not approve of Mal'akh's belief that he must destroy in order to create. In my critique of Chapter 57 (p. 80), I discussed Mal'akh in the context of the homosexual villain. However, I now believe that Dan Brown was not conforming to that old stereotype; instead, I believe that he is reflecting Joseph Campbell's concept of the *bisexual god*, which appears in the Apotheosis chapter of *The Hero with a Thousand Faces* (2008, p.138):

That father was himself the womb, the mother, of a second birth... This is the meaning of the image of the bisexual god. He is the mystery of the theme of initiation. We are taken from the mother, chewed into fragments, and assimilated to the world-annihilating body of the ogre for whom all the precious forms and beings are only the courses of a feast; but then, miraculously reborn, we are more than we were.

Having read the above, one can begin to understand Mal'akh's pains to become an androgynous, bisexual god. This also reminds me that Eliphas Levi's image of Baphomet (see p. 21) was also very androgynous, so it would appear that Mal'akh is attempting to become all that Baphomet symbolises.

The narrator states that Peter Solomon has been chose to play a vital role in Mal'akh's transformation as he had played a pivotal role in Mal'akh's mortal life. According to Mal'akh, Peter Solomon is not quite the benevolent philanthropist that he makes out to be, as he sacrificed his own son. Which, is some contexts, could make him sound like the God who sacrificed his only son, Jesus. However, Mal'akh condemns Peter Solomon's abandonment of his son as a brutal act.

Chapter 87 A 'garth' is a square surrounded by a cloister. Langdon and Katherine run to get to the sanctuary that Galloway has offered them as a CIA helicopter bears down on the cathedral. Meanwhile, Galloway stands in front of one of the cathedral's rose windows, contemplating the Rosicrucian manifestos. Incidentally, rose windows, since they are circular, are derived from the oculus, an aspect of architecture that features prominently in Dan Brown's novels. Also, some historians believe that the current design of the rose window originated in Islamic architecture, and that this feature was brought back from the Holy Land by the crusaders (1). Washington National Cathedral has three large rose windows, which represent the Creation, the Last Judgement, and the Glory of God. Galloway also reflects that Jesus' name has been hijacked throughout history by those seeking to justify their own political and bloodthirsty aims, quoting Scripture that they do not understand.

Dan Brown seems to be quoting from a new translation of the *Confessio Fraternitatis*, the second of the Rosicrucian manifestos. Thomas Vaughan did the most widely known translation in 1652 (2). Dan Brown only presents a partial version of these chapter headings. For instance, Chapter One of the *Confessio* also includes the following: "but to the ungodly that which will augment their sins and their punishments", which is a bit less benign than the segment Galloway remembers (3). I wouldn't really describe all of these chapters as prophecies either, as the context of Chapter Four seems to be more about joining the Rosicrucian movement, and gradually learning the Ancient Mysteries in a series of steps, rather like Masonic degrees, so this is more of a recruitment call than a depiction of future events. The rest of Chapter Seven is more prophetic:

Wherefore there shall cease all falsehood, darkness, and bondage, which little by little, with the great globe's revolution, hath crept into the arts, works, and governments of men, darkening the greater part of them. Thence hath proceeded that innumerable diversity of persuasions, falsehoods, and heresies, which make choice difficult to the wisest men, seeing on the one part they were hindered by the reputation of philosophers and on the other by the facts of experience, which if (as we trust) it can be once removed, and instead thereof a single and self-same rule be instituted, then there will indeed remain thanks unto them which have taken pains therein, but the sum of so great a work shall be attributed to the blessedness of our age.

Thomas Vaughan's translation of Chapter Eight also seems quite fitting in the context of *The Lost Symbol*:

As in the human head there are two organs of hearing, two of sight, and two of smell but only one of speech, and it were vain to expect speech from the ears, or hearing from the eyes, so there have been ages which have seen, others which have heard, others again that have smelt and tasted. Now, there remains that in a short and swiftly approaching time honour should likewise be given to the tongue, that what formerly saw, heard, and smelt shall finally speak, after the world shall have slept away the intoxication of her poisoned and stupefying chalice, and with an open heart, bare head, and naked feet shall merrily and joyfully go forth to meet the sun rising in the morning.

Agent Simkins then arrives to interrupt Galloway's reverie.

Chapter 88 Analyst Nola Kaye is interrupted by a call from fellow agent Rick Parrish in CIA systems security. 'Rick' means powerful and rich, while his surname depicts someone who has lived in the jurisdiction of a priest. So, if one was being conspiratorially minded, one could argue that Rick is a hidden mole for say, the Catholic Church. However, having read the end of *The Lost Symbol*, I know there's nothing particularly significant in the meaning of Rick's name. Rick's collaborative integration software has alerted him that Kaye is working on an issue related to his apprehension of Zoubianis for hacking into the CIA database. Since the keywords that Trish employed in her spider search are similar in context to the Masonic puzzles that Nola is trying to solve, she demands that Rick joins her immediately.

Chapter 89 The sanctuary that Galloway has provided for Langdon and Katherine is Washington National Cathedral College. Langdon's not sure why Katherine's heading for the kitchen though. Some of the earliest forms of writing and symbols were pictograms of objects and tools. Since such symbols are not dependent on a local dialect, such pictograms can be understood almost universally. Daniel Boulud is a well-known French chef in North America. Numerology, because of its association with divination, is now considered to be a kind of pseudomathematics. Numerology can also be seen as an early ancestor of mathematics, just as alchemy was an early form of chemistry. Some of Langdon's evidence regarding the number 33 seems to be derived from Manly P. Hall's *The Secret Teachings of All Ages*, such as the fact that God's name is mentioned in Genesis 33 times (although only 32 times in the original Hebrew), and the assertion that there is no evidence for the death of Christ at the age of 33. I can find no evidence that Joseph was 33 when he married the Virgin Mary, although it is true that Islam believes that everyone that in Heaven remains at the age of 33. Manly P. Hall's description of alchemy from *The Secret Teachings of All Ages* seems relevant here:

> Alchemy is a threefold art, its mystery well symbolized by a triangle. Its symbol is 3 times 3--three elements or processes in three worlds or spheres. The 3 times 3 is part of the mystery of the 33rd degree of Freemasonry, for 33 is 3 times 3, which is 9, the number of esoteric man and the number of emanations from the root of the Divine Tree. It is the number of worlds nourished by the four rivers that pour out of the Divine Mouth as the *verbum fiat*. Beneath the so-called symbolism of alchemy is concealed a magnificent concept, for this ridiculed and despised craft still preserves intact the triple key to the gates of eternal life. Realizing, therefore, that alchemy is a mystery in three worlds--the divine, the human, and the elemental--it can easily be appreciated why the sages and philosophers created and evolved an intricate allegory to conceal their wisdom.

Katherine says that since Newton was an alchemist, he also regarded the number 33 as being sacred. She points out that the word 'degree' can also apply to temperature. Langdon points out that 33 degrees would be quite cold, but then Katherine reminds him that Newton developed an early temperature scale, at which the boiling point of water was 33 degrees. However, as Hasok Chang points out in his article, *The Myth of the Boiling Point*, "We all learn at school that pure water always boils at 100°C (212°F), under normal atmospheric pressure. Like surprisingly many things that 'everybody knows', this is a myth... not only is it incorrect, but it also conveys misleading ideas about the nature of scientific knowledge. And unlike some other myths, it does not serve sufficiently useful functions" (1). Chang also says that Newton came up with the idea that there were actually two boiling points.

Katherine's theory is that the boiling point will reveal some incandescent writing. Luminescence does indeed occur at low temperatures, and incandescence at high temperatures. And indeed, it appears that Katherine is correct, as words appear on the pyramid.

Chapter 90 The three words on the pyramid are "Eight Franklin Square". And although Galloway had told them that the pyramid was a map, Langdon hadn't expected anything quite so specific. The arms on Langdon's Mickey Mouse watch do luminesce, and tell him that it's almost midnight, so there's not much time to arrange Peter's release. Robert calls Mal'akh's cell phone from a phone in the kitchen, and is surprised when a woman answers. The woman states that she's the partner of the security guard that called at Mal'akh's home. The security guard was found dead, but Peter was also discovered in the basement, and is receiving medical treatment. The security guard suggests that they hurry if they want to see Peter…

Chapter 91 Grabbing the pyramid, Langdon and Katherine attempt to depart to Mal'akh's house, but they are intercepted by Sato. She doesn't seem that happy when Langdon tells that the police have found Peter. Sato then reveals that she'd wanted Langdon to play along with Mal'akh, who she calls a 'lunatic'. Then Bellamy turns up, and Sato reveals that it's him who's been in contact with Mal'akh. Sato tells Bellamy to send a photo to Mal'akh's cell phone (but wasn't this phone just answered by the security guard?)
  Mal'akh is irritated to find that Bellamy has blanked out part of the puzzle in the picture that he has sent him.

Chapter 92 The CIA bring in Galloway while Langdon wonders why Bellamy is now so keen to help Sato. Mal'akh rings Bellamy and says that Peter's in the trunk of his car, something which Katherine and Langdon know to be a lie. Bellamy arranges to meet Mal'akh at Franklin Square to do an exchange. Katherine manages to persuade Sato to let her go to Peter with Agent Hartmann. Before they leave him, Galloway runs his hands down the pyramid, and asks Langdon to tell Peter that the Masonic pyramid has always held its secrets *sincerely*. Thus Langdon resumes his guardianship of the pyramid, although it's surprising that Sato didn't insist on taking it with her to Franklin Square.

Chapter 93 Alexander Graham Bell did indeed send the first wireless telephone message from Franklin School in 1880, using a device that he called a 'photophone', since it relied on using sunbeams. Bell was very proud of this invention, but it was impractical in these early days, due to the fact that the signal could be interrupted by cloud. In his interview with *New York Magazine* of the 6th of September 2009, Dan Burnstein mentioned that Bell, when he was Regent of the Smithsonian, had the body of the institution's founder, James Smithson, exhumed and reburied within the Smithsonian's grounds (1). The square is obviously named after Founding Father and inventor Benjamin Franklin, and the square must have magical scientific powers, since Charles Townes conceived the idea for the laser/maser principle while sitting on a bench in there (2).
  The CIA helicopter performs an illegal 'touch-hover' manoeuvre on the top of One Franklin Square, the fifth tallest building in DC, to allow Sato et al to disembark. The helicopter then retreats to 'silent altitude'. Sato waits for a call

from Nola with regards to the location of Eight Franklin Square, while Bellamy is sent to make his rendezvous with Mal'akh.

Chapter 94 On the way to Mal'akh's house, Langdon notices that there is now a strange substance on the pyramid: wax. However, before he can make sense of this, they arrive at the house. As Katherine rushes in, Langdon notices that there is something very very wrong…

Chapter 95 This shifts to Katherine's point of view as she suddenly starts falling for no known reason. Winded on the floor, she watches in horror as Agent Hartmann clutches at a wound in his throat. 'Hart' is another name for 'stag', so one could say that Hartmann has truly been hunted down. Mal'akh then tasers Langdon. Katherine sees that the female security guard is dead also. Mal'akh binds and gags Katherine despite her protestations that she will tell him everything about the pyramid.

An elecro-muscular disruptor is indeed a suitable weapon for a 'god' like Mal'akh to deploy, as it very much resembles a lightning bolt. Since the pyramid has been knocked over, Langdon can now see that there are markings on its base that were not there before. He then remembers Galloway's remark about the pyramid keeping its secrets sincerely, and realises that this is a reference to the old practice employed by sculptors of concealing mistakes in their work with wax. Since 'sine cera' is Latin for 'without wax', this term was supposedly used to depict works of art that had not been embellished in this way, although this etymology is the subject of debate. Note that the "mediocre thriller" that Langdon refers to is very possibly Dan Brown's *Digital Fortress*! So, this is a very tongue-in-cheek reference to a previous work. Thus Langdon realises that Eight Franklin Square is not the final answer. However, Mal'akh then violently knocks Langdon unconscious.

Chapter 96 The narrator reveals that Mal'akh had held a knife to the security guard's throat to get her to lie to Langdon. Mal'akh had then fooled Bellamy that he was not at home, but driving around with Peter's body in the trunk.

Mal'akh's TV is on in the background, allowing him to compare the televangelist's reading of the Lord's Prayer with the Hermetic philosophy. There is some mystery concerning the origins of the Lord's Prayer, as, of all the Synoptic Bibles, Mark is believed to have been written first. However, Mark doesn't include the Lord's Prayer, but Matthew and Luke (who are believed to have employed Mark as the source for their gospels, to the point of tidying up his language), do include the Lord's Prayer. This has led some historians to believe that both Matthew and Luke were also using another source that has now been lost to history (1). Mal'akh believes, as many theosophists do, that the source of the word 'Amen' is the name of the Egyptian sun god 'Amon' or 'Amun'. Miriam Lichtheim's *Ancient Egyptian Literature: Volume II: The New Kingdom* has an example of a prayer to Amun that is worth comparing to the Lord's Prayer (1976, pp. 105-106):

[Amun] who comes at the voice of the poor in distress, who gives breath to him who is wretched…You are Amun, the Lord of the silent, who comes at the voice of the poor, when I call to you in my distress You come and rescue me...Though the servant was disposed to do evil, the Lord is disposed to forgive. The Lord of Thebes spends not a whole day in anger, His wrath passes in a moment, none remains. His breath comes back to us in mercy. May your ka be kind, may you forgive, It shall not happen again.

It's true that the later Greek rulers of Egypt did regard Amun to be the equivalent of Zeus. However, most etymologists state that 'Amen' is derived from Hebrew for 'so be it', and this is the same source from where Islam derives 'Amin' (2). Then again, the Israelites did have a long period of captivity in Egypt...

It's Mal'akh's belief that when he is making sacrifices, invisible dark forces answer his demonic prayers, making him stronger. He also believes that the bigger the sacrifice, the more power he will gain. According to Mal'akh, mankind came close to transcending "his earthly bonds" in Ancient Egypt. However, greed led some men to pervert the Ancient Mysteries, and so their earliest guardians closed ranks to protect them. However, the "illuminated Adepts", in the face of this rising, potent evil, protected the Ancient Mysteries too well, so that they became lost, and the Adepts' successors began to deny the ancient knowledge as heresy. Mal'akh, of course, sees himself as the inheritor of those evil men who perverted the Ancient Mysteries.

Sufism is indeed a very mystical part of Islam that some, such as Idries Shah, thought predated the rise of Islam (3). Since 'Suf' means 'wool' in Arabic, some etymologists have thought that this branch of Islam got its name for the penchant of its followers to wear woollen cloaks in imitation of Christ. According to Wikipedia, a follower of Sufism "may be led to abandon all notions of dualism or multiplicity, including a conception of an individual self, and to realize the Divine Unity", which could almost be a Hermetic philosophy. I've already discussed how Christianity adopted the pagan days of the week, and pagan customs such as the Eucharist, and the use of frankincense in church. The *Catholic Encyclopedia* notes that in the Middle Ages, it was common to have astrological references in religious calendars (4):

> Sometimes, also, the verses thus prefixed bear an astrological import, e.g. Jani prima dies et septima fine timetur, which is meant to convey that the first day of the month of January and the seventh from the end are unlucky. It must be confessed that the traces of pagan, or at least secular, influences in many of our surviving early calendars are numerous. A very curious feature in many Anglo-Saxon documents of this class is the acquaintance which they manifest with Oriental and especially Coptic usages. For instance in the Jumièges Missal, at the head of each month we have a line giving the Oriental names for the corresponding period; e.g. in the case of April: "Hebr. Nisan; Ægypti Farmuthi; Græc. Kanthicos; Lat. Apr; Sax. Eastermonath..."

The *Catholic Encyclopedia* also acknowledges that the days of the week are derived ultimately from Egypt.

It was Caligula who originally took the obelisk that now stands in St. Peter's Square to Rome. However, it was on the orders of the Sixteenth Century Pope Sixtus V that it was placed within the grounds of the Vatican, which was, of course, the site of Langdon's first adventure, *Angels and Demons*. Mal'akh believes the Catholic Church to be the "womb of the Ancient Mysteries", and then ponders the ultimate sacrifice of Christ. Mal'akh also believes that there is no true sacrifice without blood… Since Mal'akh brings the darkness in opposition to Christ's light, he may well be the Antichrist…

Chapter 97 Sato is exasperated, as Nola can't find an "Eight Franklin Square". "One Franklin Square" is the name of the building that Sato's at the top of, but it's actual address is 1301 K Street, so Nola postulates that the street numbers may have been different when the pyramid was made, and searches for the address without a building number. When I did this search in Google, the first result was the 'Society of the Cincinnati', which is a kind of Masonic society formed at the end of the Revolutionary War, and George Washington was the first President General of the Society. However, there's not a pyramid to be seen, and this society isn't even on Franklin Square! So, the search results have obviously changed since Dan Brown wrote this chapter.

Chapter 98 Langdon, claustrophobic that he is, is terrified to have woken up within an extremely enclosed space… This fibreglass coffin very much reminds him of the time he was trapped in a well as a child, treading water. It's almost as if Mal'akh knows his fears, and has acted upon them.
  The point of view then shifts to Katherine, as Mal'akh takes her to the basement via a hidden doorway concealed by his painting of *Three Graces*. Mal'akh says that it will probably be the last thing of beauty that she sees, and that he hopes his science impresses her as much as hers' did him.

Chapter 99 Since Simkins is looking over Bellamy at ground level, Sato asks him to take a closer look at the building that Nola has located, and he sees a building that looks like a mosque. Sato says it's the Almas Shrine Temple, the headquarters of the Ancient Arabic Order of Nobles of the Mystic Shrine, otherwise known as 'The Shriners'. You have to be a Mason to join the Shriners, who are distinctive, as they wear fezzes at official functions. They are well known for founding hospitals. I've found their website, which does indeed feature a landscape of the pyramids of Giza. However, they don't mention Franklin Square in their address, just 1315 K Street, so Dan Brown may have cheated a bit here, or perhaps the Shriners modified their website to avoid unwanted hits from Robert Langdon fans?

Chapter 100 Langdon is trying to visualise that he is under a vast open sky. Mal'akh removes Katherine's gag, and then puts a finger into her mouth. He then wipes the resulting spittle on the patch of virgin skin on his head. No doubt Mal'akh thinks that he is performing a ritual of the Dark Arts, but this is the kind of thing that psychopaths always do in the movies to gross us all out. It's a kind of symbolic rape, with his finger representing a penis, and the circular Ouroboros a vagina. Katherine is even more shocked when she sees Langdon's discarded clothes. Mal'akh then reveals that Langdon's in the fibreglass box, which Katherine likens to the coffins utilised to bring back the dead from war, such as the recent conflicts in Iraq and Afghanistan. Katherine exclaims that Langdon will suffocate, but Mal'akh points out that there is a supply of air into the box, although he warns that Langdon will wish that he suffocated as he then pumps liquid into the box. After that, Mal'akh takes the time to say that drowning is a terrible death, referring to his murder of Trish and how he himself survived drowning. Langdon really thinks he's going to die as the water flows in...

Chapter 101: inside the belly of the whale – the apotheosis of Robert Langdon
Mal'akh says he's punishing them for bringing a CIA agent to his home, and demands the full address in Franklin Square, and asks what's there, as he can't go there without being caught. He then asks her what the symbols on the base of the pyramid mean, but Katherine doesn't know what he's talking about. Mal'akh then shows her the symbols that have appeared on the base. There's a whole variety of symbols: the Eye of Horus, the circumpunct split in two, ying and yang, Ouroboros, a hexagram, a pentagram, the symbols for male and female, the sun, the Christian cross, and the Ankh cross etc. Note that Dan Brown has put Katherine's thought that this represents *total chaos* into italics, as one of the most important themes in the novel is 'order from chaos'.

Mal'akh then opens a plexiglas window on the top of Langdon's crate, and asks him to decipher the symbols, telling Langdon that he only has sixty seconds...

Chapter 102 Langdon takes hope from the fact that a cornered animal can often manufacture a miraculous escape, but the symbols on the base still confuse him, as they don't derive from a single language, culture, or point in history. Despite his confusion, he does begin to detect clarity of thought emerging. However, he also has a momentary flashback to being trapped in a coffin in *Angels and Demons*. Langdon realises that the answer can't be the Almas Temple, as the Shriners were not founded until after the pyramid was made in approximately 1850. "Eight Franklin Square" could mean anything, from the grid that the symbols are on, the Masonic symbols of the square and compass. These two Masonic symbols feature on the Masonic Altar, which is indeed square. Langdon notices that the grid of symbols is 8 by 8, and that "Franklin" and the "Order" both have 8 letters. John Wallis was the English mathematician who came up with the ∞ symbol to represent infinity. Appropriately enough, he served as Parliament's chief cryptographer during the English Civil War. It's believed he derived the ∞ symbol from the Etruscan numeral for 1000 that looked like CIƆ, which also represented 'many' (1). Or he could have derived it from the last letter in the Greek alphabet, omega (ω). Putting an 8 on its side was easy enough to do in typography. Kay Lagerquist and Lisa Lenard's *The Complete Idiot's Guide to Numerology* (2004) sounds like it could contain a lot of useful lessons for Mal'akh, who appears to be a potentially destructive number 8 personality: "When the 8's ego lead, forgetting that he... is *not the power*, then failure, destruction, and reversal of fortunes often follow" (p.106). According to Lagerquist and Lenard, "Personalities with 8s often have an interest in secret societies where there's structure, organization (especially a hierarchical ladder to climb), and mystical training (Masonic Order, anyone?). They're also interested in... ancient societies..." (p.103). The website *Spiritual Numerology* also warns the 8 personality that, "You are a gambler, you have a strong desire for luxuries and you can fall for corruption. You have to find a balance between the spiritual and the material world. Learn to use your power for benefit of mankind" (2). So, Mal'akh must be a destructive 8!

Dan Brown then writes that, "A sudden womblike silence engulfed him", along with a realisation by Langdon that he's going to die. Now, this is analogy with the womb is a very important theme in *The Lost Symbol*. Remember that in Chapter 62, when Langdon emerged from the Library of Congress' conveyor belt, Dan Brown wrote that, "Langdon felt like he had just emerged from some kind of subterranean birth canal". Note also that in Chapter 30, Dan Brown mentioned "homogenized morality tales" and "archetypal hybrids", which were actually a reference to the concept of the 'monomyth', a theory that was most eloquently propounded by Joseph Campbell's book *The Hero with a Thousand Faces*. Now, by depicting Langdon in a watery casket, Dan Brown is utilising a very important aspect of the 'Hero's Journey': the 'Belly of the Whale'. This iconic element of the monomyth is derived from the famous story of Jonah's encounter with the whale. Once you read Joseph Campbell's rationale for this aspect of the monomyth, you'll realise that Dan Brown's deployment of the word *womblike* was very deliberate indeed:

The idea that the passage of the magical threshold is a transit into a sphere of rebirth is symbolized in the worldwide womb image of the belly of the whale. The hero, instead of conquering or conciliating the power of the threshold, is swallowed into the unknown and would appear to have died. This popular motif gives emphasis to the lesson that the passage of the threshold is a form of self-annihilation. Instead of passing outward, beyond the confines of the visible world, the hero goes inward, to be born again. The disappearance corresponds to the passing of a worshiper into a temple - where he is to be quickened by the recollection of who and what he is, namely dust and ashes unless immortal. The temple interior, the belly of the whale, and the heavenly land beyond, above, and below the confines of the world, are one and the same. That is why the approaches and entrances to temples are flanked and defended by colossal gargoyles... The devotee at the moment of entry into a temple undergoes a metamorphosis. Once inside he may be said to have died to time and returned to the World Womb, the World Navel, the Earthly Paradise. Allegorically, then, the passage into a temple and the hero-dive through the jaws of the whale are identical adventures, both demoting in picture language, the life-centering, life renewing act (*The Hero's Journey: Joseph Campbell on his Life and Work*, edited by Phil Cousineau, 1990).

As noted previously, there's a neat conjunction with Langdon's previous misadventure in the watery well as a child with his current predicament. Campbell would have regarded Langdon's original confinement as being womblike also, as he explored the meaning of archetypal dreams in *The Hero with a Thousand Faces* (2008, p.86):

"The dreamer is absolutely abandoned and alone in a deep hole of a cellar. The walls of his room keep getting narrower and narrower, so that he cannot stir." In this image are combined the ideas of mother womb, imprisonment, cell, and grave.

Yet this deathly womb seems to be the exact opposite of the popular image of the womb as warm, comfortable, and nourishing, so what is going on here?

Joseph Campbell's work has been criticised for being too focused on male heroes, as Wikipedia relates: "Marta Weigl rejects the idea of a 'monomyth' in which women appear only exceptionally, and then as indistinguishable from men" (3). Although, one would have thought that this was an inevitable by-product of myths developed by ancient patriarchal societies, and is thus appropriate to the extraordinary depiction of masculinity within *The Lost Symbol*, especially with regards to Mal'akh. However, there is perhaps a term from feminist theory that we can employ here, which is implicit in Campbell's work, and that is 'Couvade' or 'womb envy'. In medical terms, 'couvade' or 'sympathetic pregnancy' is a father's psychosomatic response to the pregnancy of his partner, which could include him developing a belly as large as she. Barbara Creed gives a great explanation of the feminist theory of couvade as applied to horror films in *Phallic Panic: Film, Horror and the Primal Uncanny* (2005, pp. 42-43):

> As the power to give birth was regarded most highly this became an important activity of the earliest male divinities. According to Barbara Walker, as male gods lacked a uterus they frequently gave birth from their mouths. The classical god Zeus gave birth from his head. All of the mystery cults of the early Christian period involved a baptismal re-birth through male blood. According to Walker, the male birth myth is universal.

In many of the horror films that Creed discusses, men emulate the power of the womb by say, building an android, such as the one that featured in Fritz Lang's *Metropolis*. However, Langdon isn't concerned with creating such an artefact. Yet the power of the womb is represented by his sudden enlightenment, his godlike power to open the portal to Ancient Mysteries by solving the puzzle presented before him. This startling vision is one of the best depictions of womb envy that I have ever come across. Another one that's quite similar is Paul's drinking of the Water of Life (i.e. the water of the womb) in David Lynch's *Dune*. In this movie of another typical hero's journey, Paul Muad'Dib (note the adoption of an Arabic name, just like Mal'akh) must drink the water of life to regain his prophetic powers. However, only the Bene Gesserit sisterhood has been able to previously drink the Water of Life, as it has previously killed all other men who have tried to. Paul succeeds to complete his metamorphosis into the 'Kwisatz Haderach', the messiah of Arrakis. Although this later develops misogynistic overtones, as Paul Muad'Dib is able to enter that place where no woman can go, as he warns the Bene Gesserit Reverend Mother in the movie: "Try looking into that place where you dare not look and you'll find me there staring back at you". It's also worth noting that Jesus has to be baptized by John in water before he gets the ultimate divine recommendation. So, since Langdon is so close to death, there's a considerable element of Joseph Campbell's conception of Apotheosis in this scene (*The Hero with a Thousand Faces*, 2008, p. 127):

> This godlike being is a pattern of the divine state to which the hero attains who has gone beyond the last terrors of ignorance. "When the envelopment of consciousness has been annihilated, then he becomes free of all fear, beyond

the reach of change." This is the release potential within us all, and which anyone can attain - through herohood.

So, the inclusion of the *Apotheosis of Washington* back in Chapter 21 gives another great indication of the intricate levels of meaning that Dan Brown places within his texts, as it not only reflects Mal'akh's supposed intentions, but points the way to the events of this latest chapter like a divine oracle. It's very appropriate then that Langdon's moment of inspiration is depicted as being "a bolt from above".
Langdon now realises that the talisman that Peter Solomon had given him, the capstone, can indeed "bring order from chaos". Note that therefore, Peter Solomon is, in Joseph Campbell's terms, like Galloway, a godly mentor who has presented him with a talisman that will aid him in his quest. Langdon hasn't fully completed his apotheosis though, as he begs to be let out. However, Mal'akh refuses to release him until he shares his knowledge, so Langdon complies. Yet Mal'akh goes back on his word...

Chapter 103 None of the knowledge that Langdon has acquired as an expert swimmer can help him in this situation, as it aided him in his escape from drowning in a Roman fountain in *Angels and Demons*. As yet another act of cruelty, Mal'akh forces Katherine to watch. Langdon is no longer able to hold out against the breath-hold breakpoint...

Chapter 104 Katherine's in shock after witnessing the death of Langdon. Mal'akh then transfers Katherine to his stone altar. Mal'akh again forces his finger into Katherine's mouth as a mock simulation of rape. Like most movie psychopaths, Mal'akh has placed images and text of his obsessions onto the wall. However, Katherine is most horrified when she sees the large knife next to her.

Chapter 105 Parrish informs Nola that the CIA director has a file that appears to relate to the Masonic Pyramid. Meanwhile, Sato and Simkins arrive at the conclusion that Mal'akh's not going to appear at the rendezvous, and decide to withdraw to Mal'akh's house, as they still haven't heard from Agent Hartmann.

Chapter 106 Mal'akh makes his preparations to leave, as he knows it won't be too long before the CIA realise that he had tricked them regarding the rendezvous. He thinks it could be days or even weeks before the CIA discover his secret basement and Langdon's corpse. Langdon had told him that the answer lay within "the Order Eight Franklin Square", which is a magic square, such as the one employed by Dürer in the original clue. Mal'akh would indeed be very familiar with Kameas, as Wikipedia relates that, "The most common use for these Kameas is to provide a pattern upon which to construct the sigils of spirits, angels or demons" (1), so this is something he would have utilised when deciding what tattoos to have. Benjamin Franklin did indeed pioneer the 'bent diagonal' in his Order 8 square. However, according to Harvey Heinz's online article *Franklin Squares*, "because the main diagonals do not sum correctly (one totals 260 - 32 & the other 260 + 32), it is not a true magic square" (2). The predictions that Franklin made within his yearly *Poor Richard's Almanack* were usually jokey affairs that were never meant to be taken seriously. Thus Mal'akh needs to reorder the symbols on the base of the Masonic Pyramid according to the numbers in Franklin's 8 Order Magic Square. Although Mal'akh realises that he does not fully understand the resulting rearrangement of the symbols, he has seen enough to send him on his way.

Chapter 107 Meanwhile, in the basement, Katherine mourns the loss of her research data, and then progresses to thoughts of the afterlife, and whether the soul existed. It's thought that metempsychosis could have derived in the Greek Orphic religion (1). Certainly the legendary figure at the centre of this religion, Orpheus, famously went to hell and back. The concept of metempsychosis was utilised during the Eleusinian Mysteries, and one of its earliest proponents was Pythagoras. Plato did indeed incorporate this theory of reincarnation into his work, and recounted the story of how boy called Er came back to life after being apparently dead for twelve days, and spoke of witnessing such transmigrations of souls. According to the Catholic Encyclopedia, "The Stoics taught that all existence is material, and described the soul as a breath pervading the body" (2), and did indeed call it a *apospasma tou theu*. Thus Katherine comforts herself regarding the probable death of Peter, and Langdon's death.

'Neshamah' appears in *Genesis* 2:7: "God formed man from the dust of the ground, and breathed into his nostrils the *breath* of life; and man became a living soul".   Since Noetic Science suggests that thoughts have mass, and 'Neshamah' could also mean 'intelligence', Katherine reasons that it should be possible to weigh the human soul. So she devised an experiment to prove this, which involved building a plastic airtight container (analogous to the casket currently containing Langdon) above a high-precision microbalance.   Conveniently for Katherine's experiment, her old science teacher is close to death, and, having expressed a desire to donate his body to science, volunteers to take part. After her teacher has died in the capsule, his body weight suddenly reduced slightly but measurably. Thus Peter believes that Katherine has weighed the human soul. Which is lovely from a New Age perspective, but somewhat more problematical when one considers the ethical and practical rigors of modern day science. Since scientific experiments are supposed to be repeatable, one could argue that Katherine has proved absolutely nothing, as she's not going to get the opportunity to do this unethical exercise again any time soon. It's just this kind of experiment that gives Noetic 'science' it's bad name.

The 'cosmic consciousness' is the concept that each conscious being is inextricably linked to all the others. Astral projection is the ability of the soul to leave the physical being to travel to other places on the astral plane, which is often described as an 'out of body experience'. Since it's akin to theories regarding what happens to the soul after death, it also forms part of near-death experiences, where the soul is supposedly able to leave the body and to look down upon it, before the physical body regains consciousness. 'Lucid dreaming' is the ability to recognise that you're dreaming, and to thus control the events of your dream. After the experiment, Katherine sees tears in Peter's eyes, which she sees as hope that Zachary's soul lives on.

Mal'akh then returns to the basement with Peter in a wheelchair, whom Katherine scarcely recognises. Mal'akh tells Katherine that he and Peter must travel to the 'sacred mountain', and that this is the last time that the two siblings will be together. He then again refers to the most famous knife in history, which Peter apparently recognises. Mal'akh states that he has been saving the knife for Peter. Mal'akh's sardonic humour is shown by him asking Peter to carry the bag containing the knife and the pyramid, which he just drops in Peter's lap. Mal'akh then attaches a needle to Katherine's arm, and drains her blood, using her as that very Masonic symbol, an hourglass, to ensure Peter's cooperation... He then again reminds Peter that he also abandoned Zachary in prison. Then Mal'akh departs with Peter, while Katherine still bleeds...

Chapter 108 In which Langdon's mind hovers "in an endless abyss"...

Chapter 109 The CIA arrive at Mal'akh's house, where they discover Hartmann's body and that of the security guard, but otherwise the house seems to be deserted. Sato seems most concerned that Mal'akh has taken his laptop with him. Meanwhile, Katherine can't cry out in the hidden basement, as she's still gagged. Langdon's consciousness thinks of a lost all-powerful word in Latin...

Chapter 110 Then Simkins discovers the entrance to Mal'akh's hidden basement. A canticle is a hymn derived from the Bible, although it can also refer to some ancient non-Biblical hymns. The chanting in Langdon's mind is now taking on a more apocalyptic tone...

Chapter 111: Seven Seals of Revelation? Langdon's mind floats back to a recent lecture held by Peter Solomon at Phillips Exeter Academy. Note that the academic lecture, as previously mentioned, is one of Dan Brown's favourite devices, as it literally educates the reader about complex concepts, and answers their questions at the same time. Peter's talk starts off with a slide of the Smithsonian Institution Building in DC, that none of the audience recognises. I mention James Smithson in more detail on p. 18. There is an actual office in the Smithsonian called 'Curators of Crustaceans', and there is also a picture of the two owls on page of the Smithsonian website featuring historic pictures of the Institution (1). The owls were named after the mission statement for the Smithsonian that featured in James Smithson's will: "For the Increase and Diffusion of Knowledge Among Men", which Peter mentioned earlier on in his lecture. Deism was referred to in the Twitter clues, so I discuss this theology in more detail on pp. 17-18.

One of the students challenges Peter's well-known Masonic association, baiting him with the fact that the Masons still bear witness to outdated superstitions such as the Ancient Mysteries, something that the Founding Fathers are supposed to have swept away. The quote that the student reads from the Wikipedia-like site isn't actually online, which is understandable, as this is part of the fiction and mythology that Dan Brown has created for *The Lost Symbol*, just like the legend of the Masonic Pyramid. The 'Verbum Significatium' ('the most significant word'?) would appear to be cod Medieval Latin that Dan Brown has also invented. The student recounts the legend that the verbum significatium will be unearthed at a "dark crossroads" to herald a new age of Enlightenment. Then the worlds of the best-selling adult fiction author and the best-selling children's fiction author collide, as Peter mentions that a possible derivation of the word 'Abracadabra' is from the Aramaic 'I create as I speak'. However, J. K. Rowling uses the same word in *Harry Potter* to mean 'let the thing be destroyed' (2). Although it would appear that Rowling has confused her meaning of 'Abracadabra' with another possible derivation, as the word's first recorded use was in a poem in the Second Century by Serenus Sammonicus as part of a charm to ward off illness, with the illness being the thing that needed to be destroyed. Since 'abracadabra' could have a dual meaning, this would suit the context of *The Lost Symbol*, as it could be used for good or evil (3). It's likely that Mal'akh would have come across this word in the form of 'Abrahadabra', as Aleister Crowley replaced the middle 'c' with an 'h' (4):

Abrahadabra is also referred to as the Word of Double Power. More specifically, it represents the uniting of the Microcosm with the Macrocosm—represented by the pentagram and the hexagram, the rose and the cross, the circle and the square, the 5 and the 6, etc.—also called the attainment of the Knowledge and Conversation of one's Holy Guardian Angel. In *Commentaries* (1996), Crowley says that the word is a symbol of the "establishment of the pillar or phallus of the Macrocosm...in the void of the Microcosm."

The Krita Age is also known as 'Satya Yuga', the 'Age of Truth'. However, we're now supposed to be in the immoral Age of Kali. At the end of this current Age, which could be a long way into the future, "a Divine Being is said to take birth and reestablish righteousness, thus beginning a new Satya Yuga" (5). The dawning of the Age of Aquarius was mentioned prominently at the end of *The Da Vinci Code*, and it would appear that it's Vera W. Reid's view of this age that prevails in *The Lost Symbol* (6):

Reid sees the Age of Aquarius as that time when humankind takes control of the Earth and its own destiny as its rightful heritage. As such, humankind will become the 'Son of God'. Reid believed that the keyword for Aquarius is 'enlightenment'. The destiny of humankind in the Age of Aquarius is the revelation of truth and the expansion of consciousness.

The New Age movement would also seem to regard the dawning of the Age of Aquarius to be the start of their era, as the movement does have firm roots in the Hermetic theosophical movement. According to Wikipedia (7):

The Harmonic Convergence also began the final 26-year countdown to the end of the Mayan Long Count in 2012, which would be the so-called end of history and the beginning of a new 5,125-year cycle. Evils of the modern world, e.g. war, materialism, violence, abuses, injustice, oppression, etc. would end with the birth of the 6th Sun and the 5th Earth on December 21, 2012.

However, as Dan Brown notes, some people believe that this is the date for the end of the world. Yet Peter veers more towards the enlightenment theory. An Asian student suggests that the 'truth' may be wired into everyone's DNA, which sounds like it could be a reference to the various creation myths that I mentioned throughout this book. Then again, Peter does warn that every period of enlightenment is accompanied by great darkness. Peter believes that the truth will

117

be unveiled by religion as well as science, much along Leonardo Vetra's philosophy in *Angels and Demons*. Peter then states that passion will be an important catalyst for the enlightenment, as "darkness feeds on apathy". He then tells the audience to study the last pages of the Bible, the *Book of Revelation*. According to *The Bible for Dummies* (Jeffrey Geoghegan and Michal Homan, 2003, p. 351):

> Armageddon is a Greek pronunciation of the Hebrew 'har megiddo', or "mountain of Megiddo"… in… Israel. In antiquity, all roads connecting Africa with Asia and Europe passed near Megiddo, and its strategic position ensured that many battles would be fought here, including, according to Revelation 16, the "final battle" between the forces of good and evil.

So, this may be the 'sacred mountain' that Mal'akh metaphorically referred to.

'Apocalypse' does mean 'to unveil' or 'to reveal' in Greek, so it could be a 'reveal-ation'. It's difficult to extrapolate the events of the *Book of Revelation* and compare them to todays', since they are so imbued with the context of what was happening in St. John's time. Indeed, one reading of the *Book of Revelation* is that it was based upon the persecution of Christians at the time that St. John lived, under the rule of the Roman Emperor Domitian. So, in the *Book of Revelation*, the evil superpower of St. John's era, Rome, is destroyed. If the Founding Fathers did really want the DC to become the 'New Rome', as Dan Brown asserts in *The Lost Symbol*, then this is a rather unfortunate analogy if we are really living at the 'End of Days'! This is especially so given the US's tendency to act unethically in recent wars, something that Dan Brown hints at this novel with his rather sinister depiction of Sato. Yet the *Book of Revelation* does end on an optimistic note, with the creation of a new paradisiacal Earth, with no Tree of the Knowledge of Good and Evil (eating the fruit of which led to Adam and Eve's downfall), and an abundance of the Trees of Life (which the first couple lost access to when banished from Eden, thus also losing their immortality, which Christ rectified partially by sacrificing himself on the cross). However, there could be a lot of hellfire to go through first…

It's possible that Dan Brown intended the Masonic Pyramid to be a representation of the Seven Seals of Revelation. For instance, Katherine does have to break the Solomon seal to open the stone box that contains the capstone. However, the first revelatory seal is the Freemasons' Cipher, then the code that's broken via Dürer's magic square, followed by the circumpunct in the stone box, which allows it to be transformed into a Rose Cross. And it's the Isaac Newton clue that reveals the incandescent writing, and also melts the wax on the pyramid's base. So, with Seven Seals of Revelation have been broken, the world could be in line for a true apocalypse…

Chapter 112: rescue from without Katherine is nearing unconsciousness when the CIA break their way into the hidden basement. Lactated Ringer's Solution is an isotonic with blood. According to Wikipedia, "The solution was further modified by Alexis Hartmann for the purpose of treating acidosis in children. Hartmann modified the solution by adding lactate, which mitigates changes in pH by acting as a buffer for acid. Thus the solution became known as 'Lactated

Ringer's Solution' and later, 'Hartmann's solution'" (1). So, this may be how Agent Hartmann got his name, not that the solution would be of much use to him in this chapter!

Sato opens the shutter covering the plexiglass window in Langdon's casket, and Langdon, appropriately enough during an apotheosis, thinks that he's looking into the face of God! Note that the narrator makes a point of mention the "back-to-the-womb" aspect of Langdon's sensory deprivation tank. Total Liquid Ventilation is indeed a real technology that would work well in an isolation tank, although I haven't found any such device listed on the Internet, so one can only conclude that they are not as commercially viable as Dan Brown suggests. The CIA's Directorate of Science and Technology are indeed nicknamed the 'Wizards of Langley'. TLV does have great potential for use as a diving and flying technology, especially due to its effect on dissipating g-forces in the latter. It's also interesting to see the reference to the CIA's notorious employment of waterboarding as an interrogation technique, something that has obviously encouraged Mal'akh to copy them with his very technologically advanced tank. Note that the emergence from the tank is specifically called a "rebirthing" process. So Langdon literally undergoes the rebirth that is so greatly symbolised in Masonic circles, and has gone far beyond the partial sensory deprivation that is the hoodwink of their initiation ceremonies. Unfortunately, it would appear that Langdon's rebirth will be as painful as his actual birth.

Note that when Sato gets the light switched off, Dan Brown writes that, "The Blinding Sun had vanished". This could be an allusion to sun worship, an important theme in the novel. With its depiction of a universe being split in two, chasms opening up in voids, Langdon's removal from the tank could either be read as either apocalyptic, as or an equally explosive Big Bang of Creation. Indeed, it's very much emphasised that Langdon really does feel as if he's physically being reborn from the womb, and all he wants to do is to return there... Yet, he has been reborn as an enlightened man, as he should be, according to the Masonic legend, for he now knows what is going on.

Some readers may feel cheated by Langdon's escape from death; even if, deep down in their hearts, they always knew that Dan Brown would never kill off his most lucrative character (well, not yet anyway). They may especially feel cheated by the fact that Mal'akh referred to him as dead. However, if they check back, they would discover that Mal'akh thought the hidden basement would only be found after several days or weeks, during which time Langdon would certainly have died of natural causes.

Heroes often need to be rescued by outside forces on their journeys. However, in their weakened state, they can often find that the real world has now become more than a little disorientating...

Chapter 113 Langdon is reunited with the similarly destabilized Katherine. Mal'akh can't have put hallucinogens into the tank, as Langdon is still compos mentis. When people are in an isolation tank, they can go into the theta state that occurs just before falling asleep, and just after waking up, according to studies of brain scans (1). The theta state can enhance the brain's creativity, and improve problem solving. So although Langdon no longer has access to the pyramid, it is quite possible that his prolonged exposure to this state helps in solving the puzzle.

After examining the wall containing all the clues that Mal'akh has been working on, Langdon comes to the conclusion that Mal'akh has been seeking the 'verbum significatium', 'The Lost Word', rather than a vast underground library full of the Ancient Mysteries. Sato reiterates that it's not good that Mal'akh's taken his laptop with him…

Chapter 114 When doing an online search for "33 outer columns", the first result mentions a building where these columns are each 33 feet high. Google's cache for this site dates back to the 25th of September 2009, so it's hard to say if it predated *The Lost Symbol* (1). However, this building is the House of the Temple, where the novel began… The repetition of '33' in this architecture is obviously a reference to the Masonic 33rd degree. Since Mal'akh has reached that level, he doesn't need Peter to let him in, so it raises the question of what he does need him for, as Mal'akh reminds him that, "the secret is how to die", the first line of the novel, which was employed in the context of Mal'akh's initiation.

Meanwhile, Langdon's having trouble piecing together the bits of the clue that remain in his memory, although it's encouraging that the first line includes Greek letters. Langdon suddenly remembers the first letter is a 'H', so that allows him to work out that the word is 'Heredom', which refers to a mythical mountain in Scotland. So, this must be the 'sacred mountain' that Mal'akh was referring to, rather than Armageddon. It appears that the site Langdon got the answer from could have been the House of the Temple's website, as their definition of Heredom seems identical to the one that Langdon discovers (2), although it's possible that the search results have been skewed that way since the publication of the novel.

Chapter 115 It's confirmed that 'Heredom' is the House of the Temple. Mal'akh's interpretation of the pyramid is that what he seeks is beneath the House of the Temple. So, Mal'akh needs Peter's help in interpreting the symbols on the pyramid. Mal'akh and Peter arrive in the Temple Room where he was initiated. Note that the Temple Room's *oculus* is italicised.

However, Langdon is sure that Mal'akh won't find anything, as there is no actual 'word' to find, it's just one of the many metaphors surrounding the Ancient Mysteries. This is a reference to the murder of Huram Abiff (which I mentioned on p. 32), the Architect of King Solomon's Temple, who refused to pass the word on to his assailants, and thus the word was lost. According to Langdon, the legend states that whoever has the Lost Word will understand the Ancient Mysteries. Katherine is relieved at Langdon's reiteration that there is no Lost Word for Mal'akh to inscribe upon his head, and so Peter won't be sacrificed. However, Langdon points out that Peter believes that Katherine is still bleeding to death, and would hope that Mal'akh would fulfil his promise to save her, despite all the evidence to the otherwise.

One of the agents discovers Mal'akh's blond wig, which contains a tiny video camera that Sato believes to be very important. Langdon insists on accompanying the CIA to the House of the Temple, as he states that the building is a labyrinth that they wouldn't find their way around without a guide. Although one would have thought that Warren would be guide enough.

Chapter 116 Mal'akh refuses to call an ambulance for Katherine until Peter tells him the location of the secret staircase, even although Mal'akh suspects that she is now dead. Mal'akh then shows Peter his decipherment of the pyramid's base, so that Peter now understands why Mal'akh thinks that there's a staircase beneath the central altar, with its motif from the *Book of Genesis*. However, although Peter can still make no sense of the symbols, he knows enough to believe that Mal'akh has misunderstood them.

The original reference to winding stairs comes from the *Book of Kings* (6:8) in the Bible: "The door for the Middle Chamber was in the right side of the house; and they went up with winding stairs into the Middle Chamber, and out of the middle into the third". However, beyond this slight reference, it has no basis in fact, and Peter just sees it as another allegory for the journey of man towards God, like Jacob's Ladder. The quote "to participate in the mysteries of human science" derives from the Third Degree of Freemasonry, and is a reference to the Second Degree, which features the winding staircase. The narrator states that many of Masonry's symbols refer to human physiology. So, in the legend of the Masonic Pyramid, the golden capstone (the Philosopher's Stone) refers to the mind. The winding staircase is a metaphor for the human spine, which connects the mind to the body. As Mackey's Encyclopedia of Freemasonry states, "In one of the higher Degrees of the Ancient and Accepted Scottish Rite the Winding Stairs are called cochleus, which is a corruption of cochlis, a spiral staircase" (1). Thus we learn why there are 33 degrees of Masonry. According to Wikipedia, "The name is derived from the Latin sacer, "sacred", a translation of the Greek hieron (osteon), meaning sacred or strong bone. This is supposedly because the sacrum is the seat of our organs of creation" (2). Peter reveals that, in Masonic eyes, the body literally is a temple.

Peter tries to bargain with Mal'akh by offering to show him the secret staircase after he's sent help to Katherine. Mal'akh refutes this by showing Peter the tattoo of a spiral staircase on his spine, to show that he understands the Masonic symbolism. He then also shows the tattoo of Ouroboros on his head, and the phrase *at-one-ment* is italicised by Dan Brown. Mal'akh threatens to kill Peter as well as Katherine if he doesn't accede to his demands. During the time that he was tortured, Peter did declare that the Lost Word was not a metaphor, although he probably can't remember this now. Mal'akh then tells Peter that Katherine is the least of his worries, as he gets out some myrrh, and his tattooing implements. The narrator then relates that the sacrificial knife was forged from a meteorite from the Canaan desert. Now, the Twitter clues mentioned a meteorite, the Black Stone, which is now the eastern cornerstone of the Kaaba, the ancient stone building to which Muslims pray (see p. 27). As previously discussed, according to Islamic tradition, when this stone fell from the heavens, Adam and Eve fashioned an altar from it, which became the first temple. However, this first sacrificial altar was lost in the Great Flood, yet Abraham rediscovered the stone, and ordered his son Ishmael to build a new temple to incorporate the stone. So, it's possible, and very appropriate, that this sacrificial knife was made from the same stone.

Mal'akh implies that Peter has even more to lose than he's lost already when he gets his laptop out...

Chapter 117 Langdon is surprised by the speed of the CIA's helicopters, although one would have thought that he wouldn't be astonished by such things after his little trip in the Papal chopper in *Angels and Demons*. Sato now reveals what it is that Mal'akh has on his laptop: a video of him undergoing his various Masonic degrees, featuring many powerful men. Remember that in the Prologue, Mal'akh's thoughts revealed that something had happened within the House of the Temple that had never occurred in a Masonic lodge before, so this must be the only time that an initiation ceremony has been filmed. The video reveals that he had undergone the first initiation at Potomac Lodge No. 5, which is the lodge most connected with the laying of the cornerstone for the Capitol Building and the White House. I've Googled some of the phrases from the initiation ceremony, but got no results other than those connected to *The Lost Symbol*, so it would appear that Dan Brown has used dramatic licence in his creation of them. So, it would appear that the Masons are very good indeed about keeping secret the more bizarre aspects of their initiations. Note that there is a reference to God's command that Abraham sacrifice his son, Isaac.

The ritual murder of the Third Degree is Masonry's symbolic representation of what Langdon has just been through, as it also features rebirth. In the footage, Mal'akh explicitly compares the pyramidal House of the Temple with the representation of the unfinished pyramid on the US one dollar bill, as a way of saying out that the government is run by a Masonic conspiracy. Remember that in the extract from *The Hero's Journey* quoted on p. 112, it was mentioned that gargoyles always guard the approaches to temples, so this is the role that the two sphinxes perform outside the House of the Temple. Campbell also wrote in this passage, that once the hero enters the temple, he undergoes a metamorphosis, which is hinted at in Brown's text by the reference to a 'neophyte', a term usually employed to depict a novice priest.

Langdon can now understand Sato's motives when he sees how many powerful men, including the director of the CIA, are included in the video. This will probably set off alarm bells in the reader's mind, as they know that Nola and Parrish have discovered that the CIA director is connected with a mysterious file. The video then shows the Fifth Libation, the symbolic drinking of blood from the skull, which is actually wine. However, John Quincy Adams' *Letters on the Masonic Institution* from 1847 reveal that there have been moral panics about the power of Freemasonry throughout America history. Here is his brief mention of the Fifth Libation (1):

Ashamed and afraid to go backwards, the novice suffers his love of the marvelous, his dread of personal hazard, and his hope for more of the beautiful and the true than has yet been doled out to him, to lead him on until he finds himself crawling under the living arch, or committing the folly of the fifth libation. He then too late discovers himself to have been fitting for the condition either of a dupe or of a conspirator. He has plunged himself needlessly into an abyss of obligations which, if they signify little, prove him to have been a fool; and if, on the contrary, they signify much, prove him ready at a moment's warning, to make himself a villain.

Langdon knows that these Masonic ceremonies would appear shocking to the uninitiated, not seeing beyond the memento mori to realise the rich celebration of life that they are really about, in his view. The bloodcurdlingly oaths are reminders that a man's integrity is all he can take with him when he dies. According to Langdon, the rituals have to be arcane to transcend modern culture. Yet these rituals are far more shocking than the eating of Christ's body and blood during the Eucharist, although Langdon's coy description of his 'cult' had surprised his students in Chapter 6. The Mormon baptism of the dead isn't as shocking as it first sounds, as it involves a living person being baptised on behalf of a dead loved one, so no corpses are required! The niqab is the veil that Muslim women wear over their face. Shamanism, which involves communion with the spirit world, is believed to have been a universal precursor to religion in the Stone Age (2). According to Wikipedia (3),

> Kaparot (Hebrew: כפרות, "atonements"...) is a disputed ancient Jewish ritual to save oneself from a harsh Heavenly decree by it being effected on another object. Vegetables, fish, money, and other objects have been used throughout the centuries, and this is done on the eve of Yom Kippur. The service is performed by grasping the object and moving it around one's head three times, symbolically transferring one's sins to the object. The object is then slaughtered or donated to the poor.

So Langdon finally concurs with Sato that this is a national security issue.

Chapter 118 Having shown the video to Peter, Mal'akh then begins the slow process of transmitting it over the Internet, saying that he will stop the file that would destroy the Masons if Peter gives him the Lost Word. Mal'akh wants Peter to hate him, as he believes that he'll get more energy when the 'ritual' is performed.

Nola tells Sato that the only real way to stop Mal'akh transmitting is to destroy his laptop. However, the CIA helicopter does carry an Electromagnetic-pulse gun that could do the job, but needs a direct line of sight.

Daniel Chester French and Henry Bacon were the two men who worked on both the Lincoln Memorial and the fountain in Dupont Circle, although I don't think there's any great Dan Brown mystery relating to them.

Now that he's had a chance to study the symbols a little more, Peter has begun to make more sense of them. Note that he looks up at the moon through the oculus before he speaks. And what he says is so simple and universal, that Mal'akh believes that it is indeed the answer to the Lost Word.

Meanwhile, an agent looking through Mal'akh's trash seems to have made an important discovery. Bellamy has also been doing some searching, and believes he has found the reason why Mal'akh hates the Solomons...

Chapter 119: atonement with the father? It appears that Mal'akh only needs his crow's feather to inscribe the Lost Word on the virgin skin of his head with Peter's blood, not professional needles, so it appears that this tattoo is not meant to be permanent. However, Mal'akh believes he must do this to achieve the power he has so long sought via his apotheosis. Yet this does not appear to be enough for

Mal'akh, as he still requires Peter. Mal'akh states that God ordered the sacrificial knife to be made. I can't find any reference online to the Akedah knife, so I can only conclude that this is part of Dan Brown's fiction. Conversely, it is very appropriate that Mal'akh wants to use this knife in his sacrifice, as the place where Abraham was ordered to sacrifice his son Isaac, Mount Moriah, was the same mountain where King Solomon later built his temple, the building venerated by Masons. According to some readings of the story, it was a surprise that God stopped the sacrifice of Isaac rather than the fact that he had ordered it in the first place, as the sacrifice of children was commonplace in pagan societies in those days, such as those I mentioned in connection with the god Moloch in Chapter 77. The fact that Dan Brown has chosen to revive a story involving Abraham is also quite fitting, as Abraham's a pivotal figure in all three of the main faiths: Judaism, Christianity, and Islam.

Mal'akh is insistent in his belief that there is magic and power in human sacrifice. Peter is astounded when Mal'akh says that he has been preparing to sacrifice himself, rather than Peter. Mal'akh states that the reason why he has an isolation tank is so he could prepare for his role as the 'pure white lamb'. Now, lambs were typically the kind of animals that would be sacrificed in ancient times, which is why Christ is called the 'Lamb of God', as a metaphor for his sacrifice. So, Mal'akh employs the same metaphor to liken himself to Christ, although he'd obviously be more of an Antichrist. In a neat twist on behalf of Dan Brown here, Mal'akh states that his own life is far more precious to him than Peter's, which is why he wants to perform the ultimate sacrifice. In William Harvey's article *The Altar of Freemasonry*, the fraternity's symbolic altar is described thus (1):

In the Jewish ritual the Altar had a three-fold significance: it was the place where sacrifices were made, where incense was offered, and at its horns certain classes of offenders found sanctuary. In modern Freemasonry, the whole may be moralised as the spot at which the fervent Craftsman offers the incense of Brotherly Love, Relieve, and Truth, on which he lays unruly passions and worldly appetites as a fitting sacrifice to the genius of the Order, and under the shadow of which he finds sanctuary from greed, and avarice, and other lusts that would devour him.

So Mal'akh approaches the altar from a more primeval perspective, as he desires a return to its original, bloodier function.

Yet Mal'akh may be taking things a bit too far by entrusting his execution to the left hand of a man who's just been through a terrible trauma. The left has always been literally associated with the *sinister* side of life, but also with weakness. So, Mal'akh's sacrifice could be a lot more painful and prolonged if Peter turns out to have been right handed! Then again, Mal'akh does regard chaos as being the natural order of things. Mal'akh then confronts Peter again about the abandonment of Zachary, saying that Peter is responsible for all the deaths that have occurred in his family over the pyramid. Following this, Mal'akh decries the kind of father who cannot recognise his own son... Mal'akh reveals how the prison warden beat to death a prisoner that looked similar to him after he'd bribed him, and how the body building drugs had transformed his physical appearance.

Some readers may find this revelation, that Mal'akh is Peter's son, to be a bit corny. They may also feel a bit cheated that Zachary is still alive. However, it's with a magician's sleight of hand that Dan Brown persuaded the reader that Zachary was dead, with the mention in Chapter 57 of Mal'akh's new cellmate. Since at this time, the reader had no knowledge of Mal'akh's original identity, the reader naturally assumed that Mal'akh's new cellmate was Zachary. Since then, Dan Brown has been dropping hints, such as the fact that Mal'akh knew about the Solomons' preference for black tea. Okay, so he could have picked this up from his previous meetings with Peter as an Masonic initiate, or from Peter under torture (!), but he ultimately derived this knowledge from being a member of the family. There's also the fact that Mal'akh seemed upset at learning that he'd accidentally killed Isabel Solomon, despite the fact that he'd shown no remorse after also murdering a man in order to steal his truck. In addition to this, when Peter shot Mal'akh after his first attempt to steal the pyramid, he had attempted to cross the river via *Zach's Bridge*, and unless he had done an exceptionally long reconnoitre before the attack, the only way that he could have known that there was a bridge there was if it had been named after him. There was also that reference to God's command to Abraham to sacrifice his son in Chapter 117, as Peter is obviously the forbidding father Abraham who was prepared to abandon his son in Zachary's eyes. Zachary's decision to identify himself with Moloch is also a subtle reference to parents sacrificing their children.

As an eight-year-old, I found Darth Vader's declaration of his fatherhood to son Luke to be quite corny in *The Empire Strikes Back*. As the years have passed though, I've found this scene of the father symbolically castrating his son's penis (lightsabre) to be far more compelling, due to its Freudian overtones. Dan Brown is also doing something quite clever here with regards to Joseph Campbell's concept of the monomyth, as one of the elements of the Hero's Journey is referred to as *Atonement with the Father* (a feature that George Lucas made great use of too). According to Wikipedia, "In this step the person must confront and be initiated by whatever holds the ultimate power in his or her life. In many myths and stories this is the father, or a father figure who has life and death power" (2). As Campbell himself explained it –

Atonement consists in no more that the abandonment of that self-generated double monster - the dragon thought to be God (superego) and the dragon thought to be Sin (repressed id). But this requires an abandonment of the attachment to ego itself, and that is what is difficult. One must have a faith that the father is merciful, and then a reliance on that mercy. Therewith, the center of belief is transferred outside of the bedeviling god's tight scaly ring, and the dreadful ogres dissolve... The problem of the hero going to meet the father is to pen his soul beyond terror to such a degree that he will be ripe to understand how the sickening and insane tragedies of this vast and ruthless cosmos are completely validated in the majesty of Being. The hero transcends life with its peculiar blind spot and for a moment rises to a glimpse of the source. He beholds the face of the father, understands - and the two are atoned.

Thus Dan Brown completely turns this aspect of the monomyth on its head, as Mal'akh doesn't want to abandon his id or superego, he's done everything in his power to ensure his father is not merciful to him, he's quite happy to see ogres, he revels in the chaos of the universe, and although he's close to enlightenment, he most definitely does not want atonement with his father. When you look at Mal'akh's revelation in this light, it becomes all the more deliciously perverse.

Chapter 120 Langdon gives instructions as the CIA arrives at the House of the Temple. Note that Rome's Pantheon, which featured in *Angels and Demons*, is mentioned. In Robert Langdon's first adventure, the Pantheon's oculus (or 'demon hole') became very much the subject of his attention due to his misinterpretation of a clue. As Langdon states, 'oculus' is another word for skylight, so the CIA are very excited to hear that there is a line of sight above the altar.

Chapter 121 Peter struggles to come to terms with the fact that Mal'akh is his son, Zachary. It would appear that Mal'akh has a chemical brain imbalance, possibly brought on by the abuse of drugs while he was still developing, so that his hormonal and natural rebelliousness against his father in his teenage years has never left him, as he is still obsessed with being 'abandoned', and having been forced to make a choice between 'wealth or wisdom' (when Peter actually offered him both, if he had but listened). Mal'akh places impossible stress on his father by making him choose to kill him, or lose his sister and fraternity forever.

Dan Brown prepares the reader for a scene of death by describing the House of the Temple's atrium as a 'sepulcher', i.e. a tomb. Albert Pike is also buried within the House of the Temple, and that quote of his is very famous, although I have not found the context in which he made it.

Mal'akh believes that he has finally persuaded Peter to sacrifice him. In his mind, he utters a perverse form of the Eucharist, asking demons to receive his body that he has offered up (or should that be *down*) to them.

Arriving at the Temple Room doors, Langdon and Simkins hear Peter scream. When Langdon arrives in the room, he sees what he believes to be Mal'akh in the process of delivering the fatal blow.

"Besmeared with the blood of human sacrifice", looks to be a quote from the Nineteenth Century *Primitive Church Magazine*, and is a reference to the practices of the heathen religions that the early Christians found in Britain (1).

Langdon reaches the altar and rugby tackles the assailant, as a beam of light from the helicopter pierces through the skylight. However, Langdon's confused when he sees that it's Mal'akh on the altar, and that he's just attacked Peter, who broke the Akedah knife rather than kill his own son. Although it's surprising that a knife that has lasted that long could break so easily – maybe the brittle meteorite was never up to the job in the first place, and was well, just symbolic. Langdon is momentarily alarmed when he sees a laser sight penetrating the oculus, although most readers will guess that this is the Electromagnetic-pulse gun in action, albeit apparently too late. The pilot tries to avoid putting too much stress on the glass of the oculus, but fails catastrophically.

Mal'akh uses the analogy of stars falling towards him – which is what he is was expecting at his apotheosis – to describe the shards of glass. Mal'akh is amazed that Peter refused to kill him, despite all the provocation, and yet it appears that he is indeed done for... The altar in the House of the Temple is certainly a rather splendid affair, built with black marble, although I'm not sure it's long enough to fully support a man's body from the photos I've seen.

Dr. Albert G. Mackey wrote about the symbolism of the Masonic lodge in the *Encyclopedia of Freemasonry, Part 1* (p. 363, 2003):

> If we draw lines which shall circumscribe just that portion of the world which was known and inhabited at the time of the building of Solomon's Temple, these lines, running a short distance north and south of the Mediterranean Sea, and extending from Spain to Asia Minor, will form an oblong square, whose greatest length will be from east to west, and whose greatest breadth will be from north to south. This oblong square... which thus enclosed the whole inhabited part of the globe would represent the form of the Lodge, to denote the universality of Masonry, since the world constitutes the Lodge; a doctrine that has since been taught in that expressing sentence: In every clime the Mason may find a home, and in every land a brother.

However, in an online article entitled *The Altar of Freemasonry* (2), William Harvey has extrapolated this metaphor regarding the lodge even further:

> Brethren with a larger imagination take even a broader view than Mackey, telling us that the Lodge represents the whole universe, being in length from east to west, and in breadth from north to south, and in height even to Heaven itself. And it is just because of this that the roof is frequently decorated to represent the starry firmament, an emblem of those immortal mansions to which faithful Masons hope at last to ascend, there to behold the Grand Master of the Universe who reigns for ever. To reach the celestial city the Initiate is taught that he must climb a ladder which rests upon the Volume of the Sacred Law, and of which the principal rungs are Faith, Hope and Charity – Faith in God, Hope of Immortality, and Charity towards all men.

Well, Mal'akh certainly had hoped of immortality, but he really failed at the other two. With regards to "charity towards all men", Mal'akh was the direct opposite of his philanthropic father.

Chapter 122 Mal'akh finds the irony of his predicament to be literally quite painful, and is surprised to hear the voice of Langdon, whom he had left for dead, along with Katherine. Still, Mal'akh takes comfort from the chaos he's undoubtedly caused by the dissemination of the file, and he still expects to be received as a king by his demonic brethren. However, Peter disturbs his dreams by saying that he lied about the Lost Word, and that it was not derived from the oldest language on Earth: that of symbols. Mal'akh was convinced by Peter's argument that the Lost Word was the circumpunct. However, since it has had so many resonances throughout the centuries, from symbolising Ra, alchemy and the Philosopher's Stone, the All-Seeing Eye etc., one could argue that it was hardly lost, and Mal'akh should have realised this. But that's one consequence of his having chosen wealth over wisdom. Peter tells Mal'akh that if he had revealed the true Lost Word to him, then Mal'akh, being Mal'akh, would not have understood and would not have believed him.

Chapter 84 mentioned one of Katherine's experiments, where she photographed the energy that disseminated from a faith healer's hands. Mal'akh's wounds are too numerous for Peter to heal, but the chemical reaction that is mentioned when he touches his son's head, is probably intentional on Peter's part, as he utilises his knowledge of Noetic science to lovingly ease his son's pain. Mal'akh then goes on to have an out of body experience as he dies, as his physical body gives way to entropy and is transformed, as his soul departs. And yet Mal'akh does not feel the enlightenment of apotheosis; rather the reverse, as his body is veiled by the dark. Mal'akh really did do those incantations a bit too well, as he discovers that his welcome at the gates of Hell by Satan isn't quite as warm as he'd wished...

When you consider that in Chapter 61 of *Angels and Demons*, Langdon mentioned that the Pantheon's oculus was thought by one commentator to be an entrance for demons, it makes you suspect that Dan Brown has been planning the above scene for a very long time, albeit with regards to the exit of a demon, rather than its entrance.

Chapter 123 In which Galloway senses Mal'akh's death, and is called by Bellamy, who lets him know that Peter is safe.

Chapter 124 Katherine arrives in the Temple Room, and comforts Peter over the loss of his son.

Nola informs Sato that it appears that they successfully prevented the transmission of Mal'akh's Masonic file, as the agent going through Mal'akh's trash had identified the hardware that he was using, allowing them to interrupt the file's dissemination.

Chapter 125 According to Wikipedia, "In September 1940... Truman was elected Grand Master of the Missouri Grand Lodge of Freemasonry. In November of that year, he defeated Kansas City State Senator Manvel H. Davis by over 40,000 votes and retained his Senate seat. Truman said later that the Masonic election assured his victory..." (1). Truman had a long association with freemasonry, as he was initiated back in 1909.

Katherine thanks Langdon for all he's done, and relates that Peter has just told her something wonderful that she wants to check out for herself first. Langdon notices that she looks somehow rejuvenated, despite the awful events of the night. She tells him that Peter wants to speak to him alone in the House of the Temple library.

Chapter 126 It's true that the House of the Temple's library, formed from Albert Pike's collection of books, is the oldest public reading room in DC. It's also believed to contain the biggest collection of Robert Burns material in North America, probably due to the fact that Burns was a Mason. One would have thought from the title of *Ahiman Rezon, The Secrets of a Prepared Brother*, that Ahiman Rezon was a person. However, according to the author of this Eighteenth Century book, Laurence Dermott, 'Ahiman Rezon' is Hebrew for 'the secrets of a prepared brother', except that it doesn't actually mean this at all, and they aren't actually Hebrew words (1). The book in the library that Benjamin Franklin printed by hand was *The Consitutions of the Free-Masons* (1734). According to

Heather K. Calloway, this was the first Masonic book printed in North America (2).

There's an optical illusion in the library of a pyramid with a golden capstone formed by the shadow cast by a lamp. Except the Masonic Pyramid in front of Peter is for real this time. Peter informs Langdon that the Lost Word is genuine, but Robert is still sceptical. Peter also states that Langdon has solved all the clues on the Masonic Pyramid, and asks him if he can fully read the symbols that he deciphered while solving the final clue. Langdon relates that he believes it to be a picture showing heaven and hell, with 'heredom' applying to 'heaven'. The symbols below the pyramid stand for the earth, as they are the astrological signs of the star systems that the ancients first saw in the heavens. The pyramid itself stretches to heaven, representing the lost Ancient Mysteries, and that's filled with philosophical and religious symbols, representing faiths that believe in one true god, represented by the circumpunct at the pyramid's apex. Langdon states that the staircase is the famous Masonic Winding staircase that I discussed on p. 121.

Peter agrees with Langdon's interpretation. However, he says the picture also tells another story that is "far more revealing". Given that this picture was first discussed in this chapter in the context of the apocalypse, this choice of words seems significant. Indeed, Peter says that when he was at his most desperate that night, he saw behind the Masonic Pyramid's various layers of allegory to realise exactly where the Lost Word is "buried". Albert G. Mackey's *The Symbolism of Freemasonry* (1882) has another interpretation regarding the positioning of the cornerstone in the northeastern corner:

> Now, the spiritual corner-stone is deposited in the north-east corner of the lodge, because it is symbolic of the position of the neophyte... who represents it in his relation to the order and to the world. From the profane world he has just emerged. Some of its imperfections are still upon him; some of its darkness is still about him; he as yet belongs in part to the north. But he is striving for light and truth; the pathway upon which he has entered is directed towards the east. His allegiance... is divided. He is not altogether a profane, nor altogether a mason. If he were wholly in the world, the north would be the place to find him--the north, which is the reign of darkness. If he were wholly in the order,-- a Master Mason,--the east would have received him--the east, which is the place of light. But he is neither; he is an Apprentice, with some of the ignorance of the world cleaving to him, and some of the light of the order beaming upon him. And hence this divided allegiance... is well expressed... by the appropriate position of the spiritual corner-stone in the north-east corner of the lodge. One surface of the stone faces the north, and the other surface faces the east. It is neither wholly in the one part nor wholly in the other, and in so far it is a symbol of initiation not fully developed--that which is incomplete and imperfect, and is, therefore, fitly represented by the recipient of the first degree, at the very moment of his initiation.

Mackey believed that the symbol of the cornerstone derived solely from Judaism, as it was not a common one employed in other contemporary heaven societies, and that it could also signify the Jewish Messiah in the Bible. Since the northeast corner of a building is the first to be illuminated by the morning light, so Peter suggests that Langdon should look in the northeast corner of the picture for the first source of inspiration. That symbol happens to be a downward pointing arrow, which on maps such as this one, as Peter points out, means 'South'. So, Peter says the map is pointing south of the House of the Temple.

Peter reminds Langdon that in the Masonic legend, the Lost Word is buried in DC, and that a large stone, engraved with words from an ancient language, sits on top of the entrance to the staircase. Peter then says this message in the ancient language is also written on the Masonic Pyramid, pointing to the line that begins with the Masonic square and ends with Ouroboros. However, Langdon is still mystified, but Peter insists that the large stone is hidden in plain view, and says that he will take Langdon to it.

A few minutes later, Peter and Langdon are in a CIA car with Simkins. Sato comes over and states that she has acceded to Peter's unusual request, and that he will briefly be given access, although she is coy about the location involved. She stops to thank Langdon for his help, although she rebukes him for the bullshit that she believes that he regaled her with earlier in the night. The sinister Sato, of course, played the role of red herring in the first part of the novel to perfection, and it's very likely that the Twitter clues referring to famous duplicitous CIA agents were also designed to hoodwink us into believing that she was a villain. Peter then insists on placing a Masonic hoodwink over Langdon's eyes, so that he does not see where they are going.

Chapter 127 In which Parrish reveals that the Kryptos sculpture within the grounds of the CIA's HQ in Langley, Virginia, was the topic of the redacted CIA document that Katherine tried to get access to. It would appear that Katherine's field of Noetic Science is referred to on the sculpture by the reference to "lucid memory". So, it was just a message board for folks trying to crack the sculpture's final codes. The reason why Krytos' coordinates were off by one degree on the cover of *The Da Vinci Code* is apparently revealed, as this was a way of pointing back to the sculpture itself. Readers who were hoping that Dan Brown might have solved Kryptos thus have their hopes dashed here. Even though Dan Brown does have many resources, it was always very unlikely that he would have succeeded where the CIA have failed. However, by shining more of an international light on the sculpture, he has made it more likely that it will be cracked one day.

Nola likens Kryptos to the Masonic Pyramid, since it is also a symbolon. All of the results from Googling "Masonic Kryptos" unsurprisingly point to Dan Brown's fiction, but since the sculpture contains elements such as a compass rose, it would be natural for puzzle solvers to see a Masonic link to it. So, Nola and Parrish now know that the mysterious reference to a document that only the CIA director had access to was just the solution to the Kryptos sculpture in his safe. Nola's heard that the 'WW' referred to in Kryptos may be 'William Whiston' rather than the former CIA director at the time that Kryptos was completed, 'William Webster'. However, this link with Whiston would appear to be Dan Brown's invention. According to Wikipedia, although the Eighteenth Century English theologian did lecture to the Royal Society, he was never actually a member (1), as his unorthodox views apparently upset Isaac Newton, although both seemingly believed in Arianism (2). Arius was a Christian priest whose life spanned the Third and Fourth Centuries AD. It was his view that Christ was not always the equal of God the Father and the Holy Spirit, and that he had not always existed, but had been created by God, that led to the calling of the Council of Nicea in 325 to settle the vexing question of Christ's divinity. The Holy Trinity was declared to have always existed, and Arius was excommunicated. Since Arius came from Alexandria, it's likely that Dan Brown is pointing here to the Egyptian Mystery Schools that supposedly propagated the Ancient Mysteries. With regards to William Whiston, his book *A New Theory of the Earth from its Original to the Consummation of All Things* (1696) proposed the idea that the Biblical Flood had been caused by a comet. Whiston also spent a great deal of time trying the solve the longitude conundrum, so Dan Brown may be pointing to something here with regards to the coordinates quoted in Kryptos. In addition to this, readers of *The Lost Symbol* may be interested to know that Whiston doubted the authenticity of the Song of Solomon in the Bible, and that he predicted that the world would end on the 16th of October 1736 as a result of a comet hitting the earth, which, as we know, didn't happen. He also thought that the Tatars possibly formed part of the lost tribes of Israel.

The Cyrillic Projector is linked to Kryptos, as this is another one of three James Sanborn sculptures that have employed encryption, the other being Antipodes. However, the Cyrillic Projector has been successfully deciphered, so maybe Dan Brown is mentioning this as a ray of hope that Kryptos can be deciphered too. All three sculptures use similar techniques, so could all three be related to each other as part of a bigger symbolon? However, Nola's more interested in the reputed 'Curse of the Pharaohs' that supposedly did away with Howard Carter's sponsor, Lord Carnarvon, since he accidentally gave himself blood poisoning after nicking a mosquito bite when shaving. According to David P. Silverman's *Ancient Egypt* (2003, p. 146), the story about the clay tablet warning of the pharaoh's curse was apocryphal. Howard Carter lived for a further twelve years after opening Tutankhamun's tomb, so the curse didn't affect him, and he was highly sceptical of the whole issue. Tutankhamun succeeded Nefertiti and Akhenaten, who made waves in Egyptian culture by only worshipping the sun god, Aten, a form of early monotheism. Once Akhenaten died, it's thought that the priests of the old sun god Amun regained power, and persuaded Tutankhamun to change his name from Tutankhaten.

Nola points out that one of the would-be Kryptos solvers who mentioned a pyramid got it completely wrong, as Tutankhamun wasn't buried in a pyramid. There's another reference to the imminent Mayan date for the end of the world. Thus the whole Kryptos thing, like Sato, was one big symbolonic red herring in *The Lost Symbol*.

Chapter 128: the crossing of the return threshold Langdon is trying to puzzle out the line from the Masonic Pyramid as the CIA car drives along deserted streets. The Stonemason's Square does mean "moral rectitude" (1), and we know from Maths that Sigma is most commonly used to represent 'the sum of all things'. The pyramid is, as often stated in *The Lost Symbol*, a symbol of man's reaching out towards the heavens. Delta does indeed symbolise change in Maths, and Mercury could also be symbolised as a snake in alchemy. According to About.com, "Mercury was believed to transcend the liquid and solid states. The belief carried

131

over into other areas, as mercury was thought to transcend life/death and heaven/earth" (2).

Langdon believes that they have only been driving for about ten minutes. He hears military voices, so some readers might think that they're arriving at the White House. Langdon is confused by the fact that's he's being taken inside a huge iron door into a dark stone building. Just like a Masonic initiate, Langdon has to keep his hoodwink on, and when he does remove it, there's still no light. When Peter turns on his torch, Langdon is amazed to see a square spiral staircase descending into the earth. Peter then tells Langdon to look outside via a small portal (which could be a nod to that mentioned in the legend of the Masonic Pyramid), and discovers that he's inside the Washington Monument.

Chapter 129 The Washington Monument was, of course, mentioned in the novel as far back as Chapter 1. The capstone does indeed weigh 3,300 pounds. The rarity of aluminium was also mentioned way back in Chapter 46. Langdon suddenly realises that the symbols from that line of the Masonic Pyramid are letters that stand for the Latin 'Laus Deo', which means 'Praise God', which Peter says is the Masonic Pyramid's last code, as these two words feature on the top of the Washington Monument. Peter seems to have developed Galloway's habit of dropping hints into the conversation. Langdon realises that this heavenly building is due south of the House of the Temple. Looking out through the portal, Langdon takes in the messages that are seemingly transmitted by the Capitol's neoclassical architecture, especially those commemorating previous great presidents. With his great view of the National Mall, Langdon realises that he's standing at the crossroads of America.

Peter then reminds Langdon that, according to the legend, the Lost Word is buried here. They then discuss the stone box that had contained the capstone, and Langdon mentions that he thought it resembled a cornerstone. As Albert G. Mackey has written, the concept of the cornerstone is derived from the Old Testament, and as Peter and Langdon agree, from the *Book of Psalms*. As Peter states, a true cornerstone is always buried, to symbolise a building's first step towards the heavens. This reminds Langdon that the Capitol cornerstone that George Washington dedicated has never been found. Peter also relates that many cornerstones have secret compartments in them for storing items, which has now developed into the concept of the time capsule: items from today that are supposed to be dug up and contemplated by future generations. Then Peter states that the Lost Word was definitely buried inside the cornerstone in 1848, although Langdon seems amazed that they buried a word, and he still can't believe that the Ancient Mysteries could all be buried in one place. Peter then puts in a heavy reference to the beginning of the *Gospel of St. John*: "In the beginning was the Word, and the Word was with God, and the Word was God."

Chapter 130 Starts with the opening line of the *Gospel of St. John*, as Galloway, the novel's spiritual guide, contemplates the meaning of the Word. The Wikipedia definition of the Greek word 'Logos' seems helpful here (1):

Heraclitus (ca. 535–475 BCE) established the term in Western philosophy as meaning both the source and fundamental order of the cosmos. The sophists used the term to mean discourse, and Aristotle applied the term to rational discourse. The Stoic philosophers identified the term with the divine animating principle pervading the universe. After Judaism came under Hellenistic influence, Philo adopted the term into Jewish philosophy. The Gospel of John identifies Jesus as the incarnation of the Logos, through which all things are made. The gospel further identifies the Logos as divine (theos). Second-century Christian Apologists, such as Justin Martyr, identified Jesus as the Logos or Word of God, a distinct intermediary between God and the world. In current use, Logos may refer to the Christian sense, identifying Jesus with the Word of God...

Thus, it could be argued that the 'Lost Word', from Peter's point of view, could be the teachings of Jesus. Wikipedia goes on to state that:

The author of John adapted Philo's concept of the Logos, identifying Jesus as an incarnation of the divine Logos that formed the universe... The Gospel of John begins with a Hymn to the Word, which identifies Jesus as the Logos and the Logos as divine. The first verse has been translated as declaring the Logos to be God... John's placement of the Word at creation reflects Genesis, in which God... speaks the world into being, beginning with words "Let there be light."

Indeed, so reflective is St. John of the beginning of the *Book of Genesis* that I had originally ascribed this quote from his Gospel to the beginning of the Bible!

Like Langdon and Peter, Galloway is at a crossroads, albeit he is at the Great Crossing of the Washington National Cathedral. For Galloway, the Word is to be found in all the ancient sacred books of the major religions, although the one most obviously held sacred by the founders of the Capitol was the Masonic Bible, which also contains a great deal of Masonic philosophy, as well as the more established religious text. In Galloway's eyes, few people in history have understood its true message. Newton used to scour the Bible looking for ancient scientific knowledge, and this is very much the image that springs to mind here. The rest of that quote by R.W. and Rev. Joseph Fort Newton reads (2):

We pay homage to the greatest of all books - the one enduring Book which has traveled down to us from the far past, freighted with the richest treasure that ever any book has brought to humanity. What a sight it is to see men gathered about an open Bible - how typical of the spirit and genius of Masonry, its great and simple faith and its benign ministry to mankind.

To Galloway, it's astonishing that these most studied of texts still have buried truths, but he believes that their transformative nature will soon be revealed as man reaches enlightenment...

Chapter 131 Most sources state that there are 897 steps in the Washington Monument staircase, so Dan Brown may be wrong here. However, there is certainly a copy of the Bible in the Washington Monument cornerstone, as Peter has told Langdon. Peter utilises a startling image on the wall to state that there is a large collection of knowledge hidden within the Bible, hidden by veils of allegory and symbolism. Peter then refers to the *Gospel of Mark* (4, 11-13) in the context of the Parable of the Sower. In his book *Modernism: A Cultural History* (2005, pp. 58-59), Tim Armstrong relates Frank Kermode's view of the Parable of the Sower:

> This apparently savage doctrine suggests a hermeneutic paradox: only the insider who *already has* the knowledge can decode the message. Or, since Jesus goes on to explain the parable in terms of the sowing of the word, parables are really for outsiders; insiders get straight talk.

That quotation from the *Gospel of Mark* does often appear to be used by those who believe, like Peter, that there are hidden messages in the Bible (1, 2). It's also employed by those who believe that there is an Illuminati conspiracy to rebuild the Jewish Temple on the Temple Mount (3).

Richard B. Hayes in his book *First Corinthians* (1997) argues that when St. Paul wrote of 'hidden wisdom', he was referring to the 'Cross', the 'Crucified Christ'. Paul ironically admonishes the so-called wise men of Corinth for arguing with each other, in a call for unity (p.43):

> Continuing to develop the apocalyptic dimensions of divine wisdom, Paul indicates in 2: 7-9 that the wisdom of the cross was foreordained before the ages but hidden from the rulers of this age, therefore Paul's preaching of the cross is in the form of a "mystery"... to those who can see only the power structures of the present age. This has nothing to do, as older commentators sometimes suggested, with Hellenistic mystery religions; Paul's language is indigenous to Jewish apocalyptic thought, where the "mysteries" concern the concealed will of God... These mysteries are revealed to the elect through the mediation of the prophet or seer.

So, if it's Peter's belief that the First Letter to the Corinthians contains references to the Egyptian Mystery Schools, then this view is one that is very much rebuked by Richard B. Hayes. However, Peter is very good at summarising Paul's epistle with regards to the two different levels of meaning in the parables, with "milk for babies and meat for men". It would appear that Langdon is referring to the Authorised King James edition of the Bible, as later translations, such as the New International Version, has a tendency to remove the mention of 'dark sayings' and replace them with the word 'riddles', which is a bone of contention for many admirers of the King James edition (4). However, I can't see in the *Gospel of St. John* where it forewarns "I will speak to you in parable... and use dark sayings", as surely this is just a quote from Psalm 78: "I will open my mouth in a parable: I will utter dark sayings of old". Langdon's explanation of 'dark sayings' as analogous with 'cryptic' is the one accepted by many commentators. It's interesting to see the continuing focus on the *Gospel of St. John*, as Peter continues the theme that he started back in Chapter 129.

As mentioned previously, Isaac Newton did believe that he had extracted scientific information from the Bible. Of interest to readers of *The Lost Symbol* is that Newton wrote at length about Solomon's Temple and the sacred cubit. However, he wrote it in Latin, so his musings are not readily accessible to us.

There's no real historical evidence that Sir Francis Bacon was hired by King James to create the first authorised English translation of the Bible, but this idea, and that of Bacon's authorship of Shakespeare's plays, are propounded quite firmly in Manly P. Hall's *The Secret Teachings of All Ages*, in the *Bacon, Shakespere, and the Rosicrucians* chapter. And we know that Dan Brown has read this book by Manly P. Hall since the epigraph of *The Lost Symbol* comes from *The Secret Teachings of All Ages*. Francis Bacon's 1609 book *The Wisdom of the Ancients* appears to be an examination of classical myths, but this tome is not one that is discussed widely, and may therefore not deserve the attention that Peter gives to it.

I also don't agree to the interpretation that Peter gives to the quote from William Blake's *The Everlasting Gospel* (1818). When viewed in its wider context, it reads much differently:

THE VISION OF CHRIST that thou dost see / Is my vision's greatest enemy. / Thine has a great hook nose like thine; / Mine has a snub nose like to mine. / Thine is the Friend of all Mankind; / Mine speaks in parables to the blind. Thine loves the same world that mine hates; / Thy heaven doors are my hell gates. / Socrates taught what Meletus / Loath'd as a nation's bitterest curse, And Caiaphas was in his own mind / A benefactor to mankind. / Both read the Bible day and night, / But thou read'st black where I read white.

So, William Blake is not hinting that we should read between the lines, rather he is saying that his vision of Jesus is different from the prevailing one of his day, a kind of 'you say potato, I say potato' approach to divinity. Blake was also certainly not singing from the same hymn sheet as Newton, as "he was critical of what he perceived as the elevation of reason to the status of an oppressive authority" (5). Indeed, according to Wikipedia (6),

[Blake] wrote in his annotations to the *Laocoon* "Art is the Tree of Life. Science is the Tree of Death." Newton's theory of optics was especially offensive to Blake, who made a clear distinction between the vision of the "vegetative eye" and spiritual vision. The deistic view of God as a distant creator who played no role in daily affairs was anathema to Blake, who regularly experienced spiritual visions. He opposes his "four-fold vision" to the "single vision" of Newton, whose "natural religion" of scientific materialism he characterized as sterile.

Blake went as far as to illustrate Newton as a strange godlike being drawing geometric shapes on cloth in a painting of the scientist, and he also wasn't a fan of Francis Bacon for much the same focus on scientific materialism. However, he could be more of an Enlightenment man in his other views, as displayed in his *A Vision of the Last Judgement* (1808):

Men are admitted into Heaven not because they have curbed & govern'd their Passions or have No Passions, but because they have Cultivated their Understandings. The Treasures of Heaven are not Negations of Passion, but Realities of Intellect, from which all the Passions Emanate Uncurbed in their Eternal Glory.

135

So, while there may be dangers in literal interpretations of the Bible (and Peter is probably having a go at the Creationist opposition to Darwinism here), there are also evident dangers in reading in absolutely anything and everything into the Bible.

John Adams once wrote to Thomas Jefferson that "Had you and I been forty days with Moses on Mount Sinai, and admitted to behold the divine Shechinah, and there told that one was three and three one, we might not have had the courage to deny it, but we could not have believed it" (7). This scepticism was common enough to the Founding Fathers that subscribed to Deism (see pp. 28-29), and probably inevitable in the age of scientific rationalism. Thomas Paine's *The Age of Reason*, which was sceptical of Biblical miracles and attacked the Church's grasping of political power, was embraced by the Deists in America, but was regarded as far more revolutionary and thus threatening in Britain. Benjamin Franklin famously declared that he believed in God, but had "some doubts" about Christ's divinity. In this manner, Thomas Jefferson removed the supernatural events of Jesus' life, such as the virgin birth and the Resurrection, from his version of the Bible, *The Life and Morals of Jesus of Nazareth*. Jefferson did not allow his version of the Bible to be published during his lifetime, so it was possibly presented to Congressmen in the early part of the Twentieth Century, rather than the Nineteenth. Yet one would have thought that Jefferson's actions would have stripped away the Ancient Mysteries rather than placing them at the fore, unless you regard the Ancient Mysteries to be Jesus' actual words alone. Here is what Jefferson wrote regarding his intentions:

In extracting the pure principles which he taught, we should have to strip off the artificial vestments in which they have been muffled by priests, who have travestied them into various forms, as instruments of riches and power to themselves. We must dismiss the Platonists and Plotinists, the Stagyrites and Gamalielites, the Eclectics, the Gnostics and Scholastics, their essences and emanations, their logos and demiurges, aeons and daemons, male and female, with a long train of ... or, shall I say at once, of nonsense. We must reduce our volume to the simple evangelists, select, even from them, the very words only of Jesus, paring off the amphibologisms into which they have been led, by forgetting often, or not understanding, what had fallen from him, by giving their own misconceptions as his dicta, and expressing unintelligibly for others what they had not understood themselves. There will be found remaining the most sublime and benevolent code of morals which has ever been offered to man.

Langdon is adamant in his belief that the prophets, which he likens to teachers such as himself, would not pass their messages on in code. In my conclusion to this critique of this novel, I will argue that Dan Brown is doing exactly that within the pages of *The Lost Symbol*. However, Peter argues that since the Ancient Mysteries are powerful, they can only be passed openly to the initiated, as they could be abused by evil. He then states that the Bible and the Ancient Mysteries are the same thing. Yet, Langdon can't accept this, as he argues that the Ancient Mysteries are all about the god within you, while the Bible is about the God above you. Conversely, Peter argues that when mankind separated himself from God, they lost the true meaning of the Word. He also affirms that the main message of all the ancient religious texts that the Masons revere is "Know ye not that ye are gods?"

According to Sai Baba (8),

> True ideal is to give practical knowledge of Dharma to others. One should be a hero in practice, not merely in preaching. This was the ideal of Buddha. All the Avatars and noble souls led their lives in the most exemplary manner and helped people experience divinity. Buddha said, "O man, you don't need to search for God anywhere. You are God yourself"

So, this could very well be seen as a truly empowering force for good, if you believe that you have God within you, and act accordingly, as Peter seems to be saying. Leo Tolstoy employed Jesus' saying *The Kingdom of God is Within You* for a pacifist book that later helped inspire Gandhi in his tactics against the British Empire. Peter also expounds Christian pacifist views when he rails against soldiers marching into war proclaiming that God is on their side. According to Hippolytus, Momoimus was of the Pythagorean school, although the famous quote ascribed to him could be regarded as anti-Enlightenment, since abandoning "the search for… creation" could be seen as a diatribe against science:

> Abandon the search for God and the creation and other matters of a similar sort. Look for Him by taking yourself as the starting point. Learn who it is who within you makes everything his own and says, 'My God, my mind, my thought, my soul, my body.' Learn the sources of sorrow, joy, love, hate. Learn how it happens that one watches without willing, rests without willing, becomes angry without willing, loves without willing. If you carefully investigate these matters you will find Him in yourself.

Although the above statement would sit very happily within the doctrines of Noetic Science, if not any other. Monoimus' view is pantheistic, in its depiction of God being present everywhere, something which I think was conveyed most eloquently by Shug Avery in Alice Walker's *The Color Purple*: "I think it pisses God off if you walk by the color purple in a field somewhere and don't notice it". Incidentally, Hippolytus was called an 'Antipope' because he stood in opposition to the popes of his era on theological points, not because he was regarded as evil (although one of his only surviving works is *On Christ and the Antichrist*). The Tyler is basically a doorman in Freemasonry, making sure that only members of the lodge can enter. 'Know Thyself' is saying that has come down to us from Ancient Greece, but it's uncertain who first coined this phrase, with Socrates and Pythagoras amongst the leading contenders. This legend is written on the wall of the Temple of Apollo at Delphi. According to Wikipedia, "In a discussion of moderation and self-awareness, the Roman poet Juvenal quotes the phrase in Greek and states that the precept descended de caelo (from heaven) (Satire 11.27)" (9).

Langdon is still sceptical, as he's never seen any superpeople wandering about performing miracles. However, Peter says Katherine's research may be poised to make that breakthrough. Which makes Peter's beliefs seem all that more skewed.

I mean, if Katherine can prove that faith healers really do possess supernatural powers, then Jefferson would have been wrong to remove the miracles from the Bible. Peter can't have it both ways. So, both Peter and Langdon have crossed the return threshold in their respective *hero's journeys*. As Wikipedia states, "The trick in returning is to retain the wisdom gained on the quest, to integrate that wisdom into a human life, and then maybe figure out how to share the wisdom with the rest of the world. This is usually extremely difficult" (10), especially, one might argue, when you're dealing with something as esoteric as Noetic Science.

When they're outside, Langdon suddenly notices that the Washington Monument could also represent the circumpunct. Peter says that it's probably just a coincidence, but that could apply to a lot of his own ideas. Langdon then hands Peter's ring back to him, who then theorises that the Masonic Pyramid was designed to create a fascination for the Ancient Mysteries, rather provide the answer to them. One might wonder what is truly going through Peter's mind, when one considers all the pain and anguish that his family have gone through for what is, essentially, a cryptic allusion to the Bible. This is especially so for readers naturally sceptical about Peter's claims for Noetic Science, which his family has also been inherently fighting for. It all seems quite worthless when viewed in our increasingly secular age. Yet, if it had all been reduced to a monomythical concept such as the *Force* from *Star Wars*, then we wouldn't have batted an eyelid...

Following the conclusion of their dialogue, Peter says that he now wants to show Langdon and Katherine Washington's greatest treasure...

Chapter 132 It's revealed that Peter secretly backed up all of Katherine's data, so her research has not been lost after all. Apparently, the Architect of the Capitol, Warren Bellamy, can only reveal Washington's greatest treasure and it involves an aged key.

Chapter 133 Langdon and Katherine are on the catwalk of the Capitol Rotunda that he had previously hoped to avoid in Chapter 21. The key that Bellamy has given them opens a metal door, but they have to wait for a precise time before doing so, according to Peter's instructions. Langdon takes advantage of the marvellous acoustics by only needing to whisper to Katherine despite the fact she's so far away. They then take advantage of their height to take a closer look at the *Apotheosis of Washington*, which was designed to inspire America's leaders.

Katherine suggests that Noetics is the oldest science as the ancients studied human thought relentlessly. She may have read Rishi Kumar Mishra's *The Realm of Supraphysics: Mind, Energy and Matter in the Light of the Vedas*, as that very much connects the Vedas with mind energy. New Age websites like to quote Einstein and to discuss remote healing, but beyond that, I see no link between the two. Katherine states that the Bible is a "study of the human mind"; although I'd rather say it was a study of human psychology, if one thinks along these lines. I'm not sure what part of the Bible tells us to build a temple with no tools and noise, but it does appear to be a reference to *1 Kings* 6:7 "And the house, when it was in building, was built of stone made ready before it was brought thither: so that there was neither hammer nor axe nor any tool of iron heard in the house, while it was in building". This passage, appropriately enough, deals with the building of Solomon's Temple. The rest of the quote from *Corinthians 3* is: "What? know ye not that your body is the temple of the Holy Ghost which is in you, which ye have of God, and ye are not your own? For ye are bought with a price: therefore glorify God in your body, and in your spirit, which are God's". This passage has been employed to warn people not to defile their bodies with say, tattoos, like Mal'akh. However, this is more of an injunction against fornication than anything else. The *Gospel of St. John* does indeed contain the most famous temple metaphor: "Jesus answered and said unto them, Destroy this temple, and in three days I will raise it up. Then said the Jews, Forty and six years was this temple in building, and wilt thou rear it up in three days? But he spake of the temple of his body". So, Jesus was literally describing his body as a temple, and succinctly prophesising his crucifixion and resurrection at the same time.

Langdon argues that the Messianic prophecy, in the eyes of most people, involves the building of a physical temple, something that the Masons supposedly want to in the conspiracy theories regarding them. Yet Katherine argues that the Second Coming is that of Man, when Man will build the temple of his mind. She then conjectures that the plans of the Temple mentioned in the Bible are actually a metaphor for the human brain. The part of the Bible that Langdon unwittingly quotes to support this is from the *Book of Exodus* (26:33): "And you shall hang up the veil under the clasps, that you may bring in thither within the veil the ark of the testimony: and the veil shall divide to you between the holy place and the most holy". Bill Donahue's website *Hidden Meanings* agrees with Katherine's New Age views, and states that "the term Temple used in the Bible is actually referring to the human brain" (1). "Where the mind is, there is the treasure" is indeed a quotation from the *Gospel of Mary* (Magdalene). Seeing Jesus in a vision, she asks him whether people see such visions through their soul or spirit, and Jesus answers that they see it within the mind, which is between the soul and spirit. However, he doesn't get to elaborate further, as the next part of the text is missing. So, this is another quote that Langdon and Katherine refer to very much out of its original context.

Whatever you think of Katherine and Langdon's conversation, the Rotunda is a very appropriate place for them to conduct it, especially when one considers the ideas that William Henry puts forward in his online article *The US Capitol and the Temple in Man* (2). Henry argues that the Capitol Building was built in shape of a human body, with the House of Representatives symbolising the feet, the Rotunda the womb, and the Senate as the head. Remember that the Rotunda contains the *Apotheosis of Washington*, so this is another association between the womb and man's enlightenment, just like Langdon's rebirth in the isolation tank. William Henry also regards the Capitol Building as a whole to be a temple.

The Pineal gland is very much associated with the concept of the 'third eye', something that I've always dismissed as New Age nonsense. However, there is more of a scientific basis for this, as Wikipedia relates: "Pinealocytes in many non-mammalian vertebrates have a strong resemblance to the photoreceptor cells of the eye. Some evolutionary biologists believe that the vertebrate pineal cells share a common evolutionary ancestor with retinal cells" (3). The wax like substance that Yogis secrete in their brains is probably Dimethyltryptamine (DMT). Dan Brown probably doesn't mention it by name, since this psychedelic drug is banned in most countries. Yet, as Langdon states, it does occur naturally within the body, and some scientists believe that it's connected to near-death or out of body experiences.

It's also associated with visions and hallucinations. However, I haven't found any evidence of DMT having healing properties. Katherine then associates DMT with the story of manna from Heaven in the Bible, which sustained the Israelites in the desert. As you can imagine, there have been very many attempts to identify this mysterious substance, with resin, plant lice, and lichens amongst the main candidates. According to Katherine, Manna was found throughout history as the Nectar of the Gods (which sustained the Greek gods as well as Ambrosia), the dew that was so important to Jewish agriculture, along with the Hindu 'ojas' ('fluid of life) and soma. The other possible identities that Katherine has come up with for Manna are mentioned elsewhere in this book. The *Hidden Meanings* website referred to in the previous paragraph comes up with the conjecture that Manna was the brain sugar galactose, and that the Egyptian god Osiris was actually the pineal gland. The full quotation from the *Gospel of St. Matthew* (6:22-23) is: "The light of the body is the eye: if therefore thine eye be single, thy whole body shall be full of light. But if thine eye be evil, thy whole body shall be full of darkness. If therefore the light that is in thee be darkness, how great is that darkness!" This is commonly taken to be a metaphor for illness, since if your eyes are dull, it's an indication that you're ill. The third eye is indeed also associated with the Hindu tilak and the Ajna chakra.

Katherine then states that the human mind was created in the image of God, which neatly gets around the issue of what gender (if any) God is. Therefore, we humans are the Creators. Langdon then confers upon Manly P. Hall, whose book *The Secret Teachings of All Ages* (from which this quote is derived) is so important to this novel, the title of 'philosopher'. Although Manly P. Hall did found the Philosophical Research Society, his esoteric writings aren't really considered to be amongst the philosophical canon. Katherine and Langdon agree that the ability to create reality could be very dangerous indeed in the wrong hands. Like the Vetras in *Angels and Demons*, Katherine believes that her breakthrough could transform the relationship between science and religion, once she has fully demonstrated the power of faith. Katherine answers Langdon's scepticism by saying that the power is latent within him, and needs practice and exercise to be fully realised. The common sense approach to faith healing from the American Cancer Society is (4): "Available scientific evidence does not support claims that faith healing can cure cancer or any other disease. Even the 'miraculous' cures at… Lourdes, after careful study by the Catholic Church, do not outnumber the historical percentage of spontaneous remissions seen among people with cancer. However, faith healing may promote peace of mind, reduce stress, relieve pain and anxiety, and strengthen the will to live".

Heliocentrism is the concept that the Sun is at the centre of the solar system, and that the planets revolve around it. Galileo Galilei's support of this theory, with the aid of the new invention, the telescope, got him into trouble as it conflicted with the Bible, so that's very much one Ancient Mystery that was not supported by scripture! Taking a closer look at the *Apotheosis of Washington*, Langdon begins to discern the shape of the circumpunct (since he's seeing them everywhere tonight, he'd best not go to a shooting range!) Having had another look at it myself, you can see the rough image of a circumpunct on the fresco. Katherine then reveals that her research has discovered that mental power is enhanced by the many sharing one thought, which she says is the epitome of 'at-one-ment', which would effectively create order from chaos. Katherine likens the universal consciousness with the growth of social networks online (so that's why Dan Brown placed clues on Twitter and Facebook!) Although, as I've previously mentioned, you could have regarded the Invisible College as being an early form of social connectivity between like-thinking minds. Many people have, like sheep, tweeted 'learning about Noetics' in the days since *The Lost Symbol* was published, although I've yet to discern a fundamental shift in the general worldview.

I couldn't find Plato's discourse on 'the mind of the world' or 'gathering God', so can only presume that they weren't his most popular ones. We're on safer ground with Jung's concept of the collective unconscious, which is kind of like the genetic memory of our species. You know, like the way dogs turn around in circles to sit down in a chair, an instinctual behaviour that derives from their previous wild existence on grassy plains. Katherine and Langdon are correct in the fact that Elohim is a plural word that is often used in the singular in the Bible. Katherine says that God is many because the minds of men are also many. 'E Pluribus Unum' is a motto that does indeed feature on the Great Seal of the United States, in a ribbon born by the eagle, as well as the *Apotheosis of Washington*. It's thought to depict the union of the many states into one.

Epilogue: the ultimate boon Langdon wakes up after having fallen asleep on the catwalk. Finding himself alone at the appointed hour, he follows Peter's instructions to find Katherine on a skywalk on the Capitol Dome. From there, they have a fantastic view of the Washington Monument. This obelisk was certainly the tallest structure in the world when it was completed in 1888. However, it did not maintain this record long, as the more modern, yet still pyramidal Eiffel Tower, which featured in the beginning of this novel, opened a year later. Langdon thinks that if our ancestors could see us today, then they would indeed regard us as gods, as he reviews the technological advances presented by the DC museums. Langdon then realises that the stone box that held the capstone could be a representation of the Washington Monument within the National Mall.

Katherine then points out the first rays of sunshine peaking over the tip of the Washington Monument. I'm sure that some rich tourists will be able to see this view, now that Dan Brown has so eloquently pointed it out. According to Wikipedia, it isn't true that there's a law forbidding the construction of higher buildings in DC (1). Langdon realises that Peter was cryptically referring to the Great Architect of the Universe (i.e. God) when he said that the Architect would let them see this vision. It's quite fitting that Langdon and Katherine should receive celestial enlightenment via the monuments of their nation's capital, just as the Egyptians strove to represent man's heavenly progress with the construction of the pyramids. It's even more fitting when one considers William Henry's view that the Capitol Building was constructed as a solar temple: "It is crystal clear that the builders viewed the Capitol as America's sole temple (a solemn, Solomon's Solar Temple to be exact)" (2). Langdon thinks of Jesus' prophecy that there is nothing hidden that will not come to light. And thus the lost symbol, which is now recovered, is that of our "limitless human potential"; from which Langdon derives great hope. This is the ultimate boon that Langdon has somewhat accidentally acquired during the course of his *hero's journey*. Although he has been essential to its revelation, he must now leave it to Katherine and Peter to disseminate it to humanity.

In Conclusion: Why Dan Brown isn't so dumb after all

Dan Brown is often accused of writing brainless thrillers that sink to the lowest common denominator. For instance, during a lecture to University of Maine students in 2005, Stephen King said (1):

> "If I show up at your house in 10 years from now... and find nothing on your bedroom night table but the newest Dan Brown novel... I'll chase you to the end of your driveway, screaming, 'Where are your books? Why are you living on the intellectual equivalent of Kraft Macaroni & Cheese?'"

As recounted in the beginning of this book with regards to Jodi Picoult's slating of Dan Brown, this is an accusation that is often thrown at the creator of Robert Langdon. One can understand such comments deriving from say, Salman Rushdie, but it must be quite galling for Dan Brown to get them from other authors who have absolutely no literary pretensions. In an off the cuff experiment, I decided to find out how many times "Dan Brown" was associated with the word "dumb" in a Google search, and came up 125,000 results. Obviously, that's not due to 125,000 people calling Dan Brown 'dumb', but I think it is significant that J. K. Rowling, the best-selling fiction author in the world, only came up with 98,000 results when searched for under the same terms. As a former Creative Writing tutor, Dan Brown has obviously done something right to become the best-selling author of adult novels in the world, and yet he still manages to be held in quite low regard. However, if Dan Brown really was a dumb, lowest common denominator writer, then I could have finished off this analysis of his work in a week, or even a day. But no, it took me more than three months, if you include my examination of the Twitter clues, and my rereading of Langdon's previous adventures. I hope, more than anything, that I have displayed something of the complexity of thought that went into Dan Brown's composition of *The Lost Symbol*. An original word count of close to 100,000 words for this book gives you an indication that I certainly found enough material to discuss.

There are some mistakes in *The Lost Symbol*, such as the implication that the whole of the DC area was originally called Foggy Bottom. Brown is also incorrect in his belief that the founders of the city were originally going to call it 'New Rome'; rather, the land on which the Capitol was built was already called 'Rome'. DC's full of neoclassical architecture not as a deliberate reflection of the old Rome, but because this was the style of architecture that was all the vogue in the West in the late Eighteenth Century. The statue of George Washington in the style of Zeus that stood in the Capitol Rotunda was not based on one of the Greek god from the Roman Pantheon; rather it came from the iconic sculpture of Zeus at his temple in Olympia. Dan Brown also made a mistake in the Twitter clues, misplacing the isle of Lemnos at one point. However, Dan Brown's not the only author who makes mistakes in his books, and such omissions are especially understandable in the case of *The Lost Symbol*, which was strictly embargoed, and thus can't have been thoroughly proofread. In fact I've found similar errors in practically every novel I've ever read. For instance, in the first edition of Zadie Smith's *On Beauty*, a painting upon which much of the plot pivoted was incorrectly attributed to the French philosopher Jean Hyppolite, rather than the Haitian artist Hector Hippolyte.

There are places in *The Lost Symbol* where Dan Brown reveals himself to be a sublimely clever author, such as when he features Mal'akh listening to the *Dies Irae* sequence of Verdi's requiem in Chapter 2, as it referred to his upcoming 'Day of Judgement' as a would-be anti-Christ, as well as the later revelation that this villain is castrated. The puzzles that Dan Brown sets his protagonists are also great evidence of a satisfyingly cryptic mind, an essential component for a mystery author. However, just as the Ancient Mysteries are guarded by veils of allegory, so is much of Dan Brown's fiction. For instance, there is Dan Brown's utilisation of Joseph Campbell's theorisation of the *hero's journey*, which he agreeably perverts by making the son out to be the villain, rather than the usual 'dark father'. In addition to this, Langdon's immersion in Mal'akh's isolation tank is probably the most vivid depiction of womb envy that I have ever encountered in popular culture, as he makes explicit man's traditional envy of the power of the womb.

There is also Langdon's role as teacher, which is fundamental to his adventures, as it allows him (and other characters) to interact with the audience, albeit in the form of students. This in turn, permits Langdon to have more knowledgeable companions, as they don't have to spend the whole time asking him what's going on. Indeed, since many of his protagonists are academics, one could almost view their conversations as being Platonic dialogues. For instance, there are the theoretical conversations that the sceptical Langdon holds with Peter and Katherine towards the end of the novel, which are fairly open ended, much as the dialogues that Plato presented Socrates as having with his peers. I'm not saying that Dan Brown is an insightful as Plato; merely that he employs the same devices. And yet it is Langdon that shares the sceptism of the audience in these dialogues in the face of the Solomons' fervent belief in Noetic Science. It is true that great advances are now being made in the study of human consciousness with the aid of powerful new brain scanners, as demonstrated by Professor Marcus du Sautoy in his recent BBC *Horizon* documentary, *The Secret You*. However, it was of necessity to the dictates of his plot that Dan Brown had to tie this emerging science down to its more esoteric branch. One could argue very much then, that Dan Brown acts as an educator also in this novel, teaching his readers new things. Yet, like Langdon, it's always best to keep a sceptical mind for the more incredulous details. Then again, by utilising the *hero's journey*, Dan Brown is acknowledging that it's usually the most incredible of stories that are passed on down the ages.

As Albert Pike wrote, the Magi's science was magic. Well schooled as he is in the Ancient Mysteries, Dan Brown also employs a magician's tools to make his readers look the wrong way. One only has to think of the simple mention of Mal'akh's new cellmate in Turkey as an example. The reader naturally assumes that because Mal'akh has a new cellmate, then this must be Zachary Solomon. And yet this new cellmate isn't significant at all, except for making it apparent that you should have been looking up the magician's sleeve, rather than at what his hands were doing... Indeed, there are very many instances in the novel where Dan Brown doesn't openly display all his meanings to his readers. For instance, when Zachary adopts the name of the demon Moloch, he's implicitly suggesting to his readers that they should read Milton's *Paradise Lost*, as only then will they fully appreciate why his villain has chosen this name. That's the kind of device that a literary author would use; not that Dan Brown will get any credit for it. And following the international success of *The Da Vinci Code*, Dan Brown knows that there are readers out there, who, like me, will be scrutinising his every word, and he uses this knowledge to reward such readers. And like Pavlov's dogs, we'll no doubt come back, begging for more…

References

The Build-up to The Lost Symbol

(1). http://dcist.com/2009/07/cover_of_dan_browns_the_lost_symbol.php
(2).http://www.independent.co.uk/arts-entertainment/books/news/gravity-boots-helped-me-with-da-vinci-code-brown-reveals-475472.html
(3).http://www.hmcourts-service.gov.uk/judgmentsfiles/j4008/baigent_v_rhg_0406.htm
(4). http://www.thebookseller.com/news/83123-rh-announces-dan-brown-date.html
(5).http://entertainment.timesonline.co.uk/tol/arts_and_entertainment/books/fiction/article6134742.ece
(6).http://intotheduat.typepad.com/decoding_the_lost_symbol/2009/04/symbols-lost-and-found.html
(7).http://www.thebookseller.com/news/93718-transworld-set-to-stir-up-dan-brown-frenzy.html
(8).http://www.telegraph.co.uk/culture/books/booknews/5803966/The-novelists-racing-to-beat-Dan-Brown.html html
(9).http://entertainment.timesonline.co.uk/tol/arts_and_entertainment/books/article6806777.ece
(10). http://www.independent.co.uk/arts-entertainment/books/features/two-weeks-to-save-britains-book-trade-1743363.html
(11).http://www.thebookseller.com/news/83123-rh-announces-dan-brown-date.html
(12).http://booksellercrow.typepad.com/the_bedside_crow/2009/07/dan-brown-the-lost-symbol-an-exclusive-bookseller-crow-promotion.html
(13). http://www.guardian.co.uk/books/booksblog/2009/jul/20/literary-avant-garde
(14).http://www.independent.co.uk/news/people/hit-and-run/hit-amp-run-pushy-parents-youll-go-far-1755627.html
(15). http://www.thebookseller.com/news/93718-transworld-set-to-stir-up-dan-brown-frenzy.html

Jodi Picoult's slating of Dan Brown

(1). http://www.guardian.co.uk/books/2009/may/08/jodi-picoult-da-vinci-code

The change of title

(1). http://www.pe.com/lifestyles/stories/PE_Fea_Daily_beyond1030.a0e2d.html
(2). http://www.thecryptex.com/news/solomon-key-to-lost-symbol
(3). http://entertainment.timesonline.co.uk/tol/arts_and_entertainment/books/fiction/article6134742.ece
(4).http://dan-browns-the-lost-symbol.blogspot.com/2009/07/why-solomon-key-is-now-lost-symbol.html

The publication date

(1). http://www.inquisitr.com/22337/dan-brown-returns-dbp/

The social networking clues

(1). http://www.indielondon.co.uk/Books-Review/the-lost-symbol-release-to-be-marked-by-puzzles
(2). http://www.prweb.com/releases/secret_society/Illuminati/prweb2250474.htm
(3). http://www.revisionisthistory.org/revisionist18.html
(4). http://lostsymboltweets.blogspot.com/2009/06/tweet-13-hells-legionnaire-and-solomon.html
(5). http://en.wikipedia.org/w/index.php?title=Labarum&oldid=319292324 (last visited Oct. 24, 2009).
(6). http://www.newworldencyclopedia.org/entry/Labarum
(7). http://www.ancient-symbols.com/christian_symbols.html
(8). http://www.masonicdictionary.com/tau.html
(9). http://en.wikipedia.org/w/index.php?title=Cross_of_Tau&oldid=318825266 (last visited Oct. 24, 2009).

(10). http://en.wikipedia.org/w/index.php?title=Invisible_College&oldid=319440538 (last visited Oct. 24, 2009).

(11).http://en.wikipedia.org/w/index.php?title=Rosy_Cross&oldid=320868762 (last visited Oct. 24, 2009).

(12). http://en.wikipedia.org/w/index.php?title=Rosicrucianism&oldid=316261806 (last visited Oct. 24, 2009).

(13).http://www.aftermarketjournal.com/forum/showpost.php?s=62cda2198402ab170d072edf38c665e1&p=715&postcount=2

(14).http://www.belfasttelegraph.co.uk/lifestyle/books/the-lost-symbol-new-dan-brown-book-cover-revealed-14390206.html

(15). http://www.theforbiddenknowledge.com/hardtruth/13_33_freemason_sig.htm

(16). http://www.theforbiddenknowledge.com/hardtruth/destruction_of_the_trade_centers.htm

(17). http://en.wikipedia.org/w/index.php?title=Annuit_c%C5%93ptis&oldid=317282634 (last visited Oct. 24, 2009).

(18). http://www.etymonline.com/index.php?term=Annuit+Coeptis

(19). http://en.wikipedia.org/w/index.php?title=Deism&oldid=321674527 (last visited Oct. 24, 2009).

(20).http://en.wikipedia.org/w/index.php?title=The_Rosicrucian_Cosmo-Conception&oldid=321449395 (last visited Oct. 24, 2009).

(21). http://en.wikipedia.org/w/index.php?title=Deism&oldid=321674527 (last visited Oct. 24, 2009).

(22). http://en.wikipedia.org/w/index.php?title=Smithsonian_Institution&oldid=321150569 (last visited Oct. 24, 2009).

(23). http://en.wikipedia.org/w/index.php?title=James_Smithson&oldid=313999303 (last visited Oct. 24, 2009).

(24). http://nymag.com/arts/books/features/58849/

(25).http://en.wikipedia.org/w/index.php?title=Pierre_Charles_L%27Enfant&oldid=321628591 (last visited Oct. 24, 2009).

(26). http://freemasonry.bcy.ca/anti-masonry/washington_dc/washington_dc.html

(27). http://en.wikipedia.org/w/index.php?title=House_of_the_Temple&oldid=319162393 (last visited Oct. 24, 2009).

(28). http://www.theforbiddenknowledge.com/chapter3/

(29a). http://www.jewishencyclopedia.com/view.jsp?letter=D&artid=26#69

(29b). http://www.threeworldwars.com/albert-pike2.htm

(30). http://www.millennialfreemason.com/2009/07/lost-symbol-and-dc-street-secrets.html

(31). http://altreligion.about.com/od/symbols/a/baphomet.htm

(32). http://freemasonry.bcy.ca/biography/esoterica/levi_e/levi_notes.html

(33). http://en.wikipedia.org/w/index.php?title=Taxil_hoax&oldid=317673522 (last visited Oct. 24, 2009).

(34). http://en.wikipedia.org/w/index.php?title=Eliphas_Levi&oldid=321147005 (last visited Oct. 24, 2009).

(35).http://en.wikipedia.org/w/index.php?title=Hermetic_Order_of_the_Golden_Dawn&oldid=321405637 (last visited Oct. 24, 2009).

(36). http://lorencollins.net/tytler.html

(37). http://en.wikipedia.org/w/index.php?title=Ascended_master&oldid=315698002 (last visited Oct. 24, 2009).

(38). http://en.wikipedia.org/w/index.php?title=The_White_Eagle_Lodge&oldid=318196781 (last visited Oct. 24, 2009).

(39). http://en.wikipedia.org/w/index.php?title=Count_of_St._Germain&oldid=320205904 (last visited Oct. 24, 2009).

(40). http://www.crystalinks.com/stgermain.html

(41). http://en.wikipedia.org/w/index.php?title=Unicursal_hexagram&oldid=321228435 (last visited Oct. 24, 2009).

(42). http://www.thelemapedia.org/index.php/Hexagram

(43). http://www.esotericgoldendawn.com/tradition_ciphers.htm

(44).http://en.wikipedia.org/w/index.php?title=New_Atlantis_(Francis_Bacon_novel)&oldid=321204874 (last visited Oct. 24, 2009).

(45). http://www.crystalinks.com/stgermain.html

(46). http://en.wikipedia.org/w/index.php?title=Atlantis:_The_Antediluvian_World&oldid=301731297 (last visited Oct. 24, 2009).

(47). http://en.wikipedia.org/w/index.php?title=Holy_of_Holies&oldid=319647576 (last visited Oct. 24, 2009).

(48). http://en.wikipedia.org/w/index.php?title=Black_Stone&oldid=321594745 (last visited Oct. 24, 2009).

(49). http://www.fotls.com/viewtopic.php?f=3&t=16

A critique of *The Lost Symbol*

(1). http://www.dailygalaxy.com/my_weblog/2009/05/angley-va----th.html

(2). http://en.wikipedia.org/wiki/Institute_of_Noetic_Sciences (last visited Oct. 20, 2009).

(3). http://www.noetic.org/research/files/Bleep_Study_Guide.pdf

Prologue

(1). http://www.masonicworld.com/education/files/artoct01/thecabletow.htm

(2). http://query.nytimes.com/mem/archive-free/pdf?_r=2&res=950DE4D91439E733A2575BC2A9649C946897D6CF

(3). http://www.christian-restoration.com/fmasonry/first%20degree.htm

(4). http://phoenicia.org/temple.html

Chapter 1

(1). http://www.articlesbase.com/marketing-articles/history-of-neck-tie-32032.html

Chapter 2

(1). http://en.wikipedia.org/w/index.php?title=Egyptian_soul&oldid=320948732 (last visited Oct. 20, 2009).

(2). http://www.answers.com/mal

(3). http://en.wikipedia.org/w/index.php?title=Dies_Irae&oldid=320989589 (last visited Oct. 20, 2009).

(4). http://en.wikipedia.org/w/index.php?title=Hawk&oldid=320562856 (last visited Oct. 20, 2009).

(5). http://www.theforbiddenknowledge.com/symbology/2o5.htm

(6). http://www.delandnoeticsciences.com/ForumsEvents.html

(7). http://en.wikipedia.org/w/index.php?title=Boaz_and_Jachin&oldid=315366848 (last visited Oct. 20, 2009).

(8). http://en.wikipedia.org/w/index.php?title=Boaz&oldid=320995026 (last visited Oct. 20, 2009).

(9). http://www.freemasons-freemasonry.com/larsonwilliam.html

(10). http://en.wikipedia.org/w/index.php?title=Sigil_(magic)&oldid=318486904 (last visited Oct. 20, 2009).

(11). http://www.thefreedictionary.com/artefact

(12). http://en.wikipedia.org/w/index.php?title=Demon&oldid=320978899 (last visited Oct. 21, 2009).

Chapter 3

(1). http://en.wikipedia.org/w/index.php?title=Arlington_Memorial_Bridge&oldid=312219379 (last visited Oct. 21, 2009).

(2). http://en.wikipedia.org/w/index.php?title=Foggy_Bottom,_Washington,_D.C.&oldid=317946809 (last visited Oct. 21, 2009).

(3). http://en.wikipedia.org/w/index.php?title=Jefferson_Memorial&oldid=319309578 (last visited Oct. 21, 2009).

(4). http://en.wikipedia.org/w/index.php?title=Robert_Langdon&oldid=320190540 (last visited Oct. 21, 2009).

(5). http://en.wikipedia.org/w/index.php?title=Rothschild_family&oldid=320169190 (last visited Oct. 21, 2009).

(6). http://en.wikipedia.org/w/index.php?title=Yale_University&oldid=320732479 (last visited Oct. 21, 2009).

(7). http://en.wikipedia.org/w/index.php?title=Urim_and_Thummim&oldid=320399805 (last visited Oct. 21, 2009).

(8). http://en.wikipedia.org/w/index.php?title=National_Statuary_Hall&oldid=319275499 (last visited Oct. 21, 2009).

(9). http://en.wikipedia.org/w/index.php?title=Charles_Bulfinch&oldid=319805067 (last visited Oct. 21, 2009).

Chapter 4

(1). http://www.nps.gov/history/Nr/travel/wash/fedpres.htm
(2). http://en.wikipedia.org/w/index.php?title=United_States_Capitol&oldid=320220743 (last visited Oct. 21, 2009).
(3).http://en.wikipedia.org/w/index.php?title=United_States_Capitol_Visitor_Center&oldid=319001967 (last visited Oct. 21, 2009).
(4).http://en.wikipedia.org/w/index.php?title=United_States_Capitol_Visitor_Center&oldid=319001967 (last visited Oct. 21, 2009).

Chapter 6

(1). http://en.wikipedia.org/w/index.php?title=Statue_of_Freedom&oldid=315352206 (last visited Oct. 21, 2009).
(2). http://ro-b.redorbit.com/news/oddities/37561/us_capitol_said_to_be_haunted_building/index.html
(3). http://ro-b.redorbit.com/news/oddities/37561/us_capitol_said_to_be_haunted_building/index.html
(4). http://freemasonry.bcy.ca/anti-masonry/washington_dc/washington_dc.html
(5). http://en.wikipedia.org/w/index.php?title=Augustus_B._Woodward&oldid=316846234 (last visited Oct. 21, 2009).
(6). http://en.wikipedia.org/w/index.php?title=Occult&oldid=319889521 (last visited Oct. 21, 2009).
(7). http://www.fas.harvard.edu/~memhall/sanders.html
(8). http://www.docstoc.com/docs/5911682/Atlantis
(9). http://search.barnesandnoble.com/Secret-Architecture-of-Our-Nations-Capital/David-Ovason/e/9780060953683
(10). http://en.wikipedia.org/w/index.php?title=Geomantic_figures&oldid=315398239 (last visited Oct. 21, 2009).
(11). http://en.wikipedia.org/w/index.php?title=Order_of_the_Eastern_Star&oldid=314732526 (last visited Oct. 21, 2009).
(12). http://en.wikipedia.org/w/index.php?title=Coca-Cola_formula&oldid=320149677 (last visited Oct. 21, 2009).
(13). http://en.wikipedia.org/w/index.php?title=Great_Architect_of_the_Universe&oldid=310955771 (last visited Oct. 21, 2009).
(14). http://www.easternstar.org/oeshistory.htm

Chapter 7

(1). http://newsdesk.si.edu/factsheets/msc_factsheet2009.htm

Chapter 8

(1). http://en.wikipedia.org/w/index.php?title=National_Statuary_Hall&oldid=319275499 (last visited Oct. 21, 2009).
(2). http://en.wikipedia.org/w/index.php?title=United_States_Capitol_rotunda&oldid=317923631 (last visited Oct. 21, 2009).

Chapter 9

(1). http://en.wikipedia.org/w/index.php?title=Araf&oldid=266004566 (last visited Oct. 21, 2009).
(2). http://en.wikipedia.org/w/index.php?title=Hamistagan&oldid=317158726 (last visited Oct. 21, 2009).
(3). http://en.wikipedia.org/w/index.php?title=Divine_Comedy&oldid=321072401 (last visited Oct. 21, 2009).
(4). http://en.wikipedia.org/w/index.php?title=Hermeticism&oldid=309601869 (last visited Oct. 21, 2009).
(5). http://en.wikipedia.org/w/index.php?title=Hermes_Trismegistus&oldid=320943780 (last visited Oct. 21, 2009).
(6). http://en.wikipedia.org/w/index.php?title=Hermeticism&oldid=309601869 (last visited Oct. 21, 2009).
(7). http://en.wikipedia.org/w/index.php?title=Hermeticism&oldid=309601869 (last visited Oct. 21, 2009).

(8). http://en.wikipedia.org/w/index.php?title=Hermeticism&oldid=309601869 (last visited Oct. 21, 2009).

(9). http://en.wikipedia.org/w/index.php?title=Hermes_Trismegistus&oldid=320943780 (last visited Oct. 21, 2009).

(10). http://en.wikipedia.org/w/index.php?title=Hermeticism&oldid=309601869 (last visited Oct. 21, 2009).

Chapter 11

(1). http://articles.latimes.com/2004/oct/20/entertainment/et-smithsonian20

(2). http://en.wikipedia.org/w/index.php?title=Fuel_cell&oldid=319444951 (last visited Oct. 21, 2009).

(3). http://en.wikipedia.org/w/index.php?title=Leap_of_faith&oldid=314546730 (last visited Oct. 21, 2009).

Chapter 15

(1). http://en.wikipedia.org/w/index.php?title=Electroencephalography&oldid=320729974 (last visited Oct. 21, 2009).

(2). http://www.redorbit.com/news/display/?id=126649

(3). http://www.princeton.edu/~pear/implications.html

(4). http://www.theintentionexperiment.com/the-key-to-the-lost-symbol-the-power-of-intention.htm

(5). http://en.wikipedia.org/w/index.php?title=Uncertainty_principle&oldid=320963437 (last visited Oct. 21, 2009).

(6). http://en.wikipedia.org/w/index.php?title=Quantum_mind&oldid=320197140 (last visited Oct. 21, 2009).

(7). http://en.wikipedia.org/w/index.php?title=Zohar&oldid=319960874 (last visited Oct. 21, 2009).

(8). http://www.paranormalnews.com/article.asp?ArticleID=1393

(9). http://www.crystalinks.com/sumergods.html

(10). http://en.wikipedia.org/w/index.php?title=Pythagoras&oldid=318525248 (last visited Oct. 21, 2009).

(11). http://en.wikipedia.org/w/index.php?title=Alchemy&oldid=320859903 (last visited Oct. 21, 2009).

(12). http://en.wikipedia.org/w/index.php?title=Quantum_entanglement&oldid=320876480 (last visited Oct. 21, 2009).

(13). http://en.wikipedia.org/w/index.php?title=Dharmak%C4%81ya&oldid=309804919 (last visited Oct. 21, 2009).

(14). http://prabhupadabooks.com/?g=157394

(15). http://www.dircon.co.uk/creativity/guhen/upani.htm

(16). http://www.kabbalah.com/k/index.php/p=zohar/zohar&vol=1&sec=8

(17). http://en.wikipedia.org/w/index.php?title=Sephirot&oldid=320759056 (last visited Oct. 21, 2009).

Chapter 18

(1). http://linguistlist.org/forms/langs/LLDescription.cfm?code=hmk

Chapter 19

(1). http://en.wikipedia.org/w/index.php?title=Tarot&oldid=319593433 (last visited Oct. 21, 2009).

(2). http://en.wikipedia.org/w/index.php?title=Fu_Xi&oldid=319948172 (last visited Oct. 21, 2009).

(3). http://en.wikipedia.org/w/index.php?title=Classical_element&oldid=321164107 (last visited Oct. 21, 2009).

(4). http://en.wikipedia.org/w/index.php?title=Gerald_Gardner&oldid=315583314 (last visited Oct. 21, 2009).

(5). http://www.williamhenry.net/art_temple.html

Chapter 20

(1). http://www.newadvent.org/cathen/15558a.htm

(2). http://www.visitwashingtondconline.com/washington_dc_history20.htm

Chapter 22

(1). http://en.wikipedia.org/w/index.php?title=Abaddon&oldid=321160378 (last visited Oct. 21, 2009).
(2). http://en.wikipedia.org/w/index.php?title=Michael_Parkes&oldid=319550449 (last visited Oct. 21, 2009).

Chapter 23

(1). http://en.wikipedia.org/w/index.php?title=Alcohol&oldid=320947246 (last visited Oct. 21, 2009).
(2). http://en.wikipedia.org/w/index.php?title=Runic_alphabet&oldid=321165168 (last visited Oct. 21, 2009).
(3). http://en.wikipedia.org/w/index.php?title=Alumbrados&oldid=320557332 (last visited Oct. 21, 2009).
(4). http://www.masonicinfo.com/respond.htm

Chapter 24

(1). http://en.wikipedia.org/w/index.php?title=Eleusinian_Mysteries&oldid=320104219 (last visited Oct. 21, 2009).
(2). http://en.wikipedia.org/w/index.php?title=Socrates&oldid=321039622 (last visited Oct. 21, 2009).
(3). http://en.wikipedia.org/w/index.php?title=Amulet&oldid=320978547 (last visited Oct. 21, 2009).
(4). http://www.geocities.com/endtimedeception/terrorism.htm

Chapter 25

(1). http://www.sodahead.com/entertainment/read-it-before-it-is-banned-by-the-government-article-written-by-tom-horn-with-excerpts-from-apol/question-555871/
(2). http://en.wikipedia.org/w/index.php?title=Symbol&oldid=320136091 (last visited Oct. 21, 2009).

Chapter 26

(1). http://showcase.netins.net/web/creative/lincoln/sites/uscapitol.htm

Chapter 30

(1). http://www.unexplainedstuff.com/Religious-Phenomena/Egyptian-Mystery-Schools.html
(2). http://www.opencheops.org/page3.htm
(3). http://www.cyonic-nemeton.com/IllumnitiHistory.html
(4). http://en.wikipedia.org/w/index.php?title=Monomyth&oldid=320520822 (last visited Oct. 21, 2009).
(5). http://en.wikipedia.org/w/index.php?title=Egyptian_pyramids&oldid=321056202 (last visited Oct. 21, 2009).

Chapter 34

(1). http://www.smithsonianmag.com/history-archaeology/mall_nov97.html?c=y&page=4

Chapter 35

(1).http://en.wikipedia.org/w/index.php?title=A_Journey_to_the_Center_of_the_Earth&oldid=320443276 (last visited Oct. 21, 2009).
(2). http://en.wikipedia.org/w/index.php?title=13_(number)&oldid=320030951 (last visited Oct. 21, 2009).
(3). http://www.answers.com/phalanx

Chapter 37

(1). http://en.wikipedia.org/w/index.php?title=Lazarus_taxon&oldid=317228540 (last visited Oct. 3, 2009).
(2).http://en.wikipedia.org/w/index.php?title=Twenty_Thousand_Leagues_Under_the_Sea&oldid=317575256 (last visited Oct. 3, 2009).

Chapter 38

(1). http://en.wikipedia.org/w/index.php?title=Ganesha&oldid=316214703 (last visited Oct. 3, 2009).
(2). http://en.wikipedia.org/w/index.php?title=Caput_mortuum&oldid=312763197 (last visited Oct. 3, 2009).
(3). http://freemasonry.bcy.ca/texts/gmd1999/pondering.html

Chapter 39

(1). http://en.wikipedia.org/w/index.php?title=Eye_of_Providence&oldid=317540898 (last visited Oct. 3, 2009).

Chapter 41

(1). http://en.wikipedia.org/w/index.php?title=Enigma_Variations&oldid=317546440 (last visited Oct. 3, 2009).
(2). http://www.elgar.org/1queries.htm
(3). http://en.wikipedia.org/w/index.php?title=John_Dee&oldid=315407447 (last visited Oct. 3, 2009).

Chapter 46

(1). http://en.wikipedia.org/w/index.php?title=Aluminium&oldid=317776251 (last visited Oct. 4, 2009).
(2). http://en.wikipedia.org/w/index.php?title=Age_of_Enlightenment&oldid=317050803 (last visited Oct. 4, 2009).

Chapter 50

(1). http://en.wikipedia.org/w/index.php?title=Vigen%C3%A8re_cipher&oldid=316232670 (last visited Oct. 4, 2009).

Chapter 57

(1). http://en.wikipedia.org/w/index.php?title=Manna&oldid=316128680 (last visited Oct. 5, 2009).

Chapter 63

(1). http://travel.webshots.com/photo/1255865237042336077APhMmJ

Chapter 68

(1). http://en.wikipedia.org/w/index.php?title=Melencolia_I&oldid=316586865 (last visited Oct. 6, 2009).

Chapter 69

(1). http://en.wikipedia.org/wiki/File:Albrecht_D%C3%BCrer_-_Melencolia_I_%28detail%29.jpg (last visited Oct. 6, 2009).
(2). http://www.karthikm.net/Mathemagic.aspx
(3). http://www.amazon.com/review/R390AKND71F7FI
(4). http://slate.msn.com/id/2108438/

Chapter 71

(1). http://www.theoi.com/Phylos/Heliades.html
(2). http://www.discourseunit.com/matrix/shingu_mpm_paper.doc
(3). http://www.jewishvirtuallibrary.org/jsource/judaica/ejud_0002_0004_0_04056.html
(4). http://www.goodgoshalmighty.com/essay.tl.02.htm
(5). http://en.wikipedia.org/w/index.php?title=Skoptsy&oldid=316087562 (last visited Oct. 7, 2009).
(6). http://atheism.about.com/b/2004/06/05/self-castration-in-early-christianity.htm
(7). http://www.experiencefestival.com/a/Brahmarandhra/id/100697
(8). http://en.wikipedia.org/w/index.php?title=Ouroboros&oldid=318403593 (last visited Oct. 7, 2009).

Chapter 77

(1). http://en.wikipedia.org/w/index.php?title=Johann_Weyer&oldid=318367163 (last visited Oct. 7, 2009).

(2). http://en.wikipedia.org/w/index.php?title=The_Lesser_Key_of_Solomon&oldid=318080012 (last visited Oct. 7, 2009).

(3). http://en.wikipedia.org/w/index.php?title=Grimorium_Verum&oldid=316190060 (last visited Oct. 7, 2009).

(4). http://www.straightdope.com/columns/read/2091/why-do-jews-no-longer-sacrifice-animals

(5). http://www.sacred-texts.com/grim/kos/kos52.htm

(6). http://en.wikipedia.org/w/index.php?title=Aleister_Crowley&oldid=318745213 (last visited Oct. 10, 2009).

(7). http://en.wikipedia.org/w/index.php?title=Moloch&oldid=317651961 (last visited Oct. 10, 2009).

(8). http://www.duneinfo.com/unseen/giger.asp

Chapter 78

(1). http://www.gwmemorial.org/washington.php

Chapter 81

(1). http://en.wikipedia.org/w/index.php?title=Cerulean&oldid=318830416 (last visited Oct. 10, 2009).

(2). http://en.wikipedia.org/w/index.php?title=Planetary_hours&oldid=317410886 (last visited Oct. 10, 2009).

(3). http://www.medmalexperts.com/POCM/pagan_ideas_sacred_meal.html

Chapter 82

(1). http://en.wikipedia.org/w/index.php?title=Washington_National_Cathedral&oldid=319025217 (last visited Oct. 10, 2009).

(2). http://www.theosophy-nw.org/theosnw/human/hu-sbd6.htm

Chapter 84

(1). http://www.catholicherald.co.uk/features/f0000305.shtml

(2). http://www.saisobserver.org/February-2009/western-enlightenment.html

(3). http://en.wikipedia.org/w/index.php?title=Isaac_Newton&oldid=319215076 (last visited Oct. 11, 2009).

(4). http://www.christianpost.com/article/20070619/papers-show-isaac-newton-s-religious-side-predict-date-of-apocalypse/index.html

(5). http://en.wikipedia.org/w/index.php?title=Monad_(Greek_philosophy)&oldid=308871850 (last visited Oct. 11, 2009)

(6).http://en.wikipedia.org/w/index.php?title=Jesus_Christ_in_comparative_mythology&oldid=3183051 44 (last visited Oct. 11, 2009).

(7). http://sv.wikipedia.org/w/index.php?title=Prisca_sapientia&oldid=6135596 (last visited Oct. 11, 2009).

Chapter 85

(1). http://en.wikipedia.org/w/index.php?title=Ashlar&oldid=318305399 (last visited Oct. 11, 2009).

(2). http://en.wikipedia.org/w/index.php?title=Splendor_Solis&oldid=312173766 (last visited Oct. 11, 2009).

(3). http://en.wikipedia.org/w/index.php?title=Robert_Fludd&oldid=303702834 (last visited Oct. 11, 2009).

(4). http://www.crcsite.org/affiliation.htm

(5). http://www.crcsite.org/spinoza1.htm

(6). http://en.wikipedia.org/w/index.php?title=Gottfried_Leibniz&oldid=319254908 (last visited Oct. 11, 2009).

(7). http://en.wikipedia.org/w/index.php?title=A%E2%88%B4A%E2%88%B4&oldid=315623120 (last visited Oct. 11, 2009)

Chapter 86

(1). http://en.wikipedia.org/w/index.php?title=Great_Architect_of_the_Universe&oldid=310955771 (last visited Oct. 21, 2009).

Chapter 87

(1). http://en.wikipedia.org/w/index.php?title=Rose_window&oldid=316522366 (last visited Oct. 12, 2009).
(2). http://en.wikipedia.org/w/index.php?title=Thomas_Vaughan_(philosopher)&oldid=310208072 (last visited Oct. 12, 2009).
(3). http://www.crcsite.org/confessio.htm

Chapter 89

(1). http://www.ucl.ac.uk/sts/chang/boiling/index.htm

Chapter 93

(1). http://nymag.com/arts/books/features/58849/
(2). http://en.wikipedia.org/w/index.php?title=Franklin_Square_(Washington,_D.C.)&oldid=318337389 (last visited Oct. 12, 2009).

Chapter 96

(1). http://en.wikipedia.org/w/index.php?title=Lord%27s_Prayer&oldid=318594515 (last visited Oct. 12, 2009).
(2). http://en.wikipedia.org/w/index.php?title=Amen&oldid=319238398 (last visited Oct. 12, 2009).
(3). http://en.wikipedia.org/w/index.php?title=Sufism&oldid=319342315 (last visited Oct. 12, 2009).
(4). http://www.newadvent.org/cathen/03158a.htm

Chapter 102

(1). http://en.wikipedia.org/w/index.php?title=Infinity&oldid=319560279 (last visited Oct. 13, 2009).
(2). http://www.spiritual-numerology.com/numerology-number-meaning/numerology-meaning-of-number-8.html
(3). http://en.wikipedia.org/w/index.php?title=Monomyth&oldid=319330214 (last visited Oct. 13, 2009).

Chapter 106

(1). http://en.wikipedia.org/w/index.php?title=Magic_square&oldid=319136958 (last visited Oct. 13, 2009).
(2). http://www.geocities.com/~harveyh/franklin.htm

Chapter 107

(1). http://en.wikipedia.org/w/index.php?title=Metempsychosis&oldid=315596662 (last visited Oct. 13, 2009).
(2). http://www.newadvent.org/cathen/14153a.htm

Chapter 111

(1). http://siarchives.si.edu/history/exhibits/historic/sibint.htm
(2). http://en.wikipedia.org/w/index.php?title=Spells_in_Harry_Potter&oldid=319238680 (last visited Oct. 14, 2009).
(3). http://en.wikipedia.org/w/index.php?title=Abracadabra&oldid=318664136 (last visited Oct. 14, 2009).
(4). http://en.wikipedia.org/w/index.php?title=Abrahadabra&oldid=303858314 (last visited Oct. 14, 2009).

(5). http://en.wikipedia.org/w/index.php?title=Satya_Yuga&oldid=312073170 (last visited Oct. 14, 2009).
(6). http://en.wikipedia.org/w/index.php?title=Age_of_Aquarius&oldid=319578830 (last visited Oct. 14, 2009).
(7). http://en.wikipedia.org/w/index.php?title=Harmonic_Convergence&oldid=319439605 (last visited Oct. 14, 2009).

Chapter 112

(1). http://en.wikipedia.org/w/index.php?title=Lactated_Ringer%27s_solution&oldid=316653083 (last visited Oct. 14, 2009).

Chapter 113

(1). http://en.wikipedia.org/w/index.php?title=Isolation_tank&oldid=319643372 (last visited Oct. 14, 2009).

Chapter 114

(1). http://dcpages.com/gallery/House-of-the-Temple/DSC04711.jpg.html
(2). http://www.scottishrite.org/what/educ/heredom.html

Chapter 116

(1). http://www.masonicdictionary.com/winding.html#Winding
(2). http://en.wikipedia.org/w/index.php?title=Sacrum&oldid=317694379 (last visited Oct. 14, 2009).

Chapter 117

(1). http://www.theforbiddenknowledge.com/hardtruth/lettersonthemasonicinstitutionjohnqadams.htm
(2). http://en.wikipedia.org/w/index.php?title=Shamanism&oldid=319854866 (last visited Oct. 14, 2009).
(3). http://en.wikipedia.org/w/index.php?title=Kapparot&oldid=317700054 (last visited Oct. 14, 2009).

Chapter 119

(1). http://www.lodge76.wanadoo.co.uk/the_altar_of_freemasonry.htm
(2). http://en.wikipedia.org/w/index.php?title=Monomyth&oldid=319330214 (last visited Oct. 14, 2009).

Chapter 121

(1). http://www.archive.org/stream/primitivechurch01unkngoog/primitivechurch01unkngoog_djvu.txt
(2). http://www.lodge76.wanadoo.co.uk/the_altar_of_freemasonry.htm

Chapter 125

(1). http://en.wikipedia.org/w/index.php?title=Harry_S._Truman&oldid=319610530 (last visited Oct. 18, 2009).

Chapter 126

(1). http://en.wikipedia.org/w/index.php?title=Ahiman_Rezon&oldid=228994972 (last visited Oct. 18, 2009).
(2). http://www.srmason-sj.org/web/journal-files/Issues/sep-oct05/calloway.html

Chapter 127

(1). http://en.wikipedia.org/w/index.php?title=William_Whiston&oldid=306819723 (last visited Oct. 18, 2009).

(2). http://en.wikipedia.org/w/index.php?title=Isaac_Newton%27s_religious_views&oldid=319592405 (last visited Oct. 19, 2009).

Chapter 128

(1). http://www.masonic-lodge-of-education.com/masonic-emblems.html
(2). http://chemistry.about.com/od/alchemicalsymbols/a/alchemyhg.htm

Chapter 130

(1). http://en.wikipedia.org/w/index.php?title=Logos&oldid=318511638 (last visited Oct. 19, 2009).
(2). http://www.phoenixmasonry.org/bible.htm

Chapter 131

(1). http://www.cpinternet.com/jberends/mword.html
(2). http://www.absoluteastronomy.com/discussionpost/The_last_Church-Age_Prophet_revealing_the_MYSTERY_OF_GOD_35108
(3). http://www.bengtkarlssonsbygg.eu/frukt.htm
(4).http://www.kjv-asia.com/comparing_spiritual_things_with_spiritual_dark_sayings_in_the_bible.htm
(5). http://en.wikipedia.org/w/index.php?title=William_Blake&oldid=320236057 (last visited Oct. 19, 2009).
(6). http://en.wikipedia.org/w/index.php?title=Newton_(Blake)&oldid=316298001 (last visited Oct. 19, 2009).
(7). http://www.interfaithforums.com/deist-beliefs/3161-bible-literally-true.html
(8). http://www.saibaba.ws/articles1/saibabaonbuddha.htm
(9). http://en.wikipedia.org/w/index.php?title=Know_thyself&oldid=315848548 (last visited Oct. 19, 2009).
(10). http://en.wikipedia.org/w/index.php?title=Monomyth&oldid=320520822 (last visited Oct. 22, 2009).

Chapter 133

(1). http://www.hiddenmeanings.com/serious.html
(2). http://www.williamhenry.net/art_temple.html
(3). http://en.wikipedia.org/w/index.php?title=Pineal_gland&oldid=319947286 (last visited Oct. 20, 2009).
(4). http://www.cancer.org/docroot/ETO/content/ETO_5_3X_Faith_Healing.asp

Epilogue

(1). http://en.wikipedia.org/w/index.php?title=Washington_Monument&oldid=320963478 (last visited Oct. 20, 2009).
(2). http://www.williamhenry.net/art_temple.html

In Conclusion: Why Dan Brown isn't so dumb after all

(1). http://www.independent.ie/entertainment/books/why-the-critics-are-so-wrong-about-dan-brown-1866945.html

Out now!

A Fame of Two Halves by Kevin Mahoney

For Elliot Gold, manager of the Duxford Ducks soccer team, life seems to be going from bad to worse. His job and his marriage both face imminent demise. He pins all his hopes on winning one last match. But Elliot Gold is not a lucky man! Drowning his sorrows with his parents in Malta, Elliot is suddenly offered a chance

154

to resurrect his football career with a team he renames 'The Maltese Falcons'. With the inspirational music of Spandau Ballet racing through his veins, Elliot attempts to reinvent himself. Will he woo the lovely Silvia? Can he save his parents' marriage as their union also heads for the rocks? Will he ever win again?

"a tremendous first novel - wry, funny and clever. I hope it's the first of many" - Joanne Harris, author of *Chocolat*

ISBN 9781849230360 £6.99 $10.99

The Indoor Survival Guide by Igor Vobitch

Most accidents happen within the home, but how can you avoid them? Well, help is now at hand with *The Indoor Survival Guide*. Find out how to survive nuclear bombs, murderous cadavers, wild cats, viruses, and Chinese Hopping vampires... You can find out how life first began, and maybe even learn how to live forever...

ISBN 9780953317219 £6.99 $10.99

At the age of 22, Jack is going nowhere. Stuck in a New Mexico backwater, slicing dead cattle for a living, he is ready to seize any opportunity to make something of his life. So when his workmate Ed tells him about the $25,000 stashed in a bus station locker in San Francisco, and when he meets and falls for the beautiful De S'anna, a sweet Italian supernova of sweat and lips and purple-black hair, the two events propel him into a journey of love, drugs, madness and determination as he tries to make real those two seductive mirages, the accidental fortune and the perfect love. Christopher Neilan's debut novel is a coruscating tale told in vibrant, visceral prose. Funny, sexy, poetic, thrilling and endlessly inventive, *Abattoir Jack* is a very impressive achievement.

ISBN 9780953317233 £6.99 $13.99

1102899R0

Printed in Great Britain by
Amazon.co.uk, Ltd.,
Marston Gate.